INDIANS INTO MEXICANS

INDIANS INTO MEXICANS

History and Identity
in a Mexican Town

DAVID FRYE

UNIVERSITY OF TEXAS PRESS
Austin

First edition, 1996

Requests for permission to reproduce material from this work should be sent to Permissions, University of Texas Press, Box 7819, Austin, TX 78713-7819.

∞ The paper used in this publication meets the minimum requirements of American National Standard for Information Sciences—Permanence of Paper for Printed Library Materials, ANSI Z39.48-1984.

LIBRARY OF CONGRESS CATALOGING-IN-PUBLICATION DATA

Frye, David L.
    Indians into Mexicans : history and identity in a Mexican town / David Frye. — 1st ed.
       p.   cm.
    Includes bibliographical references and index.
    ISBN 0-292-79068-6. — ISBN 0-292-72496-9 (pbk)
    1. Indians of Mexico—Mexico—Mexquitic—Social conditions.
2. Mexquitic (Mexico)—Social conditions.   3. Ethnology—Mexico—Mexquitic.   4. Indians of Mexico—Mexico—Mexquitic—History.
5. Mexquitic (Mexico)—History.   I. Title.
F1219.1.S22F79   1996
305.897'072—dc20   95-4385

Contents

Acknowledgments

The history in this book is based in part on conversations with older residents of the town of Mexquitic and in part on several months of archival work in the town, in the state capital of San Luis Potosí, in Mexico City, and in Seville. The ethnography is based on fieldwork, which Ruth Behar and I carried out for the most part in the town of Mexquitic (population about 750), with several brief trips, from a few hours to two days in length, to a dozen of the almost one hundred communities scattered about the municipio of the same name (total population in 1990: 43,053). (The "x" in Mexquitic, a bit of an affectation, is pronounced like an "s"; "Mezquitic," as it is more properly spelled, means "among the mesquite tree[s]" in Nahuatl.) We first visited Mexquitic on a brief trip in 1980 and returned to live there from November 1982 to late July 1985, with a few fairly short breaks, followed by return visits of one or two months almost every year since.

James W. Fernandez and Hildred Geertz directed the doctoral dissertation that preceded this book, and their sometimes divergent anthropological perspectives inform it in ways I hope they will recognize. I owe a debt of friendship to Teofilo Ruiz for his constant support and insightful comments. Many thanks to William B. Taylor for his pioneering work on Mexican social history and especially for his prompt, detailed, and much appreciated comments on my writing, which I hope have helped keep me historically honest. Special thanks to Lara Putnam, who read and extensively commented on the entire manuscript, and to Rosario Montoya and Barry Lyons for helpful comments on the introductory chapters. Above all, thanks to Ruth Behar, without whom this book would most literally never have been written, who endured its long genesis from fieldwork to printed page, improved it with incisive critiques, and helped me to carry through to the end. Espero que valió la pena.

I owe intellectual debts to more scholars of Mexico than are acknowledged in the notes. This research would not have been possible without the works of James Lockhart, Luis González, Judith Friedlander, Guillermo de la Peña, James Cockcroft, Rodolfo Stavenhagen, Arturo Warman, Nancy Farriss, Romana Falcón, . . . and the list goes on.

I thank the helpful staffs of the Archivo Histórico del Estado and the Biblioteca Universitaria in San Luis Potosí, especially founder and long-time director Rafael Montejano y Aguiñaga. Thanks to the staff of the Archivo General de la Nación in Mexico City, and especially to Roberto Beristain, of the Biblioteca Nacional.

I owe a special kind of thanks to the people of Mexquitic for their help. Many anthropologists have to rely on one or two principal informants for finding out what is really going on in a place; I was fortunate enough to be able to count on a good dozen families for their understanding and aid by the end of our three years in the town. (I have decided, after some deliberation, to give them pseudonyms in the book, with the exception of the priests and presidents, who are public figures.) My thanks to all, and apologies for not wishing to single out some here for special thanks.

Financial support came from a summer grant from the Latin American Studies Program of Princeton University in June 1980; a National Science Foundation Graduate Study Fellowship for 1980–1983; a Fulbright Research Award for 1983–1984 and an Organization of American States Research Award for 1984–1986, both of which funded the bulk of my research in San Luis Potosí; and a postdoctoral research award from the American Council of Learned Societies in 1989–1990. An Assistant Research Scientist appointment at the University of Michigan has given me the institutional space to finish the project. All are gratefully acknowledged.

And thanks to Gabriel, soccer player extraordinaire.

FIGURE 1. Posing before the new house, Mexquitic, 1987. (Photograph by Ruth Behar)

FIGURE 2. The house in construction, Mexquitic, 1990.

FIGURE 3.   Tending goats, Mexquitic, 1985. (Photograph by Ruth Behar)

FIGURE 4.   Gathering *nopalitos*, Mexquitic, 1985. (Photograph by Ruth Behar)

FIGURE 5. Sunday in Mexquitic: selling pulque above the town plaza, 1988. (Photograph by Ruth Behar)

FIGURE 6. Sunday in Mexquitic: selling *gordas de horno* in front of the church, 1988. (Photograph by Ruth Behar)

FIGURE 7. "La Casa del Pueblo": inside a general store, Mexquitic, 1990. (Photograph by Ruth Behar)

FIGURE 8. Stationery store, Mexquitic, 1993. (Photograph by Ruth Behar)

FIGURE 9. Stationery store, Mexquitic, 1993. (Photograph by Ruth Behar)

FIGURE 10. Dancers practicing for fiesta performance before parish church, Mexquitic, 1985. (Photograph by Ruth Behar)

FIGURE 11. Doña Bartola preparing a family grave for Day of the Dead, Mexquitic municipal cemetery, 1987. (Photograph by Ruth Behar)

FIGURE 12. Political rally, plaza of Mexquitic, 1985. (Photograph by Ruth Behar)

FIGURE 13. Sowing corn, ejido of Mexquitic, 1985. (Photograph by Ruth Behar)

INDIANS INTO MEXICANS

ONE　　　　**Introduction**

"¡Mira, un hombre blanco!"

A gang of young boys gathered around us, staring, grinning, on the dusty street that headed back to the highway and the bus that would deliver us from their attention and return us to the city of San Luis Potosí.

"Look, a white man!" *"¡El hombre blanco!"*

Why their excitement? Why their delight? *Why me?* Were they expecting handouts of gum? Or, more likely, were they simply exhilarated to discover the ease with which, by pointing me out, they could intimidate and embarrass a *gringo* from Gringolandia—and a tall, blond one, at that?

BECOMING THE OTHER

It was the summer of 1980, and Ruth Behar and I were on our first trip to the state of San Luis Potosí in north-central Mexico, traveling by bus around the *altiplano,* the high, arid central plateau of the state, to scout out a likely site for future fieldwork. Today we had spent a fruitless afternoon trying to find the president of the *ejido* community of Enrique Estrada. And here, even before we had mounted the crowded market bus that would take us to Mexquitic—the town we would return to live and work in for nearly three years—I had already been taught something essential about Mexico, and about myself. I could, I suppose, think of it as a humbling experience—to be taught at the age of twenty-three, already a graduate student in anthropology, one of the basic facts of North American social life by a bunch of unruly eight-year-olds. But the truth is that, as a white male growing up in the United States, I had never before thought of myself *as white*. Race, to the white male in the United States (at least to one growing up in the white suburbs of Dallas in the 1960s), is something that *other* people have. By pointing out my own color to me, and quite insistently, the boys of Enrique Estrada put me on notice that I was the outsider here, the one who stood out, the one whose race would never be taken for granted.

It is a lesson that I have never forgotten, one that I carried with me throughout my experiences in Mexico and back with me to the United States.

Meanwhile our search for a fieldsite continued. We did not stay in Enrique Estrada; I admit that the raucous reception by the boys had crossed that village off our list. We were drawn instead to the more circumspect people of the town of Mexquitic, seat of the *municipio* (municipality, township, or county) of the same name, set high in the arid, dust-swept, starkly beautiful hills and plateaus of north-central Mexico. There, we knew, I was a *gringo* only when our backs were turned; to our faces, I was don David, and sometimes Señor Gringuito—a more comfortable relationship for all.

Still, the lesson of the boys of Enrique Estrada gave me an early insight into my own place, as a *norteamericano,* within the Mexican society that I was presuming to study. If the town's rumor mill debated whether we were CIA agents, as some would have it, or underground Protestant missionaries awaiting our chance to corrupt the youth of Mexquitic, as others affirmed, that seemed the price I had to pay (and a small one, too) for the deep inequalities between our countries and my own implication in them. At the same time my new, personal awareness of how racial and ethnic identities are constructed, and at times hidden from sight, by social conventions gave me a new and unexpected angle on Mexican society and history. As this book developed, it grew into an ethnographic and historical study of racial ideology and politics in Mexico and of the construction of social identity as seen from the vantage point of one small rural town.

To choose a town like Mexquitic, in a northern state such as San Luis Potosí, as a place to do anthropological research goes against the received wisdom that partitions and defines Mexico. The stereotypes held by anthropologists and guidebook authors, Mexican and North American alike, would confine Indians, long considered the most proper object for the anthropological as well as the touristic gaze, to the south, the center, and a few isolated mountain hideouts of the northwest. Blacks, Mexicans of African descent, if their presence or their past in Mexico is acknowledged at all, are known to live on the coasts of Guerrero or of Veracruz.[1] The north, according to the same conventional views, is the land of haciendas and mines, mestizos and revolutionaries.[2]

Indeed, when I first went to San Luis Potosí my plan was to study the social history of the haciendas, those enormous estates which had dominated rural life in the state and in most of northern Mexico until the land reform of the 1920s and 30s broke them up into community-governed, family-run parcels called *ejidos*. I would focus on the effects that the local agrarian struggle against the haciendas and the imposition of a state-defined agrarian reform had on the local society and culture, which, I assumed, could easily be characterized as a mestizo culture. With this choice of topic—land tenure as a cultural system, I called it—and of field-site, I expected to challenge the geographic and ethnic paradigms that circumscribed ethnographic research in Mexico and that have begun only slowly to crumble in the past decade.[3] What I did not expect to find, in an apparently mestizo town, was four hundred years of history as a *pueblo de indios,* a colonial Indian town. I did not anticipate that its people would still construct their identities in terms of, against, and in the face of the colonial racial ideologies that defined "Indian," "mestizo," and "Spaniard." Nor did I expect to find haciendas whose workers, up until the end of the eighteenth century, were more often "black" than "white."

For the better part of three years I worked in and on Mexquitic, talking with people of the town and participating as well as an awkward gringo can in the life of a small Mexican community. Every week or two I would take a break from conversations and baptisms and drive the fifteen winding miles into San Luis to pass a few hours at the new State Historical Archive, where I would rummage through bundles of dusty documents scarcely touched in two hundred years, trying to read through them the late colonial history of this place that I had for the moment made my home. Talking with people and reading documents: it took me a long time and a good deal of thought before I could begin to puzzle together what I was hearing from these two, quite separate activities and see clearly what had been in front of me all along. Mexquitic's Indian past is vitally connected with the present of the town.

I was well aware of this past before we ever set foot in the town, yet it had scarcely figured in my research plan. The difficulty I had in recognizing the significance of the Indian past of Mexquitic is closely related to the difficulty others have in seeing the significance of Mexquitic itself, as an Indian town, to the general history of northern Mexico. In either case, the difficulty is rooted in an ideology that denies the *presence* of Native Americans in the north of Mexico—including those provinces of colonial Mexico now known by the names "Texas," "New Mexico," "Arizona," and "California." This semi-arid north was the land of the "Chichimecas," as Spanish colonizers followed Nahuas in naming the hunter-gatherers who roamed beyond the settled bounds of Mesoamerica. When the Spanish finally came north in search of gold and land, the Indians disappeared: killed by disease, killed in war, "reduced" to a few sad villages, or pushed into the harsh refuges of the Yaqui or Tarahumara. That is the common belief. But in fact, much of the nomadic north (San Luis Potosí, Nuevo León, Coahuila, to some degree even Texas) was subdued by Spain through the foundation of pueblos of transplanted Central Mexicans. Such was the case of the fifty families who trekked north in 1591 from the central province of Tlaxcala to found the Tlaxcalan town and build the Franciscan parish of Mexquitic. In so doing they helped begin a second chapter in the history of Native Americans in the north.

Now, back in our new home in Michigan, we visit our friend Marta, who has also moved to this cold climate from Mexquitic, her home town. Introducing us to friends of hers, Marta turns to me. "And this is David. David is writing a history of my town, of Mexquitic." Then she adds, with cutting irony and a smile, "He can tell you what kind of Indians we are." *Él los puede decir qué tipo de indios somos.* When Marta arrived in the United States seven years ago, she has told us, her new brothers-in-law would insult her, calling her *india,* when she refused to drink beer. They, born of parents from Mexquitic and Saltillo but raised speaking English in Michigan, were not referring to her color—no different from their own—but to what they saw as her rural and female Mexican traditionalism, in contrast to their own cosmopolitan freedom from antiquated convention. The fact that they were able to throw out, and she was forced to feel, the word "Indian" as an insult shows that whatever the barriers of language, culture, and upbringing that may divide Marta from her brothers-in-law, a preoccupation with the meaning of Indianness still unites them. *Indio:* a colonial category, still dripping with malice, but of ever vaguer meaning. *Indio:* not quite race, not quite culture, more a stance of otherness—or simply a lack of cool.

Sitting in Marta's apartment in a suburb of Detroit, all these thoughts quickly pass once more through my mind, and as Marta's friends walk by me to greet her husband I envision my entire project crumbling into dust.

Who am I, after all, to enter a Mexican town uninvited and, under the guise of objectivity and academic professionalism, rewrite local history? And then again, having entered, having stirred up the hornets' nest, who am I to back out now, to refuse, out of some mixture of politeness and timidity, to continue with this moral dialogue and lay out what I now see as the colonial origins of attitudes toward *lo indio?*[4] And now, sitting at my desk and writing down this incident, I again face the dilemma, in a different form. I cannot help feeling that I am exploiting a friendship by taking a casual conversation and turning it into academic prose, yet I know it would be intellectually dishonest to pass over Marta's subtle criticism in silence.[5]

Indeed, I presumed to know "what kind of Indians" the people of Mexquitic are. In my dissertation on Mexquitic, which Marta read, I wrote a narrative history of the town based on archival evidence, which I presented as an unproblematic statement of who the people of the town are today. This was a presumptuous move, founded on my insufficient understanding of what it meant, and still means, to be Indian in rural Mexico. My archival research showed without room for doubt that almost everyone in Mexquitic descends from the Tlaxcalans who settled the town in 1591. Most people in Mexquitic, on the other hand, now trace their heritage back to the nomadic, warlike Chichimecas who predated the Tlaxcalans and the rule of Spain in the region. (I will examine these conflicting origin stories in chapter 3.) More to the point, townspeople invariably phrase their connection to Native America in the past tense. "We were Chichimecas here," they tell us, or they speak of the distant past "when we were Indians." In my dissertation, I phrased the connection in the present tense. "What kind of Indians we *are.*" My history was based on a research agenda, which included the intention of showing the continuity in the native history of northern Mexico. The brief tales of townspeople about their origins reflect an ongoing struggle to define their own and their town's identity in the face of colonial ideologies of Indianness. I had delved into the "dead" past to address an academic topic and had found that topic to be still very much alive.

Yet it would be false and pointless now to suppress the version of Mexquitic that I have pieced together from documents and fieldwork. Doing so would only obscure rather than solve the ethical dilemma that arises from my use of their history for academic purposes. In writing this book I have come to the conclusion that the Indian presence in Mexquitic is denied precisely because the people of the town are forced to define their own identity in terms of a racial ideology that is ultimately colonial in origin. If I am right, then the people of the town would be well served by a history that brings that oppressive ideology into the open and thus potentially provides an opening for rethinking and redefining the bases for evaluating their identity.

By the same token, to suppress this history out of a sense that I have no right to interfere in the local process of constructing the past of Mexquitic would be to ignore the fact that some of my histories, published years ago in San Luis Potosí, have already become part of the local written record. Even more, it would exaggerate the impact that my version of Mexquitic will have in the future. For in the end I have been but one more in a series of strangers—priests, doctors, teachers, merchants—who have entered Mexquitic unbidden and have made small marks on the stories of self and past that the people of Mexquitic construct both from their own memories and life experiences and from what they choose to include of the histories written or told by others.[6]

CULTURES AND HISTORIES

Yet the struggle of identities continues, the struggle of borders is our reality still. One day the inner struggle will cease and a true integration will take place.

GLORIA ANZALDÚA (1987:63)

It now seems impossible to imagine doing any kind of ethnography without a concept of the borderlands or of border crossings.

RUTH BEHAR (1993 : 13)

More than half a century ago Simpson signaled the importance of Mexican regions in the title of his history of the country, *Many Mexicos*. Over the past two decades the new conceptualization of Mexican history promised in that title has become a reality, as Mexican historians have focused on the distinctiveness of Mexican regions and the difference they make.[7] When history is written "from the bottom up" and the people of Mexico are viewed as actors and protagonists in their own right, it becomes clear that a global history written from the center is insufficient to describe how the country as a whole became what it is today. One necessary step in this rewriting of history has been to recognize that particular groups, not abstractions, are the movers of history. The hacienda did not become a major force in the shaping of Mexican history as a generalization, but rather as *this* particular hacienda, exploiting the land in this particular way, coveting the fields of those pueblos and small cultivators, under this burden of debt and ruled over by that administrator. The colonial pueblo de indios was not an abstraction; it was *this* group of people, existing as a community through their everyday interactions, cooperations, quarrels—all understood through their own sense of self and of their history. As more localities have been studied, the deep and persistent regionalism of Mexican history has become clear. The crucial events of Mexican history, from the experience of the rural population under Spanish colonial rule to their participation in (or opposition to) the violent reforms of the Revolution, were carried out by people reacting to very specific local and regional conditions. Studying regional history in all its particularity is one key to understanding the dynamics of Mexican national history.

Anthropologists have become similarly wary in recent years of the objectivized style of ethnographic writing that once served to produce timeless portraits of such abstractions as "the Mexican peasant" and "his culture."[8] Anthropologists work with particular people in a particular time, under specific conditions of social and gender relations between fieldworker and informant. In most cases these are relations of social inequality, which in the case of a North American fieldworker in Mexico are embedded in larger patterns of political and economic inequality, all laced with differing notions of respect and of gender. An ethnography, as a social product, inevitably reflects the specific social and personal relations that went into its creation; anthropologists are now called on to reflect on those relations themselves.[9]

It is no accident that some of the most incisive critiques of objectivist anthropology have been penned by ethnographers of mixed background, with one foot in Western academia and the other in the "native" society that they are studying.[10] Over the past decade, Chicana and Chicano cultural critics have also called into question some of the certainties that underlay earlier anthropological treatments of cultures. Writing from the Borderland, or Nepantla, the Land in the Middle, as Mora calls the terrain of the insider/outsider, these poet-critics have insisted on the unresolved duality of their sense of self and of culture and in so doing have called into question the concept of culture as a largely unconscious whole.[11] "We don't identify with the Anglo-American cultural values and we don't totally identify with the Mexican cultural values. We are a synergy of two cultures with various degrees of Mexicanness or Angloness."[12] This concept of a fluid borderland identity is important for conceptualizing the meaning of Mexicanness as well, for Mexico itself comprises a vast Nepantla lying between many cultures and identities.

For my part, I did not go in search of a town that was statistically typical of Mexico—or one that was, in the Spanish sense, *típico* (picturesque, unspoiled, exotic, far from civilization)—as a privileged position from which to pronounce on Mexican culture generally. The particular and moving histories of the people who comprise Mexquitic make the town entirely one of a kind. (I hope I will be forgiven for thinking that if Mexquitic is not typical of anything, this fact alone makes it as Mexican as any town could be.) I did however go to Mexquitic with preconceived notions of history, which I would only come to reflect on many years later, in the course of writing what I at first assumed would be "the" history of the town.

One of the most widely noted and criticized hallmarks of the objectivist style in ethnographic description was the convention of the ethnographic present.[13] Of all the universalizing modes of ethnographic writing, this convention was singled out for attack at the time that I was studying anthropology in graduate school in the late 1970s. By ignoring history in the imaginary timelessness of their ethnographies, we graduate students reasoned, anthropologists seemed to imply that the cultures they described were somehow impervious to change and hence to politics. The gravest problems of ethnographic description could then be resolved by a turn to history. Seen now with more perspective, the historical turn in anthropology is actually a re-turn to history. Anthropology has long had a tormented (and not always reciprocated) relation with the discipline of history. The determinedly ahistorical turn of symbolic anthropology in the 1960s, now corrected by the latest turn to history, was but one phase of this relation. The historical turn can also be seen as a reconceptualization of history by anthropologists, for the convention of the ethnographic present was itself based on a theory of history. The object of anthropological study had been taken to be timeless tradition, to which was opposed modernity and change or, if you will, history. The rejection of this conception of history was part of the same rethinking that, from the historians' side, brought in anthropology ("history from below") and that in Mexico brought regional history into its own.

My research plan for Mexquitic, then, was decidedly historical, and this book, though it has become progressively more ethnographic, remains historical in outlook and methods. But in writing the book I had to face the irony that in my search for a panacea for an uncritically generalized concept of *Culture,* I had embraced a concept of *History* that itself was abstract and overgeneralized. What affects and molds people in their actions and interactions is not History, or even the Past, as abstract forms, but what remains of the past in people's lives. This past is to be found above all in concrete histories—the stories that people think, hear, and tell of their past, and the stories that are thrown in their face by the politically or economically powerful.

A culture, like a history, is similarly not an abstraction but something concrete. Like a history, a culture (as opposed to Culture) is a story, a description, a narrative, a thought, a piece of writing. Cultures are webs of conventions and habit that we, in dialogue with others, discern and describe as such.[14] In this sense, each of us is constantly reinventing and reassimilating our cultures, the stories we tell about our conventions and habits, through innumerable individual interactions. The construction of culture occurs at every social level and across borders of all kinds—between individuals, between groups and communities, between those imagined communities known as nations. The continual construction of culture is particularly evident, and important, in a place such as Mexquitic, where two macrocultures, first brought together by colonialism and later kept together by nationalism, are in constant contact. In the colonial era these two cultures were known as Indian and Spanish. Today (and even then) it would perhaps be more accurate to speak instead of rural and urban cultures. In a provocative study, Guillermo Bonfil Batalla refers to these cultures as *el México profundo,* "the deep Mexico," the Mexico in touch with its roots in Mesoamerican civilization; and *el México imaginario,* "the imaginary Mexico," the Mexico that denies its connection to the pre-Hispanic world and that segregates itself from the Indian world.[15]

Indian cultures, in Mexico as in the United States, are granted two historical paths, according to our different but at times converging historical ideologies. They can continue unchanged (in fact or in essence) or they can disappear, be "lost." Mexquitic, which was considered a pueblo de indios for two and a half centuries, from its foundation until the midnineteenth century, is now a mestizo town. Therefore, the logic goes, it must have lost its Indian culture to the influence of the dominant culture of San Luis. When we think with this contemporary colonial logic (and, I suggest, we all do so, in the United States as in Mexico), we seldom concern ourselves with the obvious fact that the non-Indian (Spanish, I suppose), urban culture of San Luis has no more remained unchanged than the rural culture of Mexquitic. Life in San Luis today is not the equivalent of life in sixteenth-century Seville; nor, for that matter, is life in Boston or Dallas a replica of life in seventeenth-century Bristol. But change in these cities is a given: according to our common perceptions, progress (hence change of any sort) is by definition "European" or, if you prefer, modern; "Indian" is equally identified with tradition. If an Indian pueblo has changed, we think, it can no longer be entirely Indian, since by changing it must have lost something: a sad fact, perhaps, but inevitable, as Indian peoples are ever doomed to losing their cultures under the powerful influence of mestizo/modern culture. The "Spanish" culture of urban Mexico, on the other hand, change as it will, cannot be lost to any outside influence—unless, of course, it is to that of the more powerful North American culture (again, always, the vocabulary of power).

The logic of this colonial ideology is pervasive, insidious. It is inside us, inside me. Here is the opening of the 1965 *World Book* article on the United States, a work that I read again and again throughout my childhood:

> America was largely a wilderness three hundred years ago. The story is that a squirrel might have scampered through the trees half-way across the country without touching the ground. No wheel or plow had yet touched most of America's wide, fertile prairies. Nor had a miner's pick tapped its mountains, rich in ore. Only a few American Indians, Eskimos, and Hawaiians lived here. In this great, almost empty land, western civilization won an opportunity to begin all over again.[16]

The immaculate conception. Echoes of this thinking are everywhere, even in the words of a prominent Puerto Rican historian, as quoted by a journalist for the *New York Times:* " 'We weren't Alaska, Hawaii, Arizona, or New Mexico,' Ricardo E. Alegría says. 'We weren't some sparsely settled frontier. We were a nation when the United States arrived.' "[17]

In thinking about history in Mexquitic, I return, again and again, to Herskovitz's analysis of the pernicious "myth of the Negro past, which validates the concept of Negro inferiority." Underlying this myth, Herskovitz wrote, is the core belief that "the Negro is thus a man without a past."[18] This keystone belief of colonial racial ideology would cut off African Americans from a history that, despite the myth, is nevertheless all around us and that has made America, both North and South, what it is. There is also a myth of Indian history, an inverted version of the "Negro myth," but with the same consequences: that the Indian has no present.

May this work be one small step in the dismantling of that myth.[19]

MANY MEXICOS, MANY MEXQUITICS

Mexico is made up of highly contrasting social groups and categories. . . . One often finds towns which are physically quite close to one another but which present markedly diverse lifestyles.

GUILLERMO DE LA PEÑA (1980 : 13)

Mexquitic is a town of stone and adobe, brick and cement block, set along streets paved in the 1940s with striking reddish-brown flagstones. Its streets huddle between the slopes of dry, rocky hills covered with cactus, thorny mesquite, and huizache trees, alongside a massive dam built by the national government in the 1920s and a small irrigation stream, the Río de Mexquitic, that issues from the dam when the floodgates are opened. This town of 750 inhabitants is also the county seat (*cabecera municipal*) of the municipality of Mexquitic, which covers 913 square kilometers and some one hundred communities, each with its own name, personality, and history. From the vantage point of the town, the other communities are known, collectively and with a certain urban disdain, as *ranchos,* though at least a half dozen of them are larger than the town. (Some are in fact large enough to count, rather ironically, as "urbanized" in official Mexican statistics; note that in this usage rancho is *not* the equivalent of "ranch.") But only the county seat is called a *pueblo,* in tribute to its place at the political, economic, and religious, as well as geographic, center of the municipality.

In spite of its relatively small population, the town derives a certain urban quality from the diversity of occupations and offices that it houses. It is the home of the municipal government buildings, the massive parish church and adjoining friary built under the Franciscans in the 1600s, and the municipal cemetery.[20] It also boasts an enclosed marketplace, a good two dozen shops and offices, and a full set of schools that now can take students from kindergarten through high school. The buses that stop in the town every half hour of the day on their way to San Luis, forty-five minutes away on the highway blasted through the hills in the early 1960s, also give Mexquitic an urban feel. Though they are blamed for taking away business from the local shops, the buses also bring people from other communities into the town, and they have allowed Mexquitic to become a kind of bedroom community for the students and workers who spend their days in the city. More recently, a professional couple from San Luis with no prior connection to Mexquitic has settled into a large country house built to their own design, and an engineer with ties to a San Luis

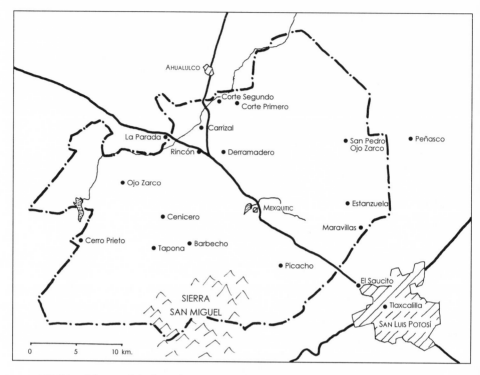

MAP 1.   The municipality of Mexquitic, showing places mentioned in text

political family has built a vacation home and opened a small public zoo just across the dam. Whether these latest urbanizations presage a gentrified future for the town remains to be seen.

As large as the ranchos may be, they are by contrast made up of more homogeneous populations of agricultural workers and day laborers, who live in uniform adobe houses along unpaved roads. Though the ranchos are slowly being electrified, and even more slowly equipped with telephone service, most are still without running water or sewers. One or two small shops, a school that might not continue past the fifth grade, and perhaps a local shrine, chapel, or even a Baptist prayer-house, round out the social amenities of the rancho. From the vantage point of townspeople, the ranchos appear rather rough and rustic; from the point of view of the communities, in turn, the town of Mexquitic can appear overbearing, overprivileged, and arrogant.

As the administrative center, the town has long been the scene of political struggles between rival elite factions within the municipality, and between the priest and the parishioners. It was also, in the centuries leading up to the Mexican Revolution, the political locus of the economic and territorial rivalry and symbiosis between the ranchos and the neighboring haciendas. I have taken these struggles—over politics, over land, and between priest and parishioners—as the defining social and historical topics of this book. This would have been a different book if I had researched it from another community in the municipality, such as Cerro Prieto to the east, Picacho to the south, or Corte to the north, just as surely as if I had worked in another Mexican region, such as the Bajío, the Huasteca, or Michoacán.

Corte, a large community on the northern border of the municipality abutting the huge hacienda of La Parada, has also been caught up in the question of territorial rivalry for at least the last two centuries, but for geographic and economic rather than administrative reasons. The location of Corte on the border between municipality and hacienda made dealing with La Parada an urgent economic and community matter, whether that meant providing the hacienda with labor and produce, defending local land against encroachment by the great estate, or, ultimately, taking the lead in the fight for agrarian reform. The centuries-long tension with the hacienda pushed the people of Corte more deeply into municipal and regional politics than any other community in Mexquitic. More *agraristas* from Corte than from any other community fought in the Revolution, and in the decades since 1910 Corte has produced more municipal presidents than any other community in this century—at least a dozen all told. This political involvement has also led to deep conflicts within Corte, including a deadly rivalry between the twin barrios of Corte Primero and Corte Segundo. Writing from Corte, I probably would have produced a more focused, more political, perhaps a more passionate account, with a greater emphasis on factionalism and on the relation between Mexquitic and La Parada than the present study has.

Cerro Prieto, on the other hand, had an entirely different history from that of Corte. Before agrarian reform Cerro Prieto was itself a small hacienda, the only one located entirely within the municipal boundaries of Mexquitic. It was also one of the few haciendas in the region not involved in territorial disputes with adjoining communities. Unlike La Parada, which depended on labor from Corte and other communities in Mexquitic for planting and harvesting its corn and wheat, Cerro Prieto was an almost self-contained industrial hacienda by the late nineteenth century. The principal crop of the hacienda was the maguey (century plant), and its one commercial product was mescal, a spirit distilled from the trunk and root of the maguey in a massive, coal-fired factory at the heart of the hacienda. The workers of Cerro Prieto—descendants of the multiracial work force that migrated to the estates around Mexquitic over the centuries—lived, as they still do, in neatly ordered adobe houses surrounding the central factory, great house, and chapel of the hacienda.

In the 1920s, when the people of Corte, Mexquitic, and other communities of the municipality were taking up arms as agraristas and petitioning for the haciendas to be carved into ejidos, the workers of Cerro Prieto refused to ask for land. "Why do we need land if we have jobs?" Crispina remembers asking. They only joined the agrarian movement in the late 1930s, when it became clear that petitioners from rival communities within Mexquitic would put an end to the hacienda and the mescal factory that employed them, in spite of their wishes. In a history written from Cerro Prieto, conflicts with the haciendas would have seemed more muted, more a matter for political rhetoric than a lived experience. The key topics, instead, would have been rural proletarianization and perhaps the discord between nationally imposed political agendas and local realities.

Picacho, too, has had relations with the regional economy different from any of these communities. This community of dispersed houses, many built in the traditional regional form with peaked roofs thatched with maguey leaves, spreads out over the dry hills between the town of Mexquitic and the city of San Luis, not far from the highway but far from the haciendas. Without access to irrigated land, Picacho has been isolated from the political struggles that come with territorial disputes—though not, of course, immune to the micropolitics of everyday disputes over family patrimonies. Yet their isolation from local resources and local struggles has forced many in Picacho to become, if anything, more involved personally in the wider Mexican economy than those of Corte or Cerro Prieto.

Many people in Picacho, hard-pressed to make a living from the products of an unforgiving landscape, have turned to producing handicrafts, such as small baskets, wooden objects, toys, and some pottery. They sell these crafts in San Luis and other cities across northern Mexico, commuting now by bus or truck, and in earlier years on foot and donkey, sometimes on journeys of hundreds of miles that last for months. In spite of their closeness to the city of San Luis, and perhaps because of their relative economic independence, the people of Picacho are thought of in Mexquitic as the "most Indian" in the municipality. A view from Picacho would have provided a more distant, detached perspective on the political struggles against haciendas, priests, and government officials, and on the establishment of the far-off ejidos of the municipality, but a more intimate perspective on questions of community, identity, and the meaning of being Indian.

This brief sketch of four communities, some of the "many Mexquitics" with their own microregional dynamics inside the reduced geographic space of the municipality of Mexquitic, is meant as a reminder that my findings are not to be read as applying wholesale to all of Mexico. Everywhere there are eddies and sidestreams in the broad sweep of Mexican history, and even adjacent communities can have quite different historical experiences and memories. The reminder is particularly apt in cases where the history of Mexquitic, as I present it, flows along lines that agree with preconceived notions of Mexican history; along the way I try to point out local cases that go against the grain of my narrative and of those preconceptions. The parish priest of Mexquitic became an ally of the hacienda owners in the late eighteenth century, fulfilling his preordained role in the class struggle then brewing, according to one common interpretation of colonial history. Yet a contemporary of his in the nearby parish of Valle de San Francisco pointed to the hacendados as the main enemies of his parishioners, and in the same years another, more famous, priest not far to the south, Miguel Hidalgo of the parish of Dolores, led his parishioners into insurrection. And again, while haciendas such as La Parada expanded into Mexquitic, usurping municipal land in the nineteenth century, other, smaller haciendas were contracting, their land bought up by prosperous small farmers from the municipality; all the local haciendas, La Parada included, depended not only on the labor but also on the produce of the small farmers of communities such as Corte for their economic survival.

What makes local studies relevant to the understanding of a national history or culture is that in their very particularity, in their eddies, their departures from and coincidences with those broader streams, they can reveal decisive forces at play that could be obscured by an overly generalized account. The political struggle over identity, in particular, occurs at a very personal level, and it is with a close focus on one community that I have come to understand something of that struggle.

In the next chapter, which forms the ethnographic introduction to this book, I draw brief portraits of some of the people of contemporary Mexquitic, in order to give a sense of how this diversity of viewpoints and historical experiences plays out on a personal level. The image of "the house as a work in progress" is introduced as a metaphor for the continual construction of the social and cultural world by the people of Mexquitic; here I raise the question of social stratification within Mexquitic and the links between economic and political power, ideology, and social identity. In the third chapter, which can stand as the historical introduction to the book, I relate the history of the founding of Mexquitic and then discuss four different historical and mythical foundation narratives as examples of the political uses of historical tales.

In chapter 4 I focus on the local political world of the late colonial Indian pueblo of Mexquitic (1764–1814). Chapter 5 deals with the elaboration of images of Indianness in the context of sometimes bitter political and social conflicts between the people of Mexquitic and their parish priest at the end of the colonial era, and the reverberations of those conflicts today. In chapter 6 the political struggles within twentieth-century Mexquitic are recounted; here I take up the theme of the local eddies in the stream of national history through an exploration of the connections and incongruities among the multiple layers of local, state, and national history. The book concludes with a chapter on the struggles over the definition and control of land from the eighteenth century to the present—conflicts that, I argue, are at the heart of the continual process of constructing local history and local identity. With the stories the people of Mexquitic tell about these efforts today, they are creating a form of discourse critical of the elite ideology that attempts to univocally set the terms of their identity.

I have modeled the title of this book, the last chosen in a long series of possible titles, after Eugen Weber's treatment of the modernization of rural France, *Peasants into Frenchmen*. The choice was based on the number of parallels between the nation-building projects in both countries. The rural majorities in both countries were made in one way or another to accommodate to national identities defined by urban minorities. In both cases, fully accepting the newly minted national identity has meant giving up something of the older local identity: a language, a regional mode of dress, a regional ethnic identity. And in both cases, people who have "passed" from one identity to the other may continue to hold their former identity, while at the same time being forced to deal with it in the terms set by a national elite. In France this was the class term "peasant," and in Mexico the racial term "Indian," but both are key terms of an imposed discourse meant to supplant specific local and regional identities.[21]

Weber looked at the national processes, forces, and actors involved in promoting and effecting the transformation of rural "peasants," mired (as the cliché goes) in the obscurity of local customs and concerns, into "Frenchmen," active members in the modern French nation. In this book

I focus more closely on the local embodiments of such national and regional processes: the parish priests, with all their personal idiosyncrasies and agendas; the local haciendas; the representatives of royal and later of national power and control. I look especially at the people of Mexquitic themselves and their own crucial part in constructing this particular corner of Mexican national identity: the struggles they endured and the struggles they initiated and carried through as they redefined their own identity, from "Indian" into Mexican.

TWO # A World in Construction

We had heard much about the economic crisis in Mexico, and we imagined the devastating effects it must have on the poor and on the rural working class. So when we moved in December 1982 to the small rural town of Mexquitic, we were surprised, and perhaps a bit heartened, to see signs of construction on almost every street of every neighborhood. New houses were going up, new additions being made. Everywhere there was the atmosphere of a housing boom, and we stopped to think: Could the economy really be so bad off? In the United States we were used to thinking of "housing starts" as an indicator, perhaps a symbol, of economic activity in general, and it was easy to transfer this way of thinking to our experience of Mexico. Yet only a few weeks of living in this town taught us that something quite different from an economic upswing was behind the apparent boom in construction.

What we noticed in those weeks was that the wall in front of Ramón and Flor's house, for which an *albañil* (builder) and two workers were breaking ground with such diligence and energy when we arrived, had then been built to a ground-level foundation and left at that. The half-finished second-story addition to Bibiano's house continued to sit unchanged from the time we arrived, as it had apparently sat for several months before. At a house on the other side of town, across the narrow stone bridge that spans the irrigation stream, Pedro suddenly began to lay cement for the second-story addition he had meant to build for over a dozen years. At other houses here and there, *castillos* of thin steel reinforcing rods rose above half-finished walls or one-story rooms, telltale signs that, sooner or later, an addition was planned.

THE HOUSE AS A WORK IN PROGRESS

What we had seen on arriving in the town, then, was not what it seemed to our unaccustomed eyes: not a housing boom, not a block of houses rising en masse from nothing, as my parents' neighborhood had arisen from a muddy field north of Dallas in a matter of three months in 1960. It was rather a collection of houses in various stages of construction. The middle-class North American route to homeowning—buying a ready-built house, taking out a mortgage, paying it off in installments—which goes hand-in-hand with the quick, large-scale construction of completed houses (and lately, of condominiums and townhouses), is simply not available to the people who live in rural Mexico.[1]

The aspect of the town as a kind of work in progress is determined by the practical solution of townspeople to the problem of building a house that costs more than they can afford to spend at any one time. Rather than buying by installments, they build by installments. The original investment, like a down payment, buys the sacks of mortar, the cement or adobe blocks (if they are not made on the spot), and the plot of land (if not inherited or granted by the ejido committee). It also pays for the indispensable services of the *albañil,* the self-trained expert in smoothing concrete, aligning blocks, attaching doors, and directing whatever other workers are needed to build the first room or two of the house. For now, two rooms will suffice, as kitchen and bedroom, even if ten sleep there. Later on, as time and money permit, more installments may be made, more rooms added. Perhaps another story and a bathroom or a new kitchen will be appended to the original plan. The entire process will take years to complete, or more likely it will never truly come to an end. There is always space for one more addition, one more improvement. And there are always new children, and children who grow up and leave. There are parents who die, inheritances to divide, a new generation that marries and brings grandchildren into the house, that moves away and sometimes moves back in. . . .

A decade after we first arrived in Mexquitic, the pace of construction had again picked up. The crisis of the 1980s was, after all, more than an abstraction or an economist's statistic; it was a serious depression that weighed on all the people of Mexico, not least on the rural population.

Mexico under Carlos Salinas in 1993 seemed to be repeating the growth, or at least the appearance of growth, of the United States under Reagan and Bush, complete with the cult of the M.B.A. and the law degree. On the middle-class and working-class streets of cities, which a few short years before were crowded with oilstained workshirts and neatly ironed *guayaberas,* dark business suits and sharp ties were the rage. The *mexicano* of Jorge Negrete ballads, *pobre pero honrado* (poor but honorable), was out; in 1993 everyone was an entrepreneur. How much of this was real, how much show and illusion, how much hope, and how much a cover for anxiety, only the uncertain future would tell.

Even as the depression of the 1980s appeared to abate, the people of Mexquitic continued to employ the ingenious solutions to constructing with limited resources that they had devised over the years, though at perhaps a quicker pace. The wall in front of Ramón and Flor's house, which took eight years to rise to the height of three feet, grew suddenly and miraculously into the ranch house, complete with bay windows and an attached restaurant in front, which Ramón had traced to us in words from the image in his mind's eye back in 1982. It is a tribute to their perseverance, and to the income of their eldest daughter, now grown and working as a lawyer in the city of San Luis. The second floor of Bibiano's house remains unfinished, its half-height brick walls and forlorn reinforcing rods having acquired an air of permanence. This family has moved on to other projects, other dreams, and completing this stage of the house is not yet among them. Pedro, on the other hand, finished his second story some years ago, began to build a bathroom on the site he had once pointed out to us, and turned the lower floor into a part-time bar where he served beer at the annual Fiesta de San Miguel. But in 1993 he and his family of ten deserted their old house and moved into a pair of half-finished rooms that Pedro is building across the highway, directly in front of the doors to the municipal cemetery. In the new house, still under construction, they are nearer to Pedro's productive ejido field, and there they can also sell refreshments and fresh-cut flowers to mourners waiting in the hot sun for a funeral to begin.

THE SPIRIT OF THE JACAL

Building a house did not always proceed in exactly this way. The style of house currently most common in the town of Mexquitic, a flat-roofed building of adobe or concrete blocks, is costly and time-consuming to build. The traditional rural house in the Mexquitic area, the *jacal* (shack), was neither. The tent-shaped jacal has triangular front and back walls, built no more than five or six feet tall, of adobe or large stones. In some cases the front wall is even omitted, leaving an open space that serves as a door. The largest part of the jacal is the roof that sweeps down to the ground on either side along an A-frame of *quiotes* (the long, lightweight, and strong shoots of the maguey), lashed together with twine or wire. Around thin *lechuguilla* shoots tied to these main supports the housebuilders bent the roofing material: the wide, fleshy leaves of the maguey, first made pliable by heating in a fire for several hours. All in all, even a large jacal took perhaps a hundred adobes or large stones and the leaves of about twenty magueys to construct. All the building materials were local products; construction took a few days.

The jacal is nevertheless a long-standing and protective shelter. The roof of maguey leaves is almost impervious to water for the first two or three years and remains watertight for at least fifteen years, as long as holes appearing in the leaves are promptly patched. We have seen jacales still in use that have been standing, as far as their inhabitants can remember, since the beginning of the century. On the other hand, because of the form of the jacal it is not possible to add additional rooms as is done with the newer kind of house. In the past, to expand the household one simply built another jacal. The typical jacal household consists of three or four jacales arranged around an empty central yard, one or two of which serve as sleeping rooms, another as a storage space, another as a kitchen.[2]

The traditional jacal has already succumbed in the town to its own association with poverty. No one who can afford to build a house will live in a jacal, which is not even termed a *casa* (house). A decade ago, about eight of the hundred or so families of Mexquitic lived in jacales. They were among the poorest of households, some with only a single, childless old man or woman—though they were well-off enough to have at least their own plot of land and jacal and not have to seek shelter with a relative or a charitable neighbor. Today, some have died and others have moved on or built block houses. Only two or three jacales remain there, though many more stand in communities such as Picacho, which have a reputation as being "more Indian." The townspeople who live in jacales no longer have the resources or the energy to work the magueys needed to keep up the repairs on the roof, so that the surviving jacales are now patched or completely re-roofed with tar paper, wood from crates, and scraps of tin and corrugated iron.

Though jacales are no longer built in Mexquitic, the spirit of the jacal resurfaces at times during the building of a new house. Early in 1985 our compadre Chuy decided to leave the jacales that he, his wife, Luz, and their six children had lived in for over a dozen years and to begin building a house of adobe. He himself was an albañil, a trade that he had learned through years of practice by building the houses of others, and that he still practiced occasionally, alongside his other trade as an itinerant vendor of exotic plants. For years he had planned to build for his family a house of their own next to their jacales, but he had hesitated because the land they lived on did not belong to him. His mother had loaned the house lot to him, and he felt he could not be certain that she would leave it to him on her death. Lately he had asked his mother several times to sell the property to him, and when she—a frail-looking woman of eighty-three years who walked three miles every morning and evening to collect the sweet, fermentable juice from her magueys—finally refused his offer, he bought a plot of land just outside of the center of town and decided to build his house there instead.

So it was that one January day Chuy left the jacales, never to return, and began digging the foundations for the new house. Luz, who suddenly found herself alone, was worried both for the safety of her children and for the health of Chuy, who apparently intended to sleep outdoors until the house was finished. She moved her family to the new site, and the very day she moved, she quickly improvised a shelter along the lines of a jacal, piling large stones and planting sections of organo cactus close together to form walls and using the corrugated tar paper that she had brought from her old outdoor kitchen to form a roof. It was in this improvised shelter that Luz, Chuy, and their six children lived for three cold and, in 1985, rainy months, until the adobe walls of one new room had risen high enough for Luz to cover it with a temporary roof and make it their home. When we left Mexquitic in late July their family still lived in this half-finished room. Chuy had by then made enough adobes to build the walls of one more room waist-high, and two more rooms were as yet just etchings in the earth.

Luz and Chuy were building their new house on the outskirts of town in a part of Mexquitic perhaps destined to be filled with new construction in the next few years. The land is flat, and it sits near the highway, the junior high school, and the waterline. It lies above the level reached by the local irrigation system, and is hence unsuitable for agriculture and inexpensive. Perhaps most important of all, it is available, since the owner of the land has divided it into lots for sale, in the style of urban developers in San Luis. The empty lots and unoccupied houses in the town itself, in contrast, are jealously held onto by a handful of relatively well-off townspeople who hope to leave them to their heirs and who think of selling their patrimony almost as a kind of betrayal or heresy. It is for the same reason, in fact, that the school is located here rather than in town.

Across the highway from Luz and Chuy's house stands the new house of Lupe and Natalio, who, like Chuy, decided to move here for family reasons, though of a different sort. Lupe and Natalio's old house, a modest concrete-block room with a dirt floor and a tar-paper roof, was built on a lot that Lupe had divided with her half-sister, María. María's family lived in what might be called jacal-house hybrids: tall adobe-walled rooms covered with the traditional slanted quiote-and-maguey-leaf roofs. This is an ingenious arrangement, since the traditional roof style is better suited than the currently fashionable flat roofs for keeping out the torrential rains that fall every few years in the usually arid altiplano of San Luis, especially when the new-style roof is made of tar paper. Yet such is the status accorded to the modern house style in Mexquitic, or rather the low status of the jacal, that the difference between Lupe's and María's houses was enough to subject Lupe's family to her half-sister's envious attentions. María is an intense person—once, according to her own testimony, she broke a large clay pot simply by looking at it and coveting the food she thought it contained—so her frequent admonitions to Natalio that the concrete blocks he made were not strong enough, and that the walls he built would never hold up, were enough to convince Lupe and Natalio to build their new, larger house elsewhere.

Like Chuy and Luz, Natalio and Lupe moved to their new house site long before they had finished constructing even the first room. As they said, the new house is so near the highway and so far from the town that they needed to keep guard over their concrete, sand, and tools to make sure these were not carted away at night. In one corner of the new lot Lupe and her children built a large room entirely of tar paper nailed onto an improvised wooden frame, and for the better part of 1983 this shelter served as a home for their family of nine. By December the new two-room house, still roofless, was complete enough to hold a *posada* indoors, as Lupe had promised her images of the *niño Dios* (the Child Jesus). When we went to visit the family Natalio would stand on the newly constructed porch in front of the house and, like Peter the Great surveying the site of Petersburg in Pushkin's poem, he would point to parts of what, to our eyes, was a dusty and unpromising chicken yard, and pronounce: "Here will be the bathroom, here the shower. I will build another bedroom over here."

LIFE IN THE "INFORMAL ECONOMY"

Living in an unfinished house: this image can serve as a metaphor for much of life in Mexquitic. Indeed, it strikes me, an outsider, as setting the dominant tone of that life. There are two sides to the image. On the one hand, it implies making do, improvising a way around the givens of one's life—ingeniously coping with the problem of raising a large family in a single small room, for instance. On the other hand, it implies living in a world which is not yet complete, not finished, but rather in the midst of a never-ending process of coming into being.

We can apply this image, for example, to the question of employment in Mexquitic. "What do the people there do?" I am asked. The inquirer wants to know, of course, what they do for a living, what their occupation is, but there is an inevitable implication—a given in North American society—that what you do for a living is somehow equivalent to what you do in general, and beyond that, that it defines who you are as a person. This attitude carries over to some extent into anthropological descriptions. We write ethnographies of hunter-gatherers, horticulturalists, and peasant farmers, in the confidence that these brief job descriptions in some way capture part of the essence of the people who fit them. But in speaking of Mexquitic I always hesitate before answering. How do you describe in a simple phrase someone who is usually a farmer but who also acts, as the situation arises, as a day laborer, a construction worker, a small-time vendor, a migrant worker, a craftsman? Here is the sense of the conditional, of making do and coming-into-being, of living in an unfinished house.

This pattern of multiple employment, and also of stretching the social bounds of different types of economic activity, became clear to me from talking with Ramón, one of the first people to warm up to us on our arrival in Mexquitic. At that time, if asked what he did for a living, Ramón would usually have identified himself as a musician—he plays a trumpet in a local group that is hired to play at fiestas in the region. But at times he would have said that he ran a pig-slaughtering business. For some eighteen years he had been buying pigs in the ranchos of Mexquitic, killing them, and selling the meat to a restaurant in San Luis.[3] He also grew flowers on a small field he had inherited from his father and sold them during the great flower-consuming holidays of All Souls (Día de los Muertos, November 2) and Mother's Day (May 10). He rented out the few other fields that he and his unmarried older sister Teresita owned in town.

Ramón was also an *ejidatario,* a member of the ejido community of the town of Mexquitic. More nonsense and misinformation has been written about the ejido than any other institution of Mexican rural life. It is regularly described in newspaper accounts, and even by Mexican government officials, as a form of communal land tenure, an atavistic throwback to Aztec or Maya ways.[4] In fact there is little that is communal and even less that is "Aztec" about the ejido. The *ejido* is a reinvention, by national officials of the 1920s, of the land tenure system of colonial *pueblos de indios*, which had been imposed on them by the Spanish colonial authority and which they adopted as their surest defense against encroachment by haciendas and other outsiders. The key feature of the ejido, as of the colonial system it was based on, is that title to the land rests in the community as a whole and cannot be bought by or sold to outsiders. The ejido, in addition, could not legally be rented to outsiders before the reforms of the Salinas administration in 1991, and ejido members meet monthly to discuss ways to improve their ejido, work they need to do in common, such as cleaning the irrigation canals, and alleged violations of ejido policy. Its "communal" nature starts and ends there. Otherwise an ejido parcel is a small plot of land, held and worked by a farming family, just like any other.

In the case of Mexquitic, it is a *very* small plot of land: either a quarter of a hectare in the tiny ejido on the outskirts of town or a full hectare of irrigated land (and several more of arid brush, which usually remains untilled) in the heart of the former hacienda of La Parada, sixteen kilometers from town. Ramón's parcel was out there. Being an ejidatario can be an economic identity in itself, and it is potentially a way of making a living if one is an apt enough farmer to make the single hectare bloom and if one doesn't have other opportunities closer to home and doesn't mind the long trek from town. Ramón, for his part, found it easier to give his ejido plot to a rich sharecropper, don Santos, from another rancho.[5]

Ramón's arrangement with Santos was the subject of frequent and rancorous debate in the monthly meetings of the ejidatarios, many of whom felt that he should not be giving out his land for another man to work when he himself was fit for labor; if he really did have to give it out, they argued, he should make his arrangements with someone from the town of Mexquitic itself, rather than letting people from other ranchos into their ejido. In private, Ramón dismissed these claims as provoked by envy—in the first year of his arrangement with Santos, he had made enough money from the deal to buy an old used truck, which was now instrumental to his pig-killing business—and said that he would never give his ejido plot to any of the men from Mexquitic, who do not work as hard, or have as good luck and as great an ability to make plants grow, as Santos. In the ejido meetings, he argued that the plot was not his at all, that it had passed from his father to his sister Teresita, and that as an older, unmarried woman she was free to make arrangements with whomever she wished to cultivate the land.

Musician, pig butcher, small-scale farmer, flower salesman, renter of ejido land—these are the employments that Ramón had in early 1983, but they did not define who he was. Whenever the opportunity arose he branched out in yet another direction. Though he sharecropped his main, irrigated ejido plot, in 1983 he decided to work a smaller nonirrigated (*temporal*) ejido field himself, or rather with the help of day laborers (*peones*), and brought in about 300 kilos of beans from it. In midsummer of 1983, during one of the periodic shortages of bread and tortillas that marked that year, Ramón suddenly dropped his pig-killing business and seized on a chance to use his truck to sell bread from San Luis in the ranchos of Mexquitic. After a week or two, though, when his source of bread from the city dried up, he quickly switched courses and sold the truck to a young man who had recently returned from the United States, for much more money than Ramón thought the truck was worth. He even daydreamed, in those days of uncertain economy and high interest rates, of retiring and living off the interest.

Ramón's wife, Flor, has been less mercurial than her husband in her careers. Most of her working day was spent in the unpaid labor of preparing food for her family, cleaning their clothes, taking care of the house, and raising the children, tasks in which she was aided by Ramón's sister, Teresita, who also formed part of the household. Otherwise, Flor stuck mainly to her vocation of selling, which, as she told us, she loved—a sentiment shared by many other women in Mexquitic. Marketing is in fact one of the few occupations open to women in rural Mexico, where gender codes keep women out of construction and hired field labor (though a number of women work in their own fields) but do not always keep them locked up in the house. Other occupations thought appropriate for women are cross-cut with classlike barriers. Domestic service is not only the most poorly paid of occupations, it is in essence an admission of poverty. As a married woman without dire economic need, Flor would disdain working *en casa ajena* (in another's house). The liberal professions, especially teaching, are now conceded to be appropriate even for married women, but they require what Flor lacks, a degree. She and Ramón are supporting their daughters' pursuit of professional careers, but Flor has made the career of selling her own.

For several months in 1983 Flor sold meals in the town's new enclosed marketplace on market days, Thursdays and Sundays, although she finally gave up this operation when it became clear that the cavernous state-built edifice was drawing even fewer customers than used to come to the open-air market in front of the church. At the same time she continued, with greater success, to resell clothes that she bought in small quantities—but at a discount—in Mexico City. Teresita, meanwhile, continued to sell rice, *mole,* and soft drinks on market days, make tortillas for sale to other women in town, and cook meals for the occasional travelers who find themselves in Mexquitic at dinnertime. The money that Teresita made from these operations allowed her to maintain a certain degree of independence and, it seems, self-respect.

In this particular family the contribution of the children to the family economy was largely limited to helping Flor with her selling and Ramón with the pig-killing, and to helping around the house. They did not add as much to the family's income as children are expected to do in many rural families, where they are employed as part of the family labor force for working the family fields or for hiring themselves out as day laborers. Instead, Ramón and Flor decided to give their children a higher education, hoping that as professionals they would eventually contribute much more to the family than as untrained workers. For two years, while the older children were in high school and university in San Luis, this meant that the whole family uprooted themselves and moved to the city (except for Teresita, who stayed behind to keep watch over the family property), where they opened a small store. But the children graduated, and Teresita, who had long suffered from diabetes but would *not* give up her daily Coca Cola, died, leaving the property unwatched. The family moved back to Mexquitic, where Flor again began selling on market days, this time calling on her culinary skills to vend tacos, *gorditas,* and tortillas at an improvised stand in front of their house. Today the family investment in education is paying off. Aided by their lawyer daughter, Flor and Ramón have transformed the market-day taco stand into the first full-time restaurant in town, with panoramic windows that look out over the plaza, the parish church, and the mesquite-covered hills that surround the town.

LIVING FROM DAY TO DAY

If there is a sense of unsettledness and of making do in the recent life histories of Ramón and Flor, with their ability to juggle many roles, to switch rapidly from one occupation to another in a continuing effort to make good each opportunity as it comes, how much more does this sense pervade the lives of others, less well-off than they? Benito, a man with a short, wiry frame and a wispy mustache that covers his nervous smile, crouches slightly as he scrambles over a rocky slope from one short-term job to the next. Micaela, more sturdily built than her husband, nurses their latest baby under her rebozo as she flips an enchilada in the hot grease and calls out to a passing customer. How do they survive and keep themselves and their nine children clothed and fed?

Micaela, like Flor and indeed almost all married women in Mexquitic, lists her primary occupation on the census form as *hogar* (the home), but in her family the older children share much of the burden of doing house-work and raising the younger ones. Micaela herself helps her parents sell produce in San Luis, both what they grow on their own land and what they buy from other farmers, riding to the market early each morning on the back of her brother's old pickup. On market days in Mexquitic she can be found in her stall in the marketplace frying *enchiladas potosinas* by the heat of a charcoal brazier, hawking her food, soft drinks, and used comic books to passersby, while one of her daughters washes the plates in a corner.

Benito is an ejidatario, but unlike Ramón he would never consider renting out his plot to an outsider for cash. He and his family use it to grow food for their own consumption, mainly beans and the sweet, starchy local variety of white corn that everyone prefers to dry, flavorless yellow store-bought corn. It is unlikely that they would make enough money from renting out his plot to buy the same amount of basic food-stuffs that they now grow there. In any case, even now that it is no longer illegal to rent out ejido land, Benito still considers it immoral and is among the first to denounce what he sees as abuses of the system. In recent years Benito and Micaela have begun with some misgivings to grow small amounts of vegetables for sale in the city as well, an operation that only became feasible after Benito dug a well, installed a gas-powered pump on his field, and joined a small cooperative that shares a tractor. Their turning to exclusively commercial vegetable farming, as about half the ejidatarios of Mexquitic have done, would bring in more money, but it is still beyond their means. Lacking a truck to get the produce to market in San Luis and elsewhere, Micaela and Benito prefer to grow for sale only as much as they can carry to market on the bus. Growing vegetables only to sell them in the field to a truck owner would, again, leave their family short of corn and beans.

Even as it is, Benito and Micaela do not produce enough corn and beans on his ejido plot to feed their family for an entire year. As a member of the ejido community of Mexquitic, Benito is entitled to just a single hectare of irrigated land, and having even that has made him the object of the intense envy of a brother who felt he should have inherited the plot instead. Since Benito inherited no other land aside from the small lot where his adobe house stands (Micaela's parents are still alive and working their fields), he works in whatever jobs he can find as a day laborer (*peón, jornalero*). Yet it would be impossible for a family of eleven to live on the wages of a jornalero, about 2 to 4 dollars a day (300 pesos in 1983, 10 to 15 new pesos in 1993) for ten to twelve hours of work. It is this aspect of his life, more than any other, that gives it the character of living from day to day, and that makes all of Micaela and Benito's other economic activities necessary.

Benito is also involved in local politics, mainly from the sidelines, and is often seen listening to the conversations of the town leaders and would-be leaders, those better-off townspeople who gather in tight circles of two or three to speak in grave whispers about who should be the next municipal president, how the town should be run, or what improvements should be made. Benito's involvement in politics has yielded him a number of low-level, unpaid community positions such as *juez auxiliar* and *juez de aguas*. In 1984 he received the first position which might be considered a job rather than an honorary appointment, as the operator of the "CONASUPO del PRI" store that was installed in the marketplace next to Micaela's enchilada stall. Over the next two years Benito, Micaela, and their children spent many hours every day tending this store, though it was far from clear whether the scant 4 percent profit they were allowed to make from sales of CONASUPO goods was enough to compensate them for their labors. It is likely that Benito thought of his running the CONASUPO as much in political terms as in economic, perhaps looking forward to a day when his faithful support of the PRI and of the leading political faction in the town of Mexquitic would be rewarded with a higher position or a steady job.[6]

AMWAY DE MÉXICO, S.A. DE C.V.

In comparison with Benito and Micaela, or even with Ramón and Flor, Yolanda and Miguel appear as pillars of stability. Few families in Mexquitic seem as established as theirs. They live, with their unmarried children and Miguel's aging parents, in an imposingly tall two-story house that overlooks the neat garden and the municipal government buildings in the very center of the town. This house, reputedly the oldest in town, had been owned and perhaps built by Miguel's grandfather, a municipal president around the turn of the century who was later gunned down at its front door in the most violent local event of the Mexican Revolution. Yolanda and Miguel are both schoolteachers, as is their oldest daughter: three regular government paychecks back up their family finances. Miguel's father is also an ejidatario, while his mother is one of the largest landowners in town, having inherited the many fields of her assassinated father. Yolanda and Miguel's oldest son, who recently completed a degree in business administration, plans to begin running the family land, including the ejido plot, as an efficient business operation.

They are also involved in the life of the community, with a strong sense of civic responsibility. Miguel's mother donated the land that the primary school of the town was built on in the 1920s, when it moved from its earlier, depressing location in the old town jail. More recently she donated land for the town's new *colegio de bachilleres* (high school). Yolanda and Miguel's oldest daughter has thrown herself with a will into the mission of bringing education and medicine to the indigenous ethnic groups of the state of San Luis Potosí. (As for her own *etnia*, to use the current official term, she sees herself quite unproblematically as a mestiza.) Miguel himself is passionately interested in the old family business—municipal politics—though he has never considered running for office himself. A stint working in the fields of central California under the *bracero* program of the early 1960s gave Miguel as large a taste as he wanted of life in the United States; he considers himself Mexican in his very essence. He is quite an expert in the Mexican popular music that helped forge a common sense of national identity among the working and middle classes of Mexico in the 1940s and 50s, though lately the stereo speakers in the entranceway of the grand old house are more likely to be blasting East L.A. rap or Madonna.[7]

But for all their solidity as citizens of Mexquitic and of Mexico, the themes of struggling to make a living and to construct a world for themselves emerge in the life histories that Yolanda and Miguel tell about themselves.

Yolanda prides herself on being the first married woman in the town to undertake a professional career. At the time, some two decades ago, teaching was thought of as a profession for married men and unmarried women. But Miguel was floundering in agriculture, which did not hold much interest for him, and wondering whether another journey to California, this time as an undocumented worker, would be his only escape. Yolanda decided to take her family's fate in her own hands. In spite of the opposition of her husband, the admonitions of her parents-in-law, and the gossip of everyone in town, she completed the course at the state normal school and undertook an arduous year of teaching in an isolated community in the Sierra Gorda, with a newborn baby at her side. Finally her hard work and determination paid off with a permanent job in Mexquitic itself. When the checks began arriving Miguel repented of his earlier attitude and followed Yolanda into teaching himself. In the years following Yolanda's success, teaching became the career of choice for both men and women, married and unmarried, in the town of Mexquitic.

But the rapid inflation of the 1980s wiped out the security of a teaching position, as the purchasing value of government salaries fell by two-thirds. With more young children to feed and the older children ready to enter college, Yolanda turned for a time to supplementing her family's income by reselling clothes bought at a discount in Mexico City, just as Flor had. The front bedroom, where Miguel's grandmother had housed a general store years earlier, filled up with racks and bundles of clothes and a small but steady stream of customers. By 1991, after the partial legalization of contraband stores in San Luis brought in a flood of cheap clothes from across the border and undercut her prices, Yolanda had abandoned the reselling business. Her oldest daughter then took over the front room and turned it into an office supply store. With two copying machines (and plans for a fax machine sometime in the future) the store is always busy, bringing in a small additional income and, as the daughter is quick to point out, providing a necessary service for the town.

The most unexpected development in Yolanda and Miguel's search to broaden their family income came in 1993, when they became distributors of Amway products. More than that: they joined the Amway team with the zeal of converts. Nothing we knew about Yolanda and Miguel had quite prepared us for this latest turn in their lives. As they eagerly explained to us about their involvement in the company, and about the benefits they expected to derive from it, we began to see how it fit in with the route they have taken to constructing their world.

Amway is a Michigan-based marketing company that rewards its "members" through a complex system of rebates for products that they and the members of their "organizations" or "multiple distribution networks" buy from a central warehouse. As a retailing network, the company heavily emphasizes attitude and motivation as the primary keys to attaining one's goals. Training for members of the Amway team consists of reading inspirational books every week, listening daily to inspirational tapes, and attending weekly and monthly meetings that draw together all the Amway members in the region (formal dress requested) for an hour of inspirational talks. Here was a link, we thought, to Yolanda's view of life: she has long been drawing inspiration in her struggles to *superar*, to improve her life and that of her children, from the books of Og Mandino (*The Greatest Miracle in the World, The Greatest Salesman in the World,* and so on). On the main bookshelf in Yolanda and Miguel's house, North American self-help books (*"I Think I Can, I Know I Can!"; There's No Such Place as Far Away*), in Spanish translation, mingle easily with schoolbooks and publications of the Department of Public Education (*Elementary Chemistry; Teacher's Guide: Geography; Fruits and Vegetables: Nutritional Properties*). When we suggested this connection to Yolanda, she heartily agreed. It seemed to her that she had been preparing for Amway all her life.

Still, as we heard Miguel praise the high quality of the Amway products (many of them pointedly "made in America"), and as we sat, entranced, through the hour-long pep talk that Yolanda gives to prospective new "members," I struggled to reconcile their Mexican nationalism with their deep involvement in a company whose very name is an acronym for "the American Way." In its values, goals, and methods, I cannot help finding Amway essentially "American"—which is to say, United States middle-class. The keystone of the ideology that the company follows and propounds is, like that of middle-class life, to deny what Foster called the logic of limited good. Or rather, in the positive terms that the company itself sets out, it is to affirm that everyone, with enough hard work and a positive attitude, can attain the American dream. Indeed, the "dream" is the key image used in the talks given for Amway. In her talk, Yolanda told us that everyone had a dream. Hers was to provide a better life for her children; her daughter's was to find a way to serve the poor children of Mexquitic. Amway, she said with great conviction, was the way to fulfill those dreams.

At the weekly meeting that we attended in San Luis, the main speaker took on the theme of the American dream directly, claiming it as a universal birthright, a right of Mexicans. When you try to involve people in Amway by speaking of dreams, he said, "they might criticize you by saying that's the American dream. But I ask you, can only Americans dream?" When I later asked Miguel how he reconciled his participation in this U.S. company with his Mexicanness, he called on this theme of universality. He did not see Amway as either Mexican or American, but as international and as the wave of the future.

Nevertheless, I did come to see how people such as Yolanda and Miguel used the organizational and ideological tools of Amway de México, S.A. de C.V., as well as the income it promises them, within the context of their lives in Mexquitic and their sense of self. The company employs the rhetoric of "helping" to refer to the way that members make money from the sales of other members below them in their "organizations": by involving others in Amway, you are not trying to make money off of them but to help them to achieve their dreams, just as they help you to achieve yours. This rhetoric seems to key into the emphasis on charity and civic involvement that characterizes Yolanda and Miguel's family. Beyond that, it serves to distance the activity of marketing Amway products from the individualistic money-grubbing commonly felt to characterize human relations in the United States. "Helping," putting the welfare of others on an equal footing with making money for oneself, is somehow "Mexican." Similarly, the inspirational books and the revival-style weekly meetings of Amway can seem very "Mexican" if they are seen in the religious context that I find them tapping into. In this way they provide a kind of rationalist alternative to the images, candles, and scapularies, the shrines, *cofradías,* and *centros* of Mexican religious culture. Or rather, they form one more of the many alternate paths, methods, goals, and interpretations that lie just under the surface of the superficially uniform Catholicism of Mexico.[8]

I also see the organizational structure of Amway being used to face, rethink, and reconstruct notions of social organization. Rural Mexico is striking for the formalism and hierarchy of its social relations. This sense of hierarchy might have its historical roots in the rigid structures of colonial Mexican society, in which class barriers were legally defined in the idiom of *casta* or race, and perhaps more distantly in the formalism of pre-Hispanic Central Mexican society. With its titles and levels of salesmanship, based on monthly sales figures, from simple member to Direct Distributor, Pearl, Emerald, and Diamond, Amway combines a penchant for hierarchy with an absolute insistence that ultimately all have an equal chance to reach the top. Anyone entering the organization at any time can climb to "Diamond" with sufficient work and determination. In other words, as Yolanda insisted, anyone, rich or poor, is equally welcome and able to triumph in Amway; it has no room for class differences—the corporation does away with them. And with them go the inherited, unerasable, castelike distinctions of race, abolished forever.

Amway also provides a structure for redefining gender roles and relations along middle-class lines. The company defines its "memberships" as familial, Yolanda explained to us. It insists, whenever possible, on the participation of both wives and husbands as equal partners. This reworking of marital relations was particularly congenial to Yolanda, revalidating as it does the story that she has told of her own life. In her Amway talk, Yolanda told us how much she prized the fact that she has always been the woman who had broken barriers and introduced new ways of doing things to Mexquitic. Just as she was the first married woman in town to get a degree and leave the house to work, she was the first in town to listen to the visionary message of Amway. When her husband opposed getting involved with what he saw as a frivolous and risky venture, Yolanda declared that she was going to go on with it, with or without him. Eventually Miguel came around, as he earlier had with her decision to pursue a career. Now she has been followed into Amway by the same group, by and large, of professional women, with their partners, who followed her into teaching. In this way, Yolanda feels, she is simultaneously constructing her own life and playing an important role in constructing the collective world of Mexquitic.

THE STRATA OF MEXQUITIC

These thumbnail sketches of the recent life histories of Flor and Ramón, Benito and Micaela, and Yolanda and Miguel illustrate the scope of possibilities open to townspeople in their struggle to make a living. They do not represent typical Mexquitic lives, not even within their respective social strata. Few people in Mexquitic employ themselves in quite as many different tasks, or switch their occupations quite as readily, as does Ramón, whose range of occupations is especially atypical of the higher social stratum in Mexquitic to which he aspires. Most of the handful of better-off families in the town employ themselves almost exclusively in agriculture and commerce. More precisely, the men of these households attend to commercial vegetable, stock, and dairy farming (on a fairly small scale by any but Mexquitic standards) and to marketing their produce in San Luis and perhaps Monterrey, while many of the women run small general stores in the front rooms of their houses.[9] Another group within the higher strata are the professionals, almost all of them schoolteachers like Yolanda and Miguel, whose regular salaries spare them the day-to-day search for work of the jornalero. Many schoolteachers are originally from better-off agricultural (and political) families, and even after the decline of the peso in the 1980s their salaries contribute to the economic stability of these families.

At the other end of the social scale are those who lack any land at all, whether ejido or private, who are not employed as schoolteachers or, say, as nightwatchmen, and who do not have the skills of the albañil, which might raise them economically and socially to a kind of middle level. These are the men who live "del puro jornal," just from day labor, and the women who work in the kitchens of other women to prepare *mole* for a baptism feast or who go out twice daily to collect maguey juice for fermenting into *pulque,* which they sell on market days on the slope behind the marketplace. Benito and Micaela are just a notch above this social level, because of his ejido plot and political connections, though in many respects Benito's life is that of a jornalero.

The very poorest are the old men and women, married or widowed, with no children living in town. They have no electricity in their jacales or one-room houses, and they eat little—the stereotypical meal of the elderly poor is *coca y bolillo,* Coca Cola and white bread—so their expenses are few. Too old for day labor, they live perhaps from selling pulque and *tunas* (prickly pears), from a little begging, or from small remittances that relatives send them. When we asked one such woman how she lived, she replied: "Yo vivo nada más de la voluntad de Dios" (I just live from God's good will).

The main marker of higher social status for a man in Mexquitic is the word "don," which under certain circumstances can be added before his given name. The female equivalent, "doña," is perhaps more ambivalent, since it is often used, either politely or euphemistically, for women of low status, at times with no name attached ("¡Oye, doña!" [Hey, lady!]). Other markers of status, for women and men alike, include the use of "usted," the formal way of saying "you," which contrasts with "tú," the informal "you" that is used to address social equals, inferiors, and younger persons (though very young children are often called "usted," as if to teach them to speak with respect).

Pedro and a companion once told us, as we joined them for a round of beers in the cool of a small store, that the criterion for being a "don" was simple: if you owned a car or truck, you were a "don"; otherwise, you were just "tú." This was, of course, a great simplification, though it holds a grain of truth. Car owners, for the most part, are schoolteachers, and most trucks are owned by the better-off families who work their own land and market their own produce. But Pedro and his friend told us this "rule" with a heavy dose of irony. Their irony was directed, in the first instance, toward us, the North American ethnographers whose social status and whose car both derived more from the economic hegemony of our country than from our own personal merit. Secondly, it was addressed towards themselves, truck owners and successful farmers who were not universally known as "don," in large part because they had a reputation of being heavy drinkers, a trait associated with lower social status. Also, a few men who are commonly called "don" do not own cars or trucks, in some cases because they are too old to learn to drive, in others because they are not in an economic position to buy one—for social status depends on more than money.

Calling a man "don" in Mexquitic can indicate a number of things: that he is relatively better off economically than you; that, even if he is not considered rich, he is at least a self-employed farmer and is not forced to search for day labor to make ends meet; that he is older; probably that you were not in the same school class together (for that would automatically put the two of you on a *tú* basis, and you would call him by a nickname); perhaps that he is an excellent orator and thus is actively sought for public or ejido office. If he is commonly known as "don," he will probably follow a certain life-style, which includes avoiding public drunkenness except on the most festive occasions, keeping the women in his family from working in the fields (housework, selling, and professional work are acceptable), having fewer and more widely spaced children, and making an effort to send all his children to school to learn a profession.

It is difficult to get a precise idea of the historical depth of this life-style or of the distinction between what we might call "don" and "tú" status. To the extent that the "don" life-style is clearly and self-consciously modeled on the perceived life-style of the middle classes in San Luis and in the United States, and that it goes together with building a new-style house for one's family, and with owning a car or truck, it is of course a recent phenomenon. Not many years ago, for example, having a large family was a sign of high status, as only a well-off family could feed and clothe a large number of children; the children, in turn, were expected to contribute to the family economy, thus maintaining their family status. Thus in 1983 there were few women in Mexquitic over the age of forty-five who had less than six living children and a number who had ten or more. Since then, however, the situation has reversed, in one of the most important demographic shifts in recent Mexican history. As schooling has become both available and necessary for maintaining status, having many children has become a drain rather than an asset, especially for the upwardly mobile family. Today there are scarcely any families in Mexquitic with more than five children, as the norm has dropped from eight children in the 1970s to three or four today, and perhaps soon to two.[10]

But this high-status life-style is also self-consciously modeled as a re-action to the perceived life-style of the rural poor in Mexquitic. Higher and lower social status in a local community are defined relative to one another, with constant reference to standards imposed from outside the community and mediated, generally, by the local elite. The "modern" life-style of the higher-status families, though manifestly recent, is thus but the latest development in a tradition of distinguishing the elite in re-lation to the rest of society in Mexquitic. Early in the colonial period, for example, there may have been a distinction between a bilingual, Spanish-speaking elite and the Nahuatl-speaking masses. In this sense the links between education and the elite may go back to the origins of the educa-tional system of Mexquitic in the Franciscan *doctrina*, the daily catechism classes that all parish children were theoretically obliged to attend (*doctrina* also meant, by extension, an Indian parish as a whole). As early as 1680 the bishop of Michoacán, in his *visita* to Mexquitic, "attended the doc-trina of the children and ordered that they be taught in Castilian, and that the Padre who was Guardian and Minister should not permit them to talk except in Castilian." [11] The elite of the pueblo henceforth communicated with the state exclusively in Spanish, serving as their own translators. In the bishop's brief decree we see summed up the links between educa-tion, the state—as represented by the religious arm of the colonializing power—and the local elite, which mediates between the colonizers and the colonized. We might also see here the beginnings of an elite identity as "ladino" (originally meaning "bilingual") rather than non-Spanish speaking, which would later be transformed into "mestizo" rather than "Indian."

In the colonial era the local elites played a key social role as mediators with the Spanish elites of the broader class system. The question of whether they were awarded elite status because of their mediating role, or whether they served as local "culture brokers" because they were already recognized as the elite, must be set aside here as a historical imponderable. It would be tempting, for instance, to link the twentieth-century Vásquez political clan with the sixteenth-century don Francisco Vásquez Coro-nado, the first Tlaxcalan governor of Mexquitic and the only founder of the town called "don," indicating a strong link to the pre-Hispanic no-bility. Yet there is little evidence of a direct connection, for of thirty-eight known governors of Mexquitic between 1714 and 1820 only one was named Vásquez (compared with eight Hernández, five López, seven with assorted surnames, and seventeen with no surname at all). The key point, however, is what Lockhart calls "the persistence of an upper group" in colonial Nahua towns: "Despite all the loss, transformation, and renaming, late colonial Indian towns still had a mainly hereditary minority group, of greater wealth, prestige, and education than most." [12] In Mexquitic as in central Mexico, the distinction between elite and nonelite is clearly present at every historical stage, even though it cannot be discerned in any given case whether the personal genealogy of the elite extends back to the early history of the town, and beyond that, to the pre-Hispanic nobility of Tlaxcala.

In the early colonial period the elite of Mexquitic mediated between the pueblo and the colonial elites as translators and interpreters. By the eighteenth century, when fluency in Spanish was almost universal in Mexquitic, literacy seems to have been the main status marker that set off the political elite of the pueblo, all of whom could at least sign their names and some of whom could write fluidly in Spanish, from the vast illiterate majority.[13] They now mediated as scribes and readers. As literacy in turn became widespread by the late nineteenth century, the distinction between high and low status might have been maintained by clothing style, by building great houses such as that of Miguel's grandfather, and by continuing to emphasize education, that key link between local society and the state that is theoretically open to all and in practice is limited to those who tear themselves away from the life-style of the poor.

These outward shibboleths of status have shifted or fallen one by one, yet the ranking continues. At some point early in this century (probably in the 1920s, though no one remembers when), the government in San Luis made it a misdemeanor to appear in the city wearing the standard garb of rural men. The plain shirts and trousers of rough white *manta* (a bleached canvaslike cloth) held up with a wide red scarf (*paño*), which once had been the outfit of the mestizo, had become the stereotyped male uniform of the "indio" by the time of the Revolution. City leaders expressed their desire to remove all traces of the Indian past by outlawing it. At first, the few men of Mexquitic who owned "real" pants and shirts could profit by renting their clothes to other men who had to go to the city for the day on business. Eventually the phrase "vestido de manta," dressed in manta, came to be a metaphor for having a backward, "Indian" mentality, but no one actually wore manta any longer. Other shibboleths had to be invented.

The stereotype of the man of lower social status held in Mexquitic is that he is hardworking but prone to bouts of drinking and fighting, squanders his money, and makes no plans for the future. He has many children, not to educate them so they will rise ahead in the future but so that they can be put to work as soon as possible. There are, of course, many living contradictions to this negative stereotype. Benito, for instance, scrupulously avoids drunkenness, has tried (so far with little success) to establish himself as a master of public oratory, and does not squander his money but is nevertheless treated as having lower social status. In his case, the facts that he must work as a day laborer, that he has many children, and that he has not yet been able to give them a proper education have been enough to negate his sobriety, his political aspirations, and his hard work, and even to negate the *quince años* party he threw for his oldest daughter.

In the case of Pedro, it is the reverse. His frequent drinking bouts, the fact that his wife works hard in the fields and that he often makes his children leave school early to work as well, and his general inattention to his children's future all negate his own hard work, his truck, the house he is building, his business acumen, and his never having been a day laborer. His lack of standing among the elite of Mexquitic is something he is acutely aware of. Have we not noticed, he asked, how the town divides when there are parties, how some people get invited to a fiesta and others aren't let into the house? Pedro has often expressed his anger at what he sees as the hypocrisy of the elite families. When one of the elite criticized him for drinking too much, he would respond by criticizing the elite for their miserliness. It just upsets them to see a poor person enjoying himself, Pedro told us. Look at Mundo: with all his money, he doesn't even know how to live, but he criticizes me for enjoying the little that I have, for drinking, for throwing a party and inviting all my friends. Pedro feels he has made a conscious decision to live as he does and that he should be accepted on his own terms. (Perhaps to prove that he did have control over his own life, Pedro swore off drinking altogether in 1992 after realizing that his occasional bouts of drunkenness were becoming a drain on the family economy.) At a party at Pedro's house, when someone asked us why we had not had any children yet, Pedro interrupted to answer for us: "Don't worry, they're just 'waiting.' First they'll finish school, then they'll get jobs, and *then* they will have children—but just two." The life-style of the elite—and of the ethnographers—was one that Pedro understood perfectly well, and rejected.

A WORLD IN CONSTRUCTION

The system of social stratification, as rigid and stifling as it can at times appear, cannot be taken as a given. Like so much else in Mexquitic, it is a world in continual construction. The distinctions between social strata are constantly being negotiated. We have seen a hint of this in Benito's attempts to insinuate himself into a higher social stratum; in the ambiguous social positions of Ramón and Pedro; even in Yolanda's turn to the teaching profession, which redefined the life possibilities for married women of higher status, as she took it upon herself to maintain her family's economic standing.

I have written here of social strata, rather than social class, because the status groups I have described do not in fact form classes in the usual sense of the term. The distinctions of social status I have presented do derive from people's positions in the local rural economy of Mexquitic. But that economy, and thus the entire status system of Mexquitic, is embedded within a regional and a national economic system. It is at those levels that true class differences emerge. The class differences between an ejidatario and part-time jornalero like Benito and an ejidatario, farmer, and part-time jack-of-all-trades like Ramón look insignificant to a banker or government functionary from the city of San Luis or from Mexico City. Yet it is his potential for forming contacts with the functionary classes (and now his children's entrance into the ranks of those classes) that gives Ramón the potential for higher status. He shores up that status by living a life-style that mimics, with a few key signs such as his sprawling multibedroom house, that of the urban professional class.

An increasingly common way in which people negotiate their position in the status system is by redefining their relation to the broader economy and in effect opting out of the local system of stratification altogether. Thus many people who live in Mexquitic now have stronger ties with the economy of urban Mexico, or that of the United States, than they do with that of rural San Luis Potosí. Some of these people, particularly schoolteachers, are indeed accorded a high status by other townspeople. The fact that this status is based on criteria external to the local economy, though, is recognized in the fact that they are referred to by the titles "profesor" or "maestro" (teacher) rather than "don." Indeed many teachers, especially the younger ones, do not otherwise take part in the stratification system. They are educated and own cars, but they hold parties and get drunk much as Pedro once did, and they do not follow distinctions based on social position when they choose their friends and drinking partners or organize their basketball teams.

Others who have found employment outside of the local economy, those with jobs in San Luis or with money from past work in the United

States, are even more anomalous in terms of the stratification system. They have money, usually enough to build a good house and often enough to buy a television, a stereo system, and sometimes a car or truck as well. Yet in their work "on the other side" they are basically employed as peones in jobs that would bring them very low status if they were part of the local economy. In fact many of these people eventually use the money they have earned to reenter the local economy on a higher level, as truck-owning commercial farmers. Others eventually leave to take up permanent residence in the city. But those who have not taken one or the other of these two paths—firmly in or firmly out of the local system— cannot, meanwhile, be accommodated in any given social strata. The anomalous position of these workers and schoolteachers is compounded by the fact that they come from families in every range of the status hierarchy, high and low. Since they generally contribute to their family economies, their social status and that of their families become intertwined.

The distinction between "high" and "low" social strata is an open secret in Mexquitic. Open because the distinction is visible, palpable, in the ways people treat and refer to each other; secret because it is denied or occulted by almost everyone in the town. Some—those on the bottom of the social scale—recognize the distinction but resist making it themselves and resist having it applied to them. More than once, when we were being introduced to a stranger by the head of one of the poorer households, they graciously showed their approval of us by saying that "ellos no distinguen" (they make no distinctions). That is, we spent our time as readily with the poorer families as with the elite. Pedro resented the fact that the elite do not treat him as an equal because he refuses to play by their rules. As he caustically pointed out, it is the families of the elite who limit their invitations to those of their own closed circles when they have a party. The poor invite everyone.

Others, those struggling to get to or stay at the top, will confirm with the certainty of an urban middle class that there is no real stratification in Mexquitic. We have seen how Amway has provided Yolanda and Miguel with a framework for asserting the potential of unlimited social mobility for all. Their daughter has told us with a shudder of the profound social inequality in the neighboring town of Ahualulco. When we noted that there was a hint of a status system in Mexquitic itself (indeed, that her own family employs servants from the poorer families in town), she protested that there was no comparison. In Mexquitic, she said (contradicting

Pedro), everyone invites everyone else to parties, while in Ahualulco the rich do not even deign to speak to the poor.

And in the lives both of those at the bottom and of those not quite at the top, one finds the houses half-built, the scrambling for a living, the children, the fiestas—the world that is Mexquitic ever coming into being.

THREE   # Founding Mexquitic

Mexquitic was founded in 1591, at the close of the Chichimeca War, to help secure the north for New Spain. In recognition of its early front-line position, Mexquitic was given the twin titles of *pueblo y frontera,* town and borderland, by which it was known for more than two centuries. Even though the line of Spanish settlement had moved far beyond Mexquitic by the end of the 1500s, as an enduring Tlaxcalan society amid an expanding hacienda economy it remained a kind of borderland well into the years when memory of the war of Spaniards and Central Mexicans against the northern nomads had receded into the semi mythical past.

THE EARLY HISTORY: PUEBLO Y FRONTERA

Spaniards had begun moving north from central Mexico in search of mineral wealth in the 1540s.[1] Their search brought them into arid mountain and grassland areas occupied by diverse bands of hunter-gatherers, whom the Spaniards collectively called Chichimecas, following Central Mexican usage. A long and bloody conflict followed this invasion, reaching a destructive crescendo in the 1580s. Nomads from across the northeast were drawn to a growing traffic of mule trains and caravans that supplied food and clothing to the fabulous mines of Zacatecas (discovered 1546) and Guanajuato (1552), returning to Mexico City laden with silver. Deadly nomadic raids on the silver highway were countered by underpaid Spanish soldiers who sought their fortunes, or just made ends meet, by capturing and enslaving entire bands of "wild Indians." Paying little regard to

whether their captives had personally taken part in the warfare, the soldiers succeeded only in provoking retaliatory Chichimeca raids, which in
turn justified further Spanish slaving incursions (*entradas*). The soldiers
sold captive Chichimecas to newly wealthy miners (for a fraction of the
price set on the lives of enslaved Africans) to be set to work in their mines
and on land they were beginning to claim and convert to ranches and
wheat fields.[2]

Between 1546 and 1591 the cycle of deceits, provocations, and reprisals
known as the Chichimeca War became a cruel way of life on the northern
frontier. Over the same decades the lands of the Chichimecas were quietly
invaded by new occupants—not Spaniards but the cattle they had introduced to the Americas, running wild from herds established in central
Mexico. By the 1570s wild Spanish cows and horses in the hundreds of
thousands roamed the Bajío or flatlands around Guanajuato. Following
the cattle came Spanish ranchers, who were quick to claim them and the
lands they grazed on, eager to profit from the sale of their hides and tallow,
and outraged by Chichimeca raids on "their" cattle and "their" lands—
incursions that they denounced in strident terms as early as 1582.[3]

By then the Crown, which had let the war fester for decades, was
caught between the intractable resistance of the hunter-gatherers to further Spanish expansion, foot-dragging by the free-lance soldiers who prof-
ited from selling captive Indians into slavery, and the demands of the new
and growing interest group of Spanish cattle ranchers to pacify their new
pasturelands whatever the cost. Towards 1590 the viceroy of New Spain
at last overturned the unofficial and unsuccessful policy of dealing with
the infidels by mass murder and mass enslavement. Ignoring the advice of
the ranchers, who supported a genocidal war of extermination against the
nomads as a reasonable alternative to enslaving them, he implemented a
more generous policy of accommodation and co-optation. Within a decade the frontier was pacified and Spanish control established as far north
as Saltillo and Monterrey.

The peace was gained by tempting the many Chichimeca *naciones*
("nations" or language groups) into congregated settlements with the offer of gifts of food and clothing—bait to lure them away from a life-style
that Spanish officials found both morally repugnant and economically incompatible with their own plans for expansion. Peace was further secured
by founding alongside each new Chichimeca settlement a pueblo of
"civilized" agriculturalist Indians from the Central Mexican province of
Tlaxcala, an early ally of Spain in the conquest of Mexico. In exchange
for the risky service to the Crown that the Tlaxcalan settlers were to per-

form, the viceroy drew up a list of promised privileges. The Tlaxcalan settlers in the north and their descendents would have the status of *hidalgos,* lower nobility free of paying taxes or tribute "in perpetuity" and at liberty to carry arms and to ride saddled horses, privileges denied to most Indians under colonial rule. No Spaniards would be granted encomiendas here, and the Tlaxcalans' fields would be free from any form of Spanish encroachment. Best of all, land would be plentiful—three leagues (twelve and a half kilometers) in every direction, to be measured from the doors of the parish churches they would build.[4]

Half a dozen new Tlaxcalan pueblos were founded in the Chichimeca heartland in 1591, the year of the peace. Chief among them was the pueblo and frontera of San Miguel Mezquitic de la Nueva Tlaxcala Tepeticpac, guardian of the northern peace and guarantor of the warlike Guachichiles, fiercest of the Chichimeca nations, as the Mexquitic elite would endlessly remind colonial officials.[5] At a ceremony in the valley of Mexquitic on November 2, 1591, witnessed by three Franciscan friars and chronicled by a Spanish scribe, the Guachichil captain Juan Tenzo gave thanks to the viceroy of New Spain for sending the Tlaxcalans, "their kin and relatives," to teach the Guachichiles "to live like men of Reason." And in his capacity as "the natural lord of these parts," Juan Tenzo made King Philip of Spain the lord of all the Guachichil territory and asked the viceregal envoy (the Tlaxcalan mestizo historian Diego Muñóz Camargo) to officially divide that same territory between the Guachichiles and the Tlaxcalans.[6]

The next two centuries brought, for the most part, slow and steady growth for Mexquitic—the Tlaxcalan pueblo, that is. The Guachichiles, whose peace and tranquility the Tlaxcalans guaranteed, had dwindled away entirely by 1700, all dead of imported diseases or gone to work in Spanish towns and mines far from the unaccustomed tedium of agriculture.[7] The social landscape in and around the pueblo was meanwhile filled in. The Tlaxcalans interpreted the viceregal concessions literally and marked out a nearly perfect circle, three leagues in radius from the door of the parish church, as the land of Mexquitic. They undoubtedly understood the Spanish word "pueblo" in classic Central Mexican style as referring to an *altepetl* (ethnic state), rather than to a compact, almost urban settlement surrounded by fields and a hinterland of woods, as the word implies in Spain.

Thus, as the pueblo grew, household groups founded ranchos throughout its territory rather than remaining in the small settlement around the Franciscan church, which Spanish officials or priests occasionally tried to treat as the head town (*cabecera*) that it only became after Independence. With time the ranchos coalesced into semi-autonomous communities themselves, in a process that reduplicated the Nahua division of altepetl into component parts. The hints of this division during the colonial years are vague, yet immediately after Independence in 1821 the northeastern section of the newly formed municipality of Mexquitic was already divided into the *cuarteles* (quarters) of Corte and Palmar, each with their own *alcalde de cuartel* (neighborhood magistrate). By the middle of the century Mexquitic had emerged with a full-blown sectional organization of fourteen *fracciones* (fractions).[8]

And the pueblo did grow. The descendents of the hundred Tlaxcalan settlers of Mexquitic in 1591 swelled to a thousand one century later, and more than eight thousand in 1792 (see appendix A).[9] The region grew as well. Soon after Indians from Mexquitic found gold in the hills twenty miles to the east in the summer of 1592, the area was overrun with migrants from central Mexico—Tarascans, Mexicanos, Otomís, and Spaniards both rich and poor with their servants and dependents—all drawn by the silver of the new Potosí, as it was called in hopeful imitation of the Andean mountain of silver. Some of the interlopers were drawn to the mines themselves, but the lack of water drove most into the valley just to the southwest of Mexquitic, where the new Spanish settlement of San Luis sprang up almost overnight, displacing Mexquitic's twin pueblo of Tlaxcalilla in the process. Tlaxcalilla in turn usurped a small slice of the new territory of Mexquitic, and if anyone had been paying attention at the time, they might have seen in these displacements an early indication of the fact that the solemn grants made in perpetuity to the Tlaxcalan settlers were but writing on paper, easily forgotten in the face of power.

Land lying west and north of the circular district of Mexquitic was soon doled out by the viceregal government to men of wealth or influence residing in the city of San Luis. The largest estate handed out in this way, the hacienda of La Parada, went to the first governor of the region, who died childless in 1617. His widow sold the estate in 1623 to the Jesuit order, which was looking for a profitable enterprise to support their recently opened college in San Luis.[10] Other San Luis Spaniards did not wait for royal grants but fanned out across the emptied countryside looking for well-watered spots for founding ore-processing plants and stands of trees to reduce to charcoal for the mines. Their carboneras dotted the woods that still separated Mexquitic from San Luis Potosí in the first century after the towns were founded.

Mexquitic was now at the center of a small archipelago of Indian pue-

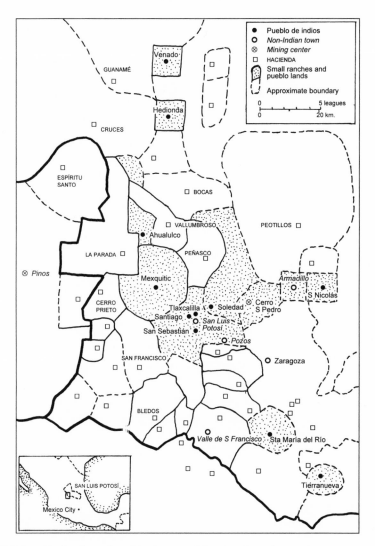

MAP 2.   Haciendas and pueblos in central San Luis Potosí around 1890

blos and barrios in a sea of Spanish ranches, haciendas, and mines
(map 2).[11] The Tlaxcalan settlers were remarkably successful in defending
their privilege of keeping non-Indians from residing or owning property
in the insular pueblos after the first wave of charcoal-makers had passed. In
the 1640s, under the leadership of their Franciscan friars, they expelled the
strangers working carboneras in the midst of the pueblo and reclaimed
ownership over the larger ranches on its edges that had been established

by such middle-level Spanish elites as the notary public Pedro Díaz del Campo and the deputy constable Francisco Díaz del Campo. These they turned into community-owned rental properties, which brought a steady income to the pueblo and maintained a certain formal distance between the Tlaxcalans and the colonial Spanish world of northern New Spain. But that success did not make Mexquitic a "region of refuge" isolated from Spanish and other non-Tlaxcalan influences. Ironically, the Tlaxcalans had been in intimate contact with the Spanish world since their arrival, and if they were able to expel the charcoal-makers that was because they had already learned that technology and were in a position to take over the charcoal market themselves. Knowledge of Spanish ways and the Spanish language was already widespread by the time an expanding population allowed the Tlaxcalans, who continued to speak Nahuatl at home until the 1840s, to solidify community control over resources. In the eighteenth century, the pueblo became more Indian than it had been earlier, but it was an Indianness deeply imbued with the Spanish-Indian ways of the colonial north.[12]

In the end it was the very ease with which outsiders could come to Mexquitic and buy, sell, or recruit labor, then return at night to the relative comfort of San Luis or move on to peddle in the next town that kept resident Spaniards and *castas* (people of "mixed race") from the town. For the most part, it was the Tlaxcalans who left their town for everyday encounters with the Spanish and casta world of colonial Mexico, selling charcoal and buying corn in San Luis and selling produce or looking for day labor on ranches and haciendas. When serious crimes were committed in the pueblo they were reported by the indigenous government to the "alcalde mayor" (chief magistrate) in the city, or on rare occasions to his commissioner (*comisario, comisionado*) in the hacienda of Bocas, north of Mexquitic. The alcalde mayor imposed Spanish *tenientes* (lieutenants) to oversee the governments of the other Indian pueblos and barrios under his jurisdiction in the wake of a regional rebellion in 1767.[13] The comisario of Bocas then began styling himself "teniente of the pueblo of Mexquitic and the district of Las Bocas," though he did not move into the town and his effect on its daily life was apparently minimal.[14]

After the parish was secularized (friars replaced by parish priests) in 1769, the rule against resident non-Indians was violated on still very rare occasions. Where the Franciscans had formed a closed, self-sufficient society, living two or three at a time in their friary without retainers, priests tended to bring in a small retinue of family members, servants, and friends. Among the latter were the two Spanish shop owners (and their families)

known to have lived in Mexquitic. Don Francisco Sánchez de Bustamante, who had lived with his extended family at the hacienda of Cerro
Prieto from at least 1775, rented a storefront in the late 1770s. Years later
his sons, who were "raised in this Pueblo since they were small, and in-
structed in its oldest customs" but had long since moved to San Luis,
served as comisionados overseeing pueblo elections when the priest was
forbidden to do so in person.

Don Agustín Navedo apparently took the rare move of moving to the
pueblo when he was named teniente de justicia ordinario around 1788.
He opened a shop, became a close friend and compadre of the priest José
Ignacio Lozano, who described him as "the only Spanish citizen of this
pueblo," and remained in Mexquitic until his death at the age of sixty-
two in 1821. (An indication of his commercial activity appears in
appendix C.) Finally, in 1783 a schoolmaster, José Manuel López García,
was sent by the alcalde mayor to teach the children of Mexquitic. The
teacher stayed for five years, after which (as he wrote years later) he "abandoned that Ministry because [he] had been offered a better destiny," but
he had meanwhile married into the Indian elite of the town and remained
interested in its affairs. On the other hand, not even the parish priests
remained in Mexquitic as they were expected to do; they were occasionally accused of living and enjoying life in the Spanish town and coming in
to Mexquitic only to say Mass on Sunday mornings, if then.[15]

The main interactions between the Tlaxcalans of Mexquitic and
Spanish-Mexican society came outside of the pueblo, where they went to
work or to sell their products. Some people—probably those living
around Picacho—specialized in making pottery for sale in San Luis. Elsewhere people dedicated themselves to cutting firewood, making charcoal,
gathering hay, or the repeatedly prohibited manufacture of mescal, all
likewise in order to provision the city and the mines. The voracious ap-
petite of city and mine for wood and charcoal, together with the sheep
and goats introduced from Spain and tended by herders in Mexquitic,
gradually devoured the oak and pine stands that once covered the south-
ern half and transformed the local ecology. By 1819 there were over
2,400 craftsmen (*artesanos*) compared with 3,300 subsistence corn farmers,
though as in the present the boundary between the two groups was probably very porous. And 480 donkeys were employed by hundreds of *arrieros*
(mule drivers) to take their firewood, charcoal, and coarse cloths and rope
to the city and to bring back "their corn from wherever they can find it
when it is lacking."[16]

People also crossed the border of Mexquitic to work in the Spanish haciendas and ranches that sprang up just beyond the three-league limit. These haciendas, which came to include a section adjacent to La Parada that the pueblo itself rented out annually to satisfy tribute obligations, belonged to the parish and the political jurisdiction of Mexquitic but were not considered part of the pueblo proper. The Tlaxcalans, "sons of the pueblo," were likewise seen by hacienda administrators as strangers on hacienda land even if they spent most of their lives living and working there. Unlike hacienda residents, who could rise to be supervisors or household help, sons of the pueblo were limited to minimally paid, back-breaking seasonal labor in the fields. And they were liable for deportation back to Mexquitic if they made trouble or if administrators simply decided they had too many workers.

No uprisings are recorded for Mexquitic during its first two centuries of existence. Not even the rebellion of 1767 affected this pueblo. That near-insurrection took as its excuse the expulsion of the Jesuit order from New Spain, but for the people of Mexquitic the Jesuits were simply the local hacienda owners. Far from rebelling, throughout these centuries the people of Mexquitic were prompt to invoke their descent from the "noble Tlaxcalans," the Spaniards' first allies, in all their dealings with Spanish officials. This tactic did not always bring them success. For instance, they lost a small but fertile section of their land to La Parada despite a lawsuit supported by their Franciscan priests in 1640 and were compensated only by an annual *censo* (rent) of seventy-five pesos; in 1712 royal officials revoked one of their most important privileges, their exemption from paying tribute to the Crown.[17]

As the memory of the Chichimeca War faded, and as the surviving Chichimecas themselves died out, the status of the Tlaxcalans of Mexquitic slowly declined. The image that their leaders promoted of themselves as a civilizing influence, a people whose Catholic faith and whose *policía humana* would bring reason to the wild Chichimecas, lost currency in the Spanish world of colonial San Luis. By 1736 the Franciscan historian Arlegui was able to write of the Tlaxcalans of San Luis Potosí that "although they have some civilization [*política*], there is still much barbarity in those of this province, and no rational style."[18] This was not yet a universal opinion at the time Arlegui wrote. Just a year earlier, during the official *visita* of 1735, the chief magistrate of San Luis congratulated the leaders of Mexquitic on the "good conduct and governance" of the pueblo, and described the Indians there as "very subdued [*reducidos*] and urbane, obedient to the precepts of justice, occupied in the labors that are theirs according to the customs of this pueblo, living moderately without getting drunk or taking mistresses." [19]

The written statements of Arlegui and of the alcalde mayor belonged to the realm of elite ideologies of the Indian. By "ideology" I mean a fairly reasoned and coherent justification of a particular group's view of the social world—in this case, a justification by the colonial elite of the relation between themselves, native peoples, and the colonial project. The reasoning involved in formulating an ideology is often stated in an "argument of images" or a "syllogism of association" rather than in formal terms, especially when expressed by people who feel no intellectual or legal need to justify themselves, and in situations where social reality and ideology largely overlap. [20] Some colonial ideologues, like Arlegui, represented Indians as barbarians, while others saw them as civilizing influences on others yet more savage, as did the alcalde mayor. But all unquestioningly placed the Indian at the bottom of society, as servants of the colony under the eternal tutelage of the elite. And such was both the legal and the actual position of native people. In a note tacked to the door of the magistrate of the Central Mexican town of Tamatlán in 1777, an irate anonymous writer elaborated the Spanish proverb *El mono vestido de seda, mono se queda* (roughly, "You can't make a silk purse out of a sow's ear") into a semicoherent allegory that expressed the anti-Indian racism of isolated local Spaniards; it is cited by William Taylor:

> The monkey, even dressed in silk, is still a monkey. Whoever
> speaks of Indians speaks of shit because the Indian is like the mon-
> key. It's as simple as that, because the Indian, like the monkey,
> utters a thousand stupidities which have neither beginning nor
> end. This is the truth and no lie. They are also very malicious
> and devilish. [21]

The same visceral disdain and fear often ran beneath more subtle expressions of elite ideology.

In the few recorded cases from the San Luis region in which Indians and non-Indians attacked each other physically and verbally, the crude view of Indians as lesser beings was put even more succinctly, in the phrase "Indian dogs." In 1599, long before the subtle devaluation of the Tlaxcalans in late-colonial elite ideology, the administrator of a mining hacienda east of San Luis complained that the owner of a neighboring carbonera had "stolen many of my Indians that have cost me many pesos to bring them from their land." The administrator sent out Juan Gómez ("the person who brings me Indians") to retrieve one of the "runaway" Indians, but the owner of the carbonera and some of his servants had chased Gómez out at sword point, shouting "Indian dog!" and threatening to kill him.[22] This incident occurred at a time and a place where labor was so scarce that workers had to be "brought" in at great cost, in dramatic contrast to the labor situation in populous central Mexico during the early conquest. It is a bitter irony that these workers were abused and treated as chattels in spite of their economic importance, and that the miners treated the name they gave the workers—Indians—as the lowest of insults.

The mistreatment of imported Indian workers in the mines of sixteenth-century San Luis did not affect the people of Mexquitic directly, because by all evidence they avoided work in the mines themselves. Their original royal charter forbade the imposition of "personal service," and they were apparently successful in fending off requests by the miners to levy forced-labor drafts (*repartimientos*) on the pueblos in the 1650s. But the existence of such demeaning attitudes in the mining region east of San Luis, which drew a multilingual, uprooted Indian work force from all over the center and near north of Mexico, was part of the broad social context that caused the Tlaxcalans to develop their own pueblos in seeming independence and maintain a fiction of difference between themselves and those other Indians. I have only found one recorded case of Spanish/ Indian violence within Mexquitic itself.[23] The most tense relations between the people of Mexquitic and non-Indians occurred because of their disputed boundary with the hacienda of La Parada, but that conflict appears in the documents in the more sedate form of a long series of lawsuits, where ideology emerges in a more reasoned and theoretically informed way than in the average street fight.

The conflicts and abrupt changes—from the struggle with La Parada to inheritance disputes within the pueblo—that were so rare in Mexquitic through the long decades since 1591 became more frequent and more intense as the eighteenth century drew to a close. These struggles were in part related to the fact that the Franciscans had been replaced in 1769 with secular priests. As we will see, secular priests occupied a different space in the local society and economy and created a different social role for themselves than the friars had.

This increase in conflict also resulted from the growth of the population. Lawsuits over land arose as population pressure slowly became a social and ecological reality. Political struggles too became routine as an ever-smaller percentage of the growing population rose into the restricted ranks of the elite, spurring fights among elite families between insiders and outsiders; also, lawsuits over politics often had a hidden basis in land disputes. Bitter conflicts between priests and parishioners—unheard of while Mexquitic was in the hands of the Franciscans—also derived in part from population growth. As the number of parishioners ballooned from around 2,500 at the beginning of the eighteenth century to perhaps 15,000 at the close (the parish included the pueblo and several surrounding haciendas), the parish priest was inevitably distanced from his flock. He came to deal with them almost exclusively through the medium of the local elites, thus mixing his own interests with their increasingly conflicted politics. The intertwining of political struggles, disputes over land, and unending conflicts with the new parish priests and their intervention in local affairs all caused changes in the society of Mexquitic of a magnitude it had not known in two hundred years. By the end of the century a large faction of the town was at the point of rebellion.

Paralleling these changes and conflicts was the deteriorating image of the people of Mexquitic held by the colonial elite. When in 1779 the priest of Mexquitic saw fit to arrest a former pueblo governor for insulting him, the alcalde mayor of San Luis not only supported the priest but ordered two companies of cavalry to march through Mexquitic "so that the Indians of said pueblo will remain subordinated in the future." The cavalry was headed by the count of Peñasco, a local *hacendado* (hacienda owner) who had been granted his title in recognition of his service to the Crown while suppressing the regional uprising of Indian towns in 1767, which Mexquitic had played no part in. The comparison between the minor fracas in Mexquitic and the earlier widespread revolt was a bit strained, but it seemed clear enough to the count, who wrote as he set out on February 6, 1779, that he was ordering his troops to

> punish the insolence of these Indians, who, so long as they do not
> see an example set, will not be restrained; and the past tumults
> were caused by the fact that don Andres de Urbina [alcalde mayor
> of San Luis Potosí in 1767] tolerated their first audacious acts.[24]

With this sweeping statement, the "noble Tlaxcalans" of Mexquitic and the seditious Tlaxcalans, Guachichiles, and Negritos of Venado, who had revolted in 1767, became all one: "these Indians," whose audacity must be nipped in the bud.

The rhetoric of Indianness was imposed on the people of Mexquitic by the ungentle hand of colonial authority and was reinforced through their involvement in the colonial system of justice and religious hierarchy. This rhetoric created the context in which the people of Mexquitic, in the long years since Mexican Independence, have conceived of their history and their identity.

ANOTHER HISTORY: THE BELLRINGER'S TALE

Making history is a way of producing identity.
                                        —JONATHAN FRIEDMAN (1992 : 837)

It was already late—late at night, late in our stay in Mexquitic. For six weeks Esperanza had been telling us her life story in long nighttime sessions, recalling it in all its poignant details as we and her children sat, enthralled and sleepy, around our kitchen table. At last the tale was finished, or rather, it had reached the present.[25] It then occurred to us to ask Esperanza, before we left Mexquitic and Mexico, to repeat for the tape recorder some of the other tales she had told us before.

"Once you told us the story of how San Miguel appeared here," Ruth said. "We would like it if you could tell us that story again."

"Well," Esperanza began, "I know it because they told it to me, not because I saw it myself. But I don't know if it really happened or not. The late Matías told it to me, to my mama—that old man who was the uncle of the wife of my uncle Miguel. That's how I learned it, but—who knows. But it's getting late, comadre, we should go now." And soon we went into our elaborate goodbyes, perhaps more elaborate than usual because we knew we would not be talking again anytime soon in this kitchen, around this table.

Still, we didn't want to leave town without this particular story. By this time I had pieced together enough of the basic history of the founding of Mexquitic to weave the story presented above, a version emphasizing the social actors and forces at play in the settling of New Spain's northern frontier four centuries before. But there were other stories about the foundation of Mexquitic circulating in the town, several of which existed side by side, neither merging together nor contradicting each other. I wanted Esperanza to retell her "miraculous" version, a religious story that stars neither conquering soldiers nor evangelizing friars nor abstract social movements, but a saint, San Miguel Arcángel (the Archangel Michael), patron of Mexquitic. She had heard it, long before, from the bellringer of the parish church, an old man who lived in her mother's household and who told many tales that strike one as "traditional." Now, as Esperanza approached the age of sixty, she had become an accomplished storyteller herself, and (especially in those days, before they had acquired a television) her children would sit and listen avidly to tales they had heard many times before, tales she retold matter-of-factly to the gringo anthropologists, tales of her childhood and adolescence, of men who married women who turned out to be blood-sucking witches, of aborted children who become imps and scamper across the bridge at midnight, of the day she saw the souls of the dead rise and wander in the cemetery at high noon, of the night La Llorona (the Weeping Woman) drove her black car through town, passing right in front of Chava's house.

So the next morning, when we walked up the steep street to Esperanza's house to say our final goodbyes and to tape the story, her children and her mother joined us to listen to the tale under the flowering canopy of the *enramada* that shelters the door of her small brick house.[26]

"This is what I remember," Esperanza begins again, "what they told me, right? What that old Matías told us. They say that over there," waving her hand to indicate the center of town, "everything was just brush, *monte*, there wasn't anything but a little trail where—"

"It was a road," her mother interjects.

"A trail, a road, whatever, where the mule drivers passed."

"The road went right here, by this bush," her mother continues. "I used to see lots of mule drivers pass by here in those days, with six, ten, a dozen burros loaded with things to sell to the people."

"They want you to tell them if you remember how all this began," Esperanza politely reminds her mother.

"No. You go ahead and tell them, however you want to."

"Right. Well, what I can remember—because it's been years since the late Matías died—is that there was nothing but the road for the mule drivers, and a couple of houses scattered around here and there in the *monte,* over near Derramadero and Carrizal. People were old-fashioned back then. They were people, like us, but they lived apart, and they were more Indian-like, you know, more Indian. The mule drivers passed through this *monte* here carrying—what was it they carried to San Luis?" Esperanza turns to her mother, who she feels is closer to that ancient time.

"Firewood, maguey juice, whatever they could find to sell."

"With three or four burros, two men—and off they go. And then they say some people were passing by, there where the church is now, right past where the altar is, and they heard arrows humming past, *rrin!* 'Hmm.

What could that be?' They couldn't figure out where it was coming from. The other one said, 'Ay, look, look at what's over there! Look, there's something swinging there in that big mesquite tree! Looks like a Christian or an animal or something, I can't tell.'

" 'Where, where?'

" 'Now I don't see anything. But I did see a person or something swinging in the mesquite.' While this was happening they stopped because they heard the arrows whistling by. It was an Indian shooting some big arrows. 'There's nothing over there.' Since they were in the *monte,* they were afraid. 'Come on, let's go.' The burros were already way ahead of them. Off they go.

"A few days later some other people passed by. On their way back, at night, they heard murmuring there in that place. Then the people there started to warn each other. 'I heard a rumor that so-and-so said he was passing by and they heard like a hum, like an arrow whistling by like, psss! And he turned around quickly and managed to see something moving in a big mesquite there.'

" 'Heavens, how strange.'

" 'Well, who knows, I passed by late at night and I heard murmuring, but I didn't see anything. Who knows what it could be.'

"Time passed, and later they learned: 'Hey, listen, so-and-so passed by alone and they say he disappeared. They just found his animals all alone over there, but he had disappeared.'

" 'Oh, it sounds like an . . .' " Esperanza, speaking in the voice of a mule driver from long ago, begins to say "an Evil Thing," but she—and her character—stops short of mentioning the Devil, even in this euphemistic phrase. " 'What could it be?'

" 'Well, who knows, he was lost and he was lost, just the animals came back alone.' Since the houses were very dispersed, they started to say, 'Who knows what it could be, or why it could be?'

"Some time later a man and a woman passed by again. 'Ah, look at what's over there, it sounded like it was snorting, it's real ugly, over there.'

" 'Yes, it must be an animal'—and again *rrinn!* it shot an arrow to kill them. But they had been warned: 'If you're going to pass by there, be careful. There to the left there's something frightening. Be sure to pass by quick and early.' Then the man said, 'I saw it. It was a, a—' " Esperanza turns again to her mother. "What did he call it, mama?"

"A *gentil,* a pagan."

"Pagan, right, so it was a pagan. But it was in the form of an Indian, a big, huge man. And it killed people and ate them. So the people just went by carefully. They figured out that it ate people, that people were disappearing. Then they said, 'No, this isn't a good thing, it must be the Evil Thing. Who knows what it is.' And it went on like that until some man . . ."

At this point, as if in response to the naming of the Evil Thing, our tape recorder stops. It takes a few minutes to get it working again. "What were we up to?" Esperanza asks.

"The man was pleading with God," I say.

"Then that man pleaded with God that the thing would disappear," Esperanza takes up the story again without skipping a beat, "since they could no longer pass by that place. And the Lord must have heard him. He must have been a very good man, and God granted what he asked for.

"Soon afterward some mule drivers were passing by, and they saw such a swarm of insects, and such a buzzing and humming! They stopped, because people always passed by there full of fear. 'What's that buzzing, what could it be?' They went over by the mesquite and saw swarms and swarms of wasps, honeybees, bumblebees, all sorts of flying insects. They froze with fright, looking. And they saw that form, the form of a man, completely covered with insects, swinging and swaying in the mesquite. Then they saw him break loose and run off like a gust of wind. And there goes the thick swarm of insects following that man! He left so fast they didn't even see which way he went. That man left and the swarm and everything left.

"They saw what they saw. 'Off it goes. It's gone. Maybe it was the Evil Thing, only God knows what it was. But now we saw that it's gone.'

"Other people still passed by full of fear. There wasn't anything in the mesquite anymore, the tree was clean. And the rumors began. 'Let's go see, they say there's nothing there anymore. The mesquite's clean.' Then people started to pass by with more confidence. 'There's nothing there now, haven't you seen?'

" 'So it's true, then, what so-and-so said.' So.

"Soon afterward a little old man passed by with a pack train. He stayed in that place while his partner went on with the animals. They were still cautious of what they had seen there. He stayed there, watching—distrustful, you know—and then he saw a big painting appear in the mesquite, moving, swinging, like it was swaying in the breeze. It's the painting that's up above the altar," Esperanza explains to us, speaking of the large painted image in the parish church of San Miguel as a kind of winged baroque Roman soldier, wielding sword and shield over a fallen dragon image of the Devil.[27]

" 'Ay, what's that up there. Some people say they saw a monkey, that they saw a man. And here I see this. What could it be?' The man just kept watching it. 'Most likely it's the figure of what those people saw. Well, I'm going to tell them I saw it.' And the little old man caught up with the other one and told him, 'Listen, it isn't true what they say, that it's gone. It's there, I saw it like this!'

" 'Then why didn't I see anything when I passed by?'

" 'I stayed there,' he said, 'and I did see it. It's a painting with these black kind of figures on it. That must be it, I think. It's not true what they say, that it disappeared.'

" 'Well, who knows.'

"A few days later the old man and the other passed by again. The other man said, 'Let's go and you'll show me, and we'll find out if you see it and I see it too.' Soon enough the man says, 'No, look, there's nothing there.'

" 'What? Well, I did see it, it was right there.'

"You may have seen it, but I don't see a thing. Nothing's going on here now. We haven't heard that so-and-so has disappeared or that such-and-such has disappeared, there's nothing now.'

"A while later the same man came back again with another pack train, and again he saw it. He said, 'Well, I'm going to go up close to see what it is.' So the little old man went up and said, 'But it's a painting, like an image.' Then he said, 'I'm going to grab it and see what it is.' And he went and grabbed the painting. That was riskier. 'Yes,' he said, 'I'm going to take it with me, to make those people believe.'

"The little old man took the painting off to his house. So then he went to tell them, 'Listen, I passed by there and I found this thing and now I have it in my house. Let's go look at it.' And off he took them to his house. He said, 'Look, come on,' and he brought them inside. 'Ah, but, it was here and now there's nothing.'

" 'No, it's not true, you're fooling us.'

" 'The painting disappeared,' the little old man said, 'but I did leave it here. Right, wife?' asking his wife, 'Right?' turning to his family. 'Didn't you see what I brought in here?'

" 'Yes, yes, it was right in here.'

" 'But how come there's nothing now? You're feeding us lies, it isn't true. We don't know if it's something good or something evil, how did it appear to you? You say it appears there in the mesquite. Hm? So?'

"So that little old man had a challenge to face. 'I'm going to go back and see if it's still there.' So the little old man came back there to the mesquite, and he found it! He said, 'Well, I'm going to leave you there.

I'm going to see a companion, to get him to come and see that it's here. I'm going to notify the judge to come see it, so that they'll believe.' He went to tell the other people that it was there, and when they got back the other person didn't see anything. He said, 'No, I don't see anything here.'

" 'Well I do, look, it's right there.'

" 'Who knows what it could be. Maybe it's for you, I don't know. But I don't see it, the mesquite is empty. So you, if you want to take it or you want to leave it here, let's see what we'll do. I can't see anything.'

" 'Well, I'm not going to take it, because it comes back, it disappears from my house. It must be some kind of image. Let's go notify the authorities and find out what it is.' They say that they did that. But what I don't really remember well," Esperanza adds, "is how they figured out its name, how did they find out it was an image of San Miguel. That's what I can't remember of what the late Matías told me.

"But in the end they found the image, and it didn't leave that place anymore. Other people came and saw it too, they said, 'Look, there it is. All right, it's true. You should take it. It appeared to you, you take it.'

"But the man was very old. He said, 'We love it, let's build it a temple. No matter how few people we are, let's build a temple and maybe it won't leave. Maybe this is an image to get rid of the Evil Thing that was here.' Well, that's what they did.

"The men began to cut down the mesquite. They start cutting off all the branches. 'Now, let's cut it down and dig it out, to pull out the roots.'

"Another one said, 'No, don't cut the mesquite down to the roots, let's try cutting it in half instead. Just part of it, and then we'll see if it's good, that's how you can tell.' That's what they did. 'Heave. And ho. And ho.' The mesquite was real thick. 'It's real hard, this mesquite is very hard.' They were almost half the way through the wood, and the painting that they had seen started to appear to them, it started to form before them in the mesquite. 'Look, it really is appearing. When you cut down a plant or a tree, you can see the heart of the tree, but not in this form. So this really does have to be an image.' By the time they were finished cutting it down it was all engraved. The painting that the old man had found was the one that they found engraved in the mesquite. Just the figure, not the painting itself."

"Of San Miguel?" Ruth asks.

"Yes, of San Miguel. I don't know how they figured out it was San Miguel, that I don't know. But I do remember that old Matías would say, 'The old-fashioned people, they were old-timey, those really good sorts of people, not like the people of today,' he said. 'Old-timey, really good people,' he said, 'they believed in everything, in everything they believed,' he said, 'and that's why . . .' " Esperanza lets the words of old Matías trail off, as if to say that being "old-fashioned" explained everything.

"So when they finished cutting down the mesquite they notified the authorities. 'Look. What should we do here? Let's not pull it out by the roots. What we ought to do, since that thing has disappeared that some people saw . . .'

" 'Yes, yes, I saw it.'

" 'But that was different. This is a saint, maybe it is an image. What should we do? We'd best build a temple, a church, and see if this is the salvation of us here who pass by here, because once we have a temple who knows but maybe what we saw might not appear again. Because for us to go on disappearing one by one, that just won't do.'

"Then the people said, 'Yes, let's build a temple.' They all were shouting. 'Let's build that temple.' They set the first stone."

THE DEVIL IN THE SHAPE OF AN INDIAN

Mythology and iconography as subjects of study are not as different as they might at first seem . . . Myth and image, as symbols, can be studied from the viewpoint of ideology.

—ALFREDO LÓPEZ AUSTIN (1993 : 1)

In her tale, Esperanza presents a thoroughly Christianized view of the origin of Mexquitic. She does so through the point of view of a popular Christianity, in which a saint or his image, rather than a priest or friar, is the link between the community and divine forces. The taming of the aboriginal wilderness comes not through conquest by soldiers, or through deft diplomacy, or through the sufferings of missionaries, but by divine and saintly intervention, which is interpreted and acted on by the community. The construction of a temple around the saint's image, organized and undertaken by the people themselves without prompting or interference by Church authorities, is the sign that the pueblo has come into existence. The images in the tale present an argument about the identity of the people who founded Mexquitic and their claim to the land.

Much of the iconography, the structural elements from which Esperanza constructs the tale, derives from late medieval legends of saintly apparitions in Iberia and neighboring Western European countries.[28] In particular, two key moments in the tale are commonplaces in Iberian legends and are also incorporated into the familiar legend of the apparition of the Virgin Mary of Guadalupe just north of Mexico City. First, the saint's image appears repeatedly in a deserted spot to a godly man, but it remains invisible to others. Second, the finder of the image repeatedly attempts to bring the image home (or to another church), yet the image returns with mysterious determination to its original location, where it is at last made visible to all. This fact is interpreted as a sign that the image—the saint— wishes for its temple to be built on that spot.

But in Esperanza's version, the saintly apparition tale of San Miguel is prefaced by an inverted, demonic disapparition tale. This diabolic preface to the story can be seen as a homegrown interpretation of the origin of Mexquitic in the aftermath of the Chichimeca War.[29] The cannibalistic man-ape swinging in the tree, the "bad Indian," the "pagan," the "Evil One," would then represent the Chichimecas, who were routinely accused of cannibalism by the Spaniards. The evil presence in the mesquite tree, like the sixteenth-century Chichimecas, attacks and destroys commerce along the road. In this telling, though, he is finally chased off by the will of God and not by Spanish soldiers, nor is he accommodated and co-opted by royal gifts. And he is kept away by the appearance, swinging in the same tree, of the image of San Miguel.

The "Evil Thing" that swung in the mesquite tree is, significantly, the only character in Esperanza's story who is identified as an Indian (rather than described as *indiado*, "Indian-like"). The people in the story alternate between calling this savage presence a man and calling him an animal. Esperanza, in telling the story, alternates between calling him an Indian (often the "bad Indian," *el indio malo*) and calling him the Devil in the form of an Indian. The image of the "bad Indian" acts within the story to define the other actors, the mule drivers who become the founders of Mexquitic, as implicitly "other." The latter are, the narrative implies, separate and distinct from this grotesque embodiment of all the negative stereotypes of the Indian. And, indeed, of all negative qualities, for this "Indian" is revealed in the end as none other than the Devil itself, the very same demon that is depicted in the painting of San Miguel.

The importance of this identification between the "bad Indian" and the Devil explains why Esperanza kept trying to remember, as she told her story, "how they figured out to call it San Miguel Mexquitic." When she returned to this question after finishing the tale, her son ventured to suggest, "Well, they called it 'Mexquitic' because of the mesquite tree."

"Right," Esperanza agreed, "but how did they figure out that the image was San Miguel? That's what I can't remember. Because when they found that painting and took a good look at it and fixed it up to put up on the altar, it *already* had a picture of the Evil Thing there. There it is. San Miguel is here, holding something like a wheel, and holding a sword or something, and then down under him is—with your pardon—*el chamuco,* the Devil, which he is dominating. So they must have understood that it was San Miguel in his battle against the demon. I think that must be how they decided his name. That is why the more Indian-like people back then believed that the Evil Thing had been there. And that San Miguel beat him, and drove him off. Eh? And that's why the temple is there, and it is San Miguel Mexquitic."

Thus the painted image of San Miguel defeating the demon turns out to be, in Esperanza's tale, an allegory of its own discovery, as well as a symbol of the victory of the people of Mexquitic, through their patron saint, over their savage predecessors in this land. The image of San Miguel first swinging in the mesquite and then being engraved in the very heart of the tree trunk (which people insist is still conserved behind the altar of the church) is an almost glyphic symbol as well of the founding of the pueblo, for "San Miguel Mezquitic" can be interpreted literally as "San Miguel in the mesquite tree."

In contrast to the demonic "thing," who Esperanza identifies as *an* Indian, the people who flee the demon, then return to discover San Miguel and build his church, have little fixed identity. Usually they are simply an unspecified "they"—an "inchoate pronoun" in search of predication.[30] "They" discover and name the features of the world at an inchoate time, which might as well be at the beginning of the world. Esperanza describes them only as mule drivers (*arrieros*), occupied in a constant coming-and-going between their own wasteland (*monte*) and the incongruously already-existing San Luis. Beyond this peripatetic identification, Esperanza describes them as "old-fashioned" and "old-timey" (*gente antigua, gente de anterior*). These last two attributes, as heavily connotated as "traditional" or "primitive" in our own lexicon, are underlined with other heavy adjectives: *indiados,* "Indian-like," and *más indios,* "more Indian." These descriptions are not labels, like "Tlaxcalan," "Guachichil," or "Indian," but adjectives. Esperanza uses *estar* ("to be," referring to a temporary or relative condition) rather than *ser* ("to be," referring to a state of being): "*estaban más indiados verdad, así, más indios así.*" "Indian" is not their essence, their identity, but their condition.

The difference between the two ambiguous, equivocal, and overlapping usages of "Indian," as adjective and as noun, condition and essence, was demonstrated graphically in a bit of conversation we had with Atanasia:

Atanasia: They call us "Indians" here.
Ruth: Who?
Atanasia: The people from over there [pointing toward San Luis].
   Well, sure, we *are* Indians—we don't have money, we don't have anything, what can you do? [31]

Here Atanasia "confesses" to being an "Indian," but not in the sense that the people of San Luis would use it of her, as an identity, an essence. Instead, she concisely argues, if she conforms to their stereotypes of the "Indian" it is because she has no money.

In Esperanza's parenthetical comments on her own story, she gives a connotative slant to their ambiguous attributes as "old-fashioned" and "Indian-like." Being "more Indian" could mean any number of things, refer to any number of stereotypes of the Indian, but Esperanza tries to restrict its connotative range by linking the attribute with specific images: they lived in dispersed houses, and they were "good," religious, more believing than people today. Their "Indianness" is summarized in the word *ajeno,* which might be translated as "strangers" but which I have rendered as "living apart." They lived apart from each other, in their dispersed houses in the monte, and their way of life was also apart, different, from "ours" (the people of Mexquitic today) since we do not live in scattered houses, nor are we as firm believers as they were.

The vague identity constructed for the founders of Mexquitic serves to justify their authority in the area and their occupation of the land. The mule drivers lived dispersed in the wilderness—here again we see their inchoate origins. In the beginning the social world was without form, though not void. They were willing believers, as is necessary for the progress of the story, for how else could they see San Miguel in the mesquite? But this is also a legitimizing attribute. Among the many and varied stereotypes of the Indian, the storyteller chooses to emphasize that of Indian religiosity, not only because it can be seen as positive but because it lends authority to the implied contract between San Miguel and the people who founded Mexquitic. In short, "they," the mule drivers, are pictured as living in what is now Mexquitic since the mythic time before the foundation of the pueblo. That is to say, they are autochthonous, they have been given this land from the beginning.

Esperanza concluded her story on a note of pride at Mexquitic's primacy in the region of San Luis Potosí:

"And that's all. They built the temple. Because Mexquitic here is the first church that was founded of all the churches in San Luis Potosí. The very first. This is the capital of San Luis Potosí. Some say the capital, others say the cradle of San Luis Potosí. Because this is the first church founded. They built the high altar in front of the mesquite, and they built it all, all built in the old days. Because there are churches in San Luis, but not like this one. Maybe they're more beautiful, better made or better built, but not like this one. And this one also has its plaque, there on the wall, haven't you seen? It has it all, in what year and everything."

"Yes," Ruth and I responded. Having come into Mexquitic to investigate its past and its culture, we had naturally seen and read that historical plaque on our first visit to the town.

Esperanza's son commented, "That's about the Guachichiles."

"Yes, well," Esperanza admitted, "the *indiados*. There used to just be Indians here."

CONTESTED TALES

Between Esperanza's mythic tale of the origins of Mexquitic and the secular social history of its foundation I have written, a number of other origin tales coexist rather peacefully. One prominent alternative is the version expounded by Philip Wayne Powell in numerous publications. If my origin tale is a secular social history emphasizing the groups and forces behind the colonial settling of northern New Spain, I would characterize Powell's as secular heroic histories. In them Powell treats the Chichimeca War as an epic struggle of "civilization" against "savagery," and its successful conclusion as the victory of a single man Captain Miguel Caldera, and his diplomacy. The most significant social component of the epic, in Powell's account, is that Caldera was a mestizo, a son of a Spanish soldier and a Guachichil woman. Powell weaves into his story of the conquest of northern Mexico a subtext in which the victory of Caldera and his methods (particularly the policy of peace in exchange for gifts of food, a policy which Powell identifies with the person of Caldera) stand allegorically for the victory of mestizo Mexico over both Spaniard and Indian. In this allegory, the savagery of the warlike Chichimecas and the civilization of the warmongering Spanish soldiers lead equally to destruction; only the mestizo civilization of Caldera, mediating between the two, leads to peace and prosperity for the northern borderlands. The allegory is not incidental to Powell's tale. It is the driving force behind his historical investigations and his narration.[32]

Powell's secular heroic tale of the settling of New Spain's northern frontier is counterbalanced by a number of religious heroic tales. The latter tell, in varying style and detail, of how the Chichimecas were pacified and the northern space settled as a direct result of the evangelization by Franciscan friars in the late sixteenth century. These religious foundation stories can be traced back to the early Franciscan chronicle of Torquemada (1615), who wrote within a few years of the events he recounted. Torquemada's brief account of the settling of San Luis and environs, a chronological series of short notices of martyrs and missionaries, received an almost novelistic elaboration at the hands of Arlegui (1737), a Franciscan based in Santa María del Río. Arlegui's tales, in turn, were popularized by the San Luis historian Velázquez (1897 and 1946), who fixed on one of the dozens of hagiographies in Torquemada and Arlegui that of Fray Diego de la Magdalena, and made of him a frontier friar-hero, a Franciscan counterpoint to Powell's mestizo captain Miguel Caldera. From the vague statements of Torquemada, Velázquez surmises that Fray Diego was present at the foundation of every mission in the north from Nombre de Dios in 1555 onward. He places Fray Diego at the side of Caldera during the subjugation of the Guachichiles, and prefers "to believe that [Caldera] worked under the inspiration of that man, who through the force of meekness and gentleness alone mastered their rebellion and barbarity." He also sends Fray Diego off with Caldera to Mexico City, to the negotiations that ended the war and suggests that it was the friar who proposed sending the Tlaxcalans to "civilize" the Guachichiles.[33]

This missionary version has been adopted by the priests of Mexquitic at least since the time of Padre Albino Escalante, an amateur historian and parish priest (1912–1923) who lifted the story of Fray Diego from Velázquez's early work and localized it by placing the friar squarely at center stage during the founding of Mexquitic.[34] It was apparently Escalante who commissioned the portrait of Fray Diego that now hangs in the priest's house. His promotion of Fray Diego has found a receptive audience among later parish priests, who often refer to the pioneer Franciscan in their sermons. One of Escalante's successors, Padre Herminio, went so far as to have a statue representing Fray Diego erected in the church courtyard in the early 1940s.

In fact, a kind of silent conversation is being eternally played out, perhaps unnoticed by anyone, before the church in Mexquitic. On one side of the courtyard stands the crumbling concrete statue of Fray Diego, which represents the religious heroic version of the founding of the town. He faces with outstretched arms the plaque which Esperanza spoke of, which is attached to the face of the church itself in commemoration of the secular heroic version. The plaque was placed there, on the preeminent domain of official religion in the town, by a secular authority (the representative for Mexquitic in the state congress) on a secular occasion (May 5, anniversary of the Battle of Puebla and a prime nationalist holiday). And it was placed there at the height of the conflict between church and state in Mexico, just a month before the churches were closed throughout the country and the Cristero revolt began.

> This pueblo and monastery of Mexquitic were founded
> in the year 1590 after the surrender of
> the Guachichil and Chichimeca Indians in 1589,
> and that of San Luis in 1592, when the Chief Magistrate
> Don Miguel Caldera, who resided in this pueblo,
> rode out from this place accompanied by the
> future founders of San Luis on March 4, 1592,
> on learning of the mines of San Pedro, a discovery
> which determined the foundation of San Luis
> in a spot which only a few days before had been
> just a camping grounds of the barbarous Chichimecas.
> San Miguel Tepeticpac, 5 May 1926
> Respectfully, The Pueblo of Mexquitic, Rep. Rutilio Alamilla[35]

The dialogue is indeed a mute one, for it takes place between two ideologies that few people in Mexquitic have any direct stake in. The secular heroic story of the foundation of Mexquitic is given voice by those interested in playing up the role of the representatives of secular authority in civilizing the region, just as religious leaders who have promoted the religious heroic tale, beginning with the Franciscans, have an interest in playing up their own importance. Most people in Mexquitic do not fall into either of these categories, but they too have used the story of the foundation of their town to legitimize their own authority.

Throughout the colonial period the political leaders of Mexquitic frequently referred to themselves and their pueblo as descending from the Tlaxcalan "conquerors" of the region, calling upon their ancestral service to the Crown to bolster their claims for land, territorial jurisdiction, or whatever privileges they could wrest from a grudging provincial elite. These days, townspeople readily relate to visitors a common version of the foundation story, which bypasses the Tlaxcalans and instead traces their ancestry directly to the "Guachichiles and Chichimecas" of the plaque. This revised standard version, with its implicit argument that the people of Mexquitic have an autochthonous right to the land of Mexquitic, has taken root at the same time as a revolutionary ideology that lends value to such pre-Hispanic claims to land while devaluing claims that rest on the authority of the Spanish kings.[36] The story itself is an easy synthesis of the two theoretically competing versions given above, and those who tell it cite both the plaque and the statue as authoritative texts. A few people, such as don Pedro, also cite occasional newspaper articles. His version, as excerpted in my fieldnotes, is as follows:

> Mexquitic was the cradle of San Luis. It was founded in 1590 by Captain Caldera and Juan Oñate. There were two tribes here, the Guachichiles and the Chichimecas—the people of Santa María del Río are of the same stock [*raza*] as the people of Mexquitic. They were barbarian tribes [*tribus bárbaras*]; Fray Diego de la Magdalena came to conquer them, through the Gospel, because the Spaniards couldn't do it.[37]

Several key themes run throughout all tellings of this brief foundation story. They place the "Guachichiles and Chichimecas," thought of sometimes as rival tribes and sometimes as a single conglomeration, squarely at the center of the action. These "barbarous tribes" were not mere obstacles to be removed from the path of progress; rather, they were the primordial inhabitants of the region ("there were two tribes here"), and subsequently the prime actors in the foundation of the town. In fact those who tell this story make the tacit assumption that "we" descend from "them," that these Chichimecas and Guachichiles were not only the original founders of the town but the ancestors, directly or indirectly, of the people of Mexquitic today. When don Raúl greeted us on the street recently after our long absence from the town, he treated us to a spontaneous speech on his pride in belonging to the "brown race," the "race of bronze or copper," and in the Chichimecas, "our ancestors": "I feel a certain satisfaction in considering myself a descendent of the indigenous people of this place." [38]

The same pride is evident in the story's characterization of the Guachichiles as indomitable barbarians. Caldera could found their town, but he couldn't conquer them; Fray Diego could subdue them, but it was not really Fray Diego that succeeded, it was the force of Christianity—and perhaps they were not ever truly subdued. People of Mexquitic who tell the story of their town's foundation have combined the secular heroic and the religious heroic versions of the story to create a heroic social version, in which they themselves, in the person of their Guachichil predecessors, play the role of collective hero. The same tale can even be combined, without any sense of contradiction, with a miraculous origin tale such as Esperanza's, or the more common version told to us by doña Lala:

> The friars had brought *el señor* San Miguel from San Miguel el Grande, that is to say San Miguel de Allende, and they say that they were coming in search of a place that would be for him. They stopped over there by the river, where there were a few large elms, and that is why they called it "La Parada" ("the stopping-place"), because [San Miguel] stopped there. . . . Back then there was a beautiful forest here, and the water ran beautifully in the river. And the friars passed by here, carrying the image of *el señor* San Miguel, searching for a place for him, and when they had passed by here they discovered that they were no longer carrying him. They went to search for him and couldn't find him, until they found him at last here in a mesquite. This was like a sign that here was where he wanted to stay.[39]

Here the friars of the religious-heroic version, unnamed, have to take their cues from San Miguel, the patron saint who stands for the pueblo as a whole, and who through his miraculous actions creates and thus lays claim to a human geography, giving names to space. Apart from the friars, the founders of the town remain, as in Esperanza's tale, an inchoate "they." Doña Lala went on to recite much the same secular story told by don Pedro, referring to "don Miguel Caldera" as "the first president" of Mexquitic. "I really like to talk about these histories [*historias*]," she told us, as she launched into the familiar story of the "Guachichiles and Chichimecas." This time I contradicted this story as an experiment, maintaining that the people of Mexquitic were actually descended from Tlaxcalans (*tlaxcaltecas*). Doña Lala eventually accepted the possibility that this was true, because it would answer the problem of where the word *teco* comes from. "That is what the people from San Luis call everyone from Mexquitic," she explained. "As an insult: oh, you're from there, from the rancho, you're just a *teco*. But if we're tlaxcal*tecas,* that explains it: tlaxcal*teca, teco.*"

"But why do they call you that?" I wanted to know.

"Just as an insult, because we're from the ranchos. And you know that there's lots of maguey here, people live pretty much from magueys, from collecting aguamiel and making pulque, and over there in Ahualulco there aren't many magueys, so over there they call us 'sweet shins' [*corvas dulces*]—you know when you get the juice it runs all over you and gets your feet wet, so that's why they named us 'sweet shins.' " [40]

Thus the Tlaxcalan identity of the people of Mexquitic, which was for so long used with pride and insistence by the leaders of the pueblo to defend themselves, their rights, and their lands against outside assault, has degenerated into a kind of vestigial ethnic epithet, "teco," which calls forth the entire gamut of racist stereotypes held about "indios" in Mexico—stereotypes with histories that stretch back to the sixteenth-century conquest. And the people of Mexquitic themselves have shed their former identities as "indios" and as Tlaxcalans. In exchange they take on, in the stories they tell of the origins of their pueblo, a somewhat vaguer identification as the descendants—whether through kinship or through a kind of spiritual connection does not enter the stories—of the barbarous Guachichiles. The Guachichiles, in this telling, were never conquered and therefore cannot be painted with those stereotypes that depict Indians as base, servile, defeated. And they were an autochthonous people, with a clear right to the land that the ejidos of Mexquitic now occupy.

After Esperanza finishes telling the story of founding Mexquitic, she begins to mull over some of its implications.

"And that's what that little old man told me, I don't really remember well anymore. But I tell you, that's how they say this history was. That's how it appeared. But more recent things, no, because all this was about the old-fashioned people who were Indians. Indians, Indians, Indians, they were the Indian people. Because the church was built by the Indians. That's it."

"And you don't remember seeing Indians here in Mexquitic?" Ruth asks.

"No," Esperanza insists.

"People who spoke another language?"

Esperanza, certain that *she* has never heard of such a thing, turns to her son: "Do you?"

"My grandmother does," her son suggests.

Esperanza doubts this. "No, my mama doesn't, my mama—well, who knows, I don't, who would think. Well, maybe my mama. . . . But what I don't know, about the Indians, how did they die, how did they stay, how did the Indian who built the church die, only God knows. People started getting a little civilized, some of them, others who are us, you know, because we here, they tell us we are 'Indians.' "

"Who tells you that?"

"Well—you hear it, everywhere. San Luis, everywhere, they say that here we are . . ."

"In Ahualulco they're called 'tecos,' " her son interrupts.

" 'Tecos.' And here?"

" 'Indians,' " Esperanza and her son respond in unison. "This is where *la indiada* [i.e., the Indians, as a homogenous group] was civilized," her son added.

"Eh. Here we are the Indians," Esperanza explains. "And then one grew up, from the relatives of those Indians, right, our parents, our grandparents, our parents' grandparents, and, God only knows, so on. But when I came to know this place—well, the pueblo was already here. All these houses were here." [41]

FOUR   # Colonial Politics

In the middle years of the sixteenth century, as the *altepetl* (ethnic states) of central Mexico were reconceptualized as pueblos de indios, they gradually adopted Spanish-style municipal governments. Lockhart has described the process by which the dynastic rulers of the altepetl were transformed into *gobernadores* (governors), around whom municipal councils were then created.[1] Mexquitic was founded after this transformation had been completed. Central Mexican altepetl had for a time adopted the Spanish term *cabildo* for the new form of indigenous governments, but by the 1600s that term was reserved for the municipal governments of Spanish towns. Here, the local government during the colonial period was called simply the *república de indios* (Indian polity) which in its broadest sense referred to the entire Indian sector of society in Spanish America. This was appropriate, if somewhat circular, because by 1591 (and throughout the next 230 years of colonial rule) the Indian sector was by definition contained in exclusively Indian towns, while the main trait used to distinguish a pueblo de indios from its mixed-race or Spanish counterpart was precisely its government by a república de indios.

Just as the Tlaxcalans of Mexquitic seem to have translated the title of *pueblo* into their own terms, treating their newly founded town as a kind of neo-altepetl, there is some evidence that they treated their first Spanish-appointed governors as quasi-dynastic rulers, with lifetime, or at least long-term, rule.[2] By the end of the seventeenth century, however, yearly terms were the customary rule in Mexquitic as in central Mexico, and it was rare and greatly protested for a governor to get away with re-election two years in a row by the small circle who formed the electorate.

THE REPÚBLICA OF MEXQUITIC

The officers of the república of Mexquitic were elected on December 31 for terms of one year, which began that same night when the stroke of midnight divided the old year from the new. The passing of the staff of office (*vara de justicia*) to the new officers concretely symbolized the transference of power and authority.[3] Elections were held in the small Franciscan friary adjoining the church and were supervised by the priest. That arrangement figured prominently in lawsuits after the Franciscans were replaced by parish priests in 1769 and after the supervision of local elections by priests was outlawed in the 1780s.

The electors (*vocales*) were limited to two groups of local notables. One was former local officials, *republicanos antiguos,* who preserved their authority and even some power in a manner more reminiscent of Mesoamerican than of Spanish governing traditions.[4] The other was the nobles, *principales* or *caciques*—a word still evolving from its original meaning of "Indian chiefs" to its modern meaning, "political bosses"—who traced descent from the ancient nobility of Tlaxcala. Principales were distinguished in documents of the colonial period by being given the title "don," which in Spain at that time was restricted to members of the nobility. By 1800 the title "don" was applied equally to principales and to former officials, and indeed the distinction between the two groups of notables was extremely vague, since most elected officials were drawn from the ranks of the principales (and presumably most principales were elected to some position or other at some point in their career). Altogether the notables comprised a small, self-perpetuating elite, and as the pueblo grew over the course of the colonial period this elite came to represent a shrinking proportion of the total population. In the disputed election of 1804, the governor was chosen by twenty-two out of thirty-six electors; another thirty-seven principales and former officials (*republicanos pasados*) protested that they had been excluded from the vote.[5] Thus the electorate in 1804 comprised at most seventy-three men, less than 1 percent of the pueblo population of 10,200.

The república formed part of a system of prestige and authority like that enshrined by anthropologists of Mesoamerica as the "cargo system" or the "civil-religious hierarchy."[6] But the república was not merely a means for producing and maintaining prestige within the pueblo; it was first of all the recognized civil governing structure. The twelve officers of the república, in ranked order, were: governor and lieutenant governor (*gobernador, teniente de gobernador*), first and second magistrates (*alcalde de primer voto* and *de segundo voto*), first and second regents (*regidor de primer voto* and *de segundo voto*), chief constable and lieutenant constable (*alguacil mayor, teniente de alguacil mayor*), and four constables (*alguaciles*). The república also had a notary (*escribano de república*), a literate member of the indigenous elite who, though not an elected official, performed essential legal functions such as writing wills and communicating with the Spanish government in San Luis.

The governor was clearly the most important elected official, serving as both mayor and judge for the pueblo. His power, based on both his moral authority as the recognized head of the pueblo and on the power of the colonial state, was real. He decided civil and criminal cases that arose between the "sons of the pueblo," that is, the citizenry of Mexquitic, and he forwarded the more delicate cases involving outsiders to the alcalde mayor of San Luis, with his commentary. It was his duty to represent the interests of the pueblo in any disputes with powerful outsiders, whether neighboring hacendados or the parish priest. He was in charge of renting out community land to outsiders and collecting tribute, he could levy taxes to cover extraordinary expenses (such as lawsuits), and he had final control over the community treasury, which held more than 3,000 pesos by the end of the colonial era. Finally, he had the formidable power to grant or to take away agricultural land within the pueblo boundaries. The other major officers of the república, the alcaldes, regidores, chief constables, and lieutenants, met at council regularly at the will of the governor, working with him and through him. At the other end of the hierarchy were the alguaciles, also known as *ministros de vara* (staff ministers, a translation of the Nahuatl title *topile*, "staff-holder"). They formed a kind of amateur police force and served as manual laborers for their superiors, much as the "comandantes" in Mexquitic today do, and, apart from the alguacil mayor and his lieutenant, had no voice on the council.[7]

In addition to the governing civil hierarchy there was a lay religious hierarchy in Mexquitic, about which much less is known, for it left no records. It was apparently intertwined to some extent with the civil service ladder, in the style of more recent civil-religious hierarchies, for its elected head official, the *fiscal mayor*, appears in one document ranked just behind the governor and lieutenant governor in prestige and authority. But this was a very rare appearance of the fiscal in colonial documentation, and in practical terms the civil business of governing the town and the religious business of enforcing Church policy were kept separate. Other religious officials, the ministros and *fiscales topiles,* were the religious equivalent of alguaciles. Their duties were limited to maintaining order within the Church and attending to the needs of the priests.

This system also included the only known elective office for women, *tenanche* (from Nahuatl *tenantzin,* literally "[someone's] mother [honorific]"). The tenanches—apparently unranked, though such information might not have been picked up by the male-oriented documents—were in charge of keeping the church and the saints swept and clean. They may also have had some control over lay religious finances, for a 1776 petition complains that the governor had been taking away money "from the tenanches of the pueblo, [and] from the *cofradías* or *hermandades.*"[8]

The *cofradías* (religious brotherhoods) just mentioned formed one of two other religious systems, which are incorporated into the modern civil-religious hierarchies that are described elsewhere in Mesoamerica. Here, however, these systems operated with apparent autonomy both from the general religious hierarchy and from the civil government. *Mayordomos* (stewards) administered the cofradías, which proliferated in eighteenth-century Mexquitic. Like other officials, mayordomos were probably elected annually and awarded both prestige and some power, for several cofradías owned land and flocks of sheep; mayordomos also held authority over organizing their members to celebrate their cofradía's patron saint.[9]

The other lay religious system revolved around the great annual fiesta and fair of San Miguel and other major feast days. These were week-long affairs that attracted parishioners from all over Mexquitic, unlike the more limited celebrations sponsored by cofradías. The *fiesteros* who were elected to organize and fund them, and particularly the head fiestero or *patrono,* took on that burden (*cargo*) primarily for the prestige that the position gave.[10] For the fiesta patron had to spend liberally and was given no secular power in return, if we can believe the description given by store owner don Agustín Navedo in his legal fight with a local shoemaker who claimed not to have enough money to pay his debts:

> That he does have it is obvious: every year he begs for, and gets, for his pretensions, the most costly cargos such as that of Patron of the pueblo, in which he has served for more than four years now for his pretensions, without anyone obliging him to do so: and this makes him far from able to allege poverty [*miseria*] and insolvency, because in that case how could he ask for cargos that produce

nothing but insufferable expenses, such as (aside from the dues for the mass of the patron saint) renting clothes and horses, feeding all the people who are involved from the beginning of the rehearsals: on the days of Santiago and Santa Ana: the day of the patron saint, and the octave that they call the fiestas, when each individual spends more than a hundred pesos from the beginning to the end of these performances? [11]

There was an academic controversy in the 1960s and 1970s over the function of the fiesta and cargo systems of Mesoamerica. The opposing positions in this debate, which was never fully resolved, were succinctly stated by Chance and Taylor: "Is the hierarchy best regarded as a community defense against exploitation by outsiders, or as an instrument devised by the very same outsiders to subjugate and exploit the Indian population?" [12] When the alcalde mayor of San Luis attempted to cancel the annual bullfights in Tlaxcalilla in 1698, the governor of that pueblo/suburb responded with an argument that cut both ways. The fame of the fiestas of Tlaxcalilla, he argued, attracted people from all over the region to live there, most of whom found work during the year in the mines and ore-processing plants (*haciendas del beneficio de sacar plata*) of San Luis Potosí. But it was, he went on, only because the people of Tlaxcala looked forward to the fiestas and had to pay for the expenses entailed that they bothered to work in the mines at all:

[T]he sons of this Pueblo work with reputation and effort in the said Mines and Haciendas so that they will each be able to fulfill the cargos which they are given, and accept voluntarily, for the celebration of said fiestas; because if they are not permitted to hold the fiestas, it may cool the fervent desire and vigilance with which they work in the Mines and ore-processing Haciendas, in which there are so many life-threatening dangers; and they only endure in the said Ministry and labor of Mining in order to be able to celebrate that fiesta with polish [*con lustre*], because for their everyday food and clothing they can make do with the products of their land, gardens, and fields, from whose fruits they can easily obtain honestly their clothing and food. [13]

On the surface, the governor's argument that the fiestas "bring to Mining extraordinary benefits" supports the view that the fiesta/cofradía system was an elite imposition that buoyed up the class structure of colonial

Mexico. But what are we to make of the fact that it was the local Spanish elite, in the person of the alcalde mayor, who tried to abolish the fiesta? And it was the Indian governor of Tlaxcalilla who defended it, drawing an image of industrious Indian fiesteros and wielding that image as both shield and threat. As with any petition, the rulers of Tlaxcalilla phrased it in a way they felt would appeal to the Spanish authorities; it does not necessarily follow that their petition reflects their own feelings about the fiestas. The view of the fiesta system as an elite imposition could itself be seen as an elite interpretation imposed on the indigenous reality, while the use of that view by the governor could be a creative, indigenous use of colonial representations to support an independent local sense of religiosity.

Perhaps the key point in this scenario, however, is one ignored by both sides in the academic controversy. This is the role of the governor who lodged the petition and of his successors who, over the course of a century, continued to defend their town's right to hold a fiesta as they saw fit. It was long taken for granted by both anthropologists and historians that governing hierarchies represented the corporate interests of entire Indian towns, which were taken to be egalitarian, leveled communities. Even Gibson, following the common knowledge of the time, asserted that "the traditional leaders lost power" in Indian society, that "after the sixteenth century few individuals stand out in either [colonial or Indian] society, and the history becomes one of localized groups."[14] It is now clear, however, that the governors "and other officers of the república," as the documents put it, formed persistent elites within Indian towns that did not die out, were not exterminated by the conquering Spaniards, and were not uniformly absorbed into the mass of peasants, as various scenarios have theorized. The local elites continued throughout the colonial period to promote the interests of their towns, which they viewed as indistinguishable from their own interests.

Just what those interests were, and how they related to the broader social order of New Spain, can be hard to discern at times, as in the case of the fiestas of Tlaxcalilla. But the elites did not always present a unified front; frequently the elite of a town such as Mexquitic was internally divided, and each side took to the colonial justice system with claims of truly representing the neglected "sons of the pueblo." Hundreds of such petitions and civil suits fill the eighteenth-century shelves of the state historical archives in San Luis, for these persistent elites were riven also by factionalism. In this chapter I will use one set of petitions as a window on the workings of the república in Mexquitic and on the contested symbols of the colonial order that formed the terrain on which such disputes were waged.

"THAT HE LOOK ON US AS A FATHER"

The small political world of Mexquitic was turned upside down in 1764 by scandals and accusations against its governor, don Nicolás Francisco López. The scandals of that year added up to the first in a series of disputes between governors and groups claiming to represent the *común,* that is, all the sons of the pueblo. Later disputes proved more wrenching, more expensive to prosecute, and much more protracted, spanning the years 1776 to 1780 and 1797 to 1814. In the 1764 case—recorded in three short documents produced over a span of six months—we can see in abbreviated form the key themes that surfaced in the longer disputes.

On March 30, 1764, the alcalde mayor of the city of San Luis was presented with a petition by the provincial *defensor de indios y pobres,* a public official charged with the legal defense of Indians and the poor—a significant conflation of categories.[15] The petition was filed on behalf of María de Jesús and her husband Juan Obispo, "both Indians of the Pueblo of San Miguel Mexquitic." Juan Obispo had recently been wounded by three Indians from the neighboring pueblo of Tlaxcalilla while trying "to defend some magueys . . . located in the territory of the pueblo of Mexquitic." Magueys are commonly used as boundary markers between fields, so that by defending them Juan Obispo was metaphorically defending his field and, since it lay on the border, his pueblo as a whole from outside encroachment. The petition was not against the men from Tlaxcalilla, however, but against the governor of Mexquitic.

The petition stated that when María de Jesús went to complain about the three men before her governor she found him "completely drunk and out of his senses, and when she put in her complaint he began to mistreat her with insulting words." He sent for her wounded husband and for their son, and, when they were brought, "instead of giving them the consolation he should, their governor don Nicolás Francisco López ordered, with ignominy, cruelty, and tyranny, that his lieutenant Pedro Antonio shear his whole head with scissors, making use of powers which are not his, nor his to confer, since such punishments belong only to the superior judge." Cutting off the long braids that all Indian men in New Spain wore in accordance with both tradition and sumptuary laws was a deeply offensive form of punishment. The petition underlines the offense by using the word *tusar,* ordinarily reserved to speak of shearing an animal. Next, "as his intoxication held his senses captive, not satisfied with such a heinous and outrageous punishment," the governor ordered both Juan Obispo and his son arrested "to alleviate his guilt, and demonstrate his intrepidness and arrogance."

It was presumably at this point that María de Jesús contacted the defensor, who skillfully drew up the petition. The document worked in two ways to point to the guilt of the governor. With a forward-moving narrative thrust it told the story, moved to a brief demonstration of the culpability of the governor and the lieutenant for their actions, and concluded with a formal request that the case be heard and that the two officials be punished. This narrative structure was bolstered by a piece of evidence filed with the petition, one of the braids said to have been "shorn" from Juan Obispo. At the same time, the petition worked by repetition, accumulation, and insinuation. The defensor laced the account with a string of accusatory motifs: repeated insinuations of the governor's drunkenness, the eclipse of his reason, his cruelty and arrogance. Interwoven with these accusations were other rhetorical strings. These included stock references to the "superior wisdom" and the "most proven skill" of the judge who should hear the case. But they also, tellingly, include the theme of the proper, paternal relation of an Indian governor to the "sons" of his pueblo, which the current governor had abrogated through his cruelty, arrogance, and pride, "instead of giving them the consolation he should"; "[governors] should look at the sons with the Love and Charity which befits their poverty, and not with all the outrages which the poor sons of this Pueblo experience."

The arguments of the defensor apparently had some effect, since some of what he asked for was actually carried out. The governor and lieutenant governor were arrested and brought to San Luis to testify. It seems the matter ended there, however. There is no record that other witnesses were called, nor that the two officials were meted out "the proper punishment, to serve as a lesson to them, and an example to others."

Five months later a second complaint over the governor's imperiousness was presented to the alcalde mayor by Mónica de la Cruz and two other women, all identified as widows from the pueblo of Mexquitic (a translation of the entire petition appears in appendix D). There are broad parallels between the story the widows told in this petition and the one the defensor put forward in the preceding. Both asserted that an offense had occurred to a son of the pueblo, and both centered around the way the governor overturned expectations by doling out "mistreatment" where "consolation" was in order. But there are also numerous differences between the two compositions. The first was, after all, composed by a lawyer and the second by one of the widows from Mexquitic—no doubt with the assistance of an unnamed scribe. Where the lawyer's petition relied on the cumulative effect of a narrative filled with constant insinuations of the governor's deficiencies, the widows' was boldly and directly accusatory. The three widows opened their petition by accusing "our governor, don Nicolás López de la Puerta," of trying "to take away the [house] sites that we have always occupied, in which we live as daughters of said pueblo." Yet their argument was based on an understanding of the local setting that the officials in San Luis may have lacked, perhaps making it appear disjointed and elliptical to them. By the same token, exploring its ellipses can lead us back into the widows' worldview.

They followed their initial direct accusation of the governor with a long digression into the offices of the religious hierarchy that they and their sons and daughters had filled, as tenanches, fiscales topiles, ministros, and *pastores,* [16] "which we have all done without anybody objecting." It is not clear whether the Spanish officials who read and ignored the petition understood the relevance of lay religious office here. For them, I suspect, this was merely a rambling and tangentially related interlude, but for the widows it was a key element in their argument that the governor's attempt to take away their land was unjust. Title to land within the boundaries of Mexquitic was held by the pueblo as a whole, not by families or individuals. As the head of that legal corporation the governor did have the authority to take away a piece of land, even a house site, from any of its members, but he could only do so legitimately for a compelling moral reason. By attempting to take away the widows' land he was either impugning their morality or, worse, implying that they were not true daughters of the pueblo.

The fact that they had filled these minor positions in the religious hierarchy, without objections, implied that everyone had tacitly recognized their membership in the pueblo and their right to a share of land; the offices were the widows' credentials as upstanding citizens. The plaintiffs' apparent need to establish their credibility as citizens also underscores a general impression that they were fringe figures in the pueblo. As women and as widows, they were socially marginal.[17] They lived far from the center of the pueblo, on the border with the haciendas. Their sons made a living not in the pueblo or on their own land, but by migrant work in the surrounding Spanish estates, and so were marked as economically marginal. These facts must have loomed large in the widows' perceptions of their case, and perhaps in the local discussions of it as well.

Where the first petition wove in references to the governor's character, stated as abstractions ("ignominy, and cruelty, and tyranny"), the widows' tendency was to refer to the specific acts that had earned him his reputation ("that he might shear him as he is used to doing and has done with others"). This tendency is even more pronounced in the second half of the petition, which turns from the narration of the widows' own case to a general indictment of the governor's administration. At first this additional complaint against the governor seems to have been included only to demonstrate what a scoundrel he was, and perhaps to place the widows' case in the context of a generally mismanaged local administration. Only at the end of the segment does the purpose of its inclusion become clear. The widows were using this example of the governor's mismanagement of the pueblo patrimony—for them a major public event—as metaphor for their own private plight. Just as the governor played into the hands of the great landowners and squandered community lands while arrogantly ignoring the views of former governors and other sons of the pueblo, they argued, so he tried to take away the widows' own homesteads (at the landowners' behest, they implied) without attending to their pleas. In conclusion, "he should guard over this property" of the community—an indisputable duty of office from their point of view—"just as he should leave us in our house."

As the widows entwined the governor's alleged official mismanagement and their allegorical use of it in their conclusion, what began as a civil suit against the governor suddenly bloomed into a wide-ranging criminal suit against his entire term of government. Here, too, there is an allegorical argument behind what may have seemed to the authorities in San Luis a disorganized barrage of accusations. Just as the governor called meetings of the local notables (as he was obliged to do by custom) but ignored what those elders had to say, so he ignored the widows' wishes by ordering them to move. The widows indicted him for his lack of respect for "the elders" (*los viejos*), a category in which they implicitly included themselves when they asked "likewise . . . that he not mistreat us."

This same context highlights the ambiguity of their final request: "and that he look on us as a Father." This is a key motif of these petitions and in fact of colonial discourse about authority figures in general. For example, priests are called "fathers" in Mexico, both when they are referred to by name ("el padre Marcelino") and when they are talked about generally ("the padre said Mass").[18] The ambiguity of speaking of the governor as a father in this context is that, in so doing, the petitioners are invoking an image of patriarchal, or at least paternalistic, authority, and at the same time demanding that this authority respect and listen to his "sons," who are also his "elders."

It is not surprising to find that when Indians addressed colonial authorities, they used this loaded image of their own subordination as a counterbalance to their potentially insubordinate criticism of their governor. The governor (like the priest and other officials) was a "father," his subjects were "sons"—in fact, since colonial law declared all Indians legal minors, not only "sons" but literally "children." The governor was therefore hierarchically superior, in a position to carry out colonial policy, sit in judgment, grant mercy, and mete out punishment. But quite another argument underlies a second image, a second social relation that was often drawn on in the petitions—not of fathers and sons, but of fathers and stepfathers. By bringing in the figure of the stepfather, petitioners subtly transformed the terms of the original image and shifted the terrain of its argument: as a father, not a stepfather, the governor had not only the right to sit in judgment but also the duty to love and be charitable. The patriarchal overtones of the image of the father were reinterpreted to put factional struggles in moral, not hierarchical, terms.

The same terms continued to be used well after the end of the colonial period. Thus when the workers of the hacienda of Bocas, just north of Mexquitic, rebelled against the hacienda administrator in 1853, they wrote to the governor of San Luis Potosí in an attempt to forestall the use of troops to quell the rebellion: "We are looking for a father, not a stepfather."[19] The position of the administrator in the hacienda was in many ways similar to that of the governor in the pueblo: the administrator was an employee, like other employees, the governor a villager like other villagers, yet both were charged by their own superiors with maintaining order in their domains. Rebellions, too, tended to be aimed at administrators and governors rather than at the hacienda system or the colonial political structure behind them.

In the end, the petition of the widows was ignored. Perhaps I should not make too much of this fact; after all, such was the fate of innumerable petitions to the colonial authorities, perhaps a majority of them. But the contrast with the previous petition, presented by the defensor and resulting in a short spell in the provincial jail for the governor, is notable. It is as if the alcalde mayor was not able to make heads or tails of the form in which the widows presented their case. The contrast with the final, major petition, also presented by the defensor, is even more striking, for that one resulted at last in the governor's ouster from power.

THE GOVERNOR'S DEMISE

This third petition and its accompanying documents form the largest file in the don Nicolás case. They reveal a few telling details about the governor himself and about the local factions behind the suit. In them we can discern a bit about the three main groups of actors involved: the Indians of Mexquitic, the defensor, and the government officials in San Luis.

The petition was presented by the defensor de indios y pobres on behalf of the former governor don Juan de los Santos (who was also mentioned in the widows' suit) and several other former officials. The defensor cited the two general complaints around which all three suits revolved: don Nicolás's treatment of his fellow citizens and his mismanagement of the pueblo. In spite of the governor's spell in the provincial jail, the defensor stated,

> instead of reforming, every day and every moment he continues to disturb my parties more and more, with which he has made all the Sons restless, embarrassing them [lit., making them blush] with whippings and shearing them; and, what most needs rectifying, the damage which he is causing to this pueblo in its territory and its community funds.

In order to curtail this "cancer," the defensor insisted, the governor should be jailed once more and testimony should be taken from the governor and other witnesses on these charges. Into this request the defensor slipped a comment on the governor's lack of "respect for other Sons of the Pueblo who are more elder than he," along with references to his own earlier petition and "that of the widows."

The request was granted and the cane of office was temporarily handed over to the lieutenant governor of Mexquitic. The defensor then submitted, as was customary in colonial court cases, lists of questions to be put before the governor, the witnesses for the plaintiffs, and the preceding governor, who was treated as an accomplice in some of the alleged irregularities. The five questions put to don Nicolás involved the specifics of the administrative charges against him: Why did he lend the land titles of Mexquitic to the president of Tlaxcalilla? Had he allowed the hacienda of Cerro Prieto to take a piece of land from the pueblo and move the boundary markers? Why had he not given an account of the community funds to the local officials and notables "as is the custom," and what had he done with those funds? Where had he spent the money earned from the sale of wool of the local religious brotherhoods? And why did he order the widows to move?

The governor, in his replies, was equally straightforward in denying any culpability. He had loaned the document to his fellow governor "in a friendly way, as a brother"—here he extended the familial metaphor of fathers and sons to relations between governors. He did not let Cerro Prieto take over any land, nor did he move any markers; he had nothing to do with the new boundary marker, which was built by and for the count of San Mateo, owner of the hacienda. Giving accounts to the local notables was the business of the preceding governor, just as accounting for the sale of wool was up to the mayordomos of the brotherhoods. And, finally, he had ordered the widows to move because the Jesuit *padre rector* who administered La Parada had asked him to do so, on account of the damage caused by a son of one of the widows.

The questions the defensor wrote to be asked of the witnesses, by contrast, were long, leading, and heavy with innuendo (this too was standard procedure in colonial trials, as anyone who has read such a document will recognize). One of them will suffice to give a sense of their style:

> 2. Item. Whether they know and are aware that the governor is out of his mind day and night, and for this reason whenever his intoxication incites him he goes to the jail of the pueblo and whips and shears the imprisoned Sons that he has locked up, with no more cause than his own drunkenness; whether they are aware that whenever someone asks for justice from him they find him inebriated and instead of keeping justice he mistreats them verbally [*de razones*] and on many occasions he orders them whipped, and in this way they never obtain justice, so that, in every way and circumstance, my parties are living in utter dismay under the said don Nicolás Francisco López.

While the defensor questioned the governor on fiscal and administrative matters, he asked the witnesses for the plaintiffs to comment on the governor's mistreatment of the sons of the pueblo and his arrogance. The defensor did treat fiscal matters in the third question to the witnesses, but he couched them in the same terms of arrogance and personal mistreatment:

Whether they know and are aware that when he is requested to account for the community funds and is asked where he has the money, he answers that "he knows that very well" and that "they shouldn't meddle in that." For it is well known that the said don Nicolás sells sheep and goats to pay off his debts [*para salir de sus drogas*], and then in order to return the cattle he charges the Sons, taking from each of them according to the size of their small herds.

The correspondences between the concerns of the questions asked of the witnesses and those of the petition presented by the widows are striking. Perhaps these questions reflected more closely the concerns, and even the words, of the petitioners themselves. Don Nicolás's failure to present accounts was wrong not in itself but because it manifested his arrogance toward his fellow principales. His malfeasance in using community funds and cofradía flocks for private purposes was overshadowed by his single-handed imposition of taxes on the pueblo (and on the better-off members of it). Throughout the accusations we can detect a corpus of linked concepts that are being drawn upon. What was heinous, according to these concepts, was not the governor's mismanagement itself but the fact that it resulted from his irrationality, cruelty, arrogance, and lack of respect for his elders.

The witnesses the defensor brought to San Luis to testify were all, like the petitioners themselves, former officials. Two witnesses were in fact related both to current governor don Nicolás and to former governor don Juan de los Santos, who headed the list of petitioners.[20] This was indeed a small and intermarried elite. After their testimony was completed, a final witness, also a cousin of don Nicolás, was called: the previous governor, to be interrogated about having given don Nicolás money from the community treasury and fiesta funds the year before, all without giving accounts to the principales.

The exgovernor defended his actions. He had entrusted don Nicolás with collecting the royal tribute in the pueblo because he himself had fallen sick during the epidemic that ravaged Mexquitic in 1763 and was unable to complete his term, and he had done so considering don Nicolás a "man of good will" (*en confianza de hombre de bien*). In fact he apparently still held this view of don Nicolás, for among all the witnesses only he denied the various accusations and defended the governor:

Of all the other questions that have been asked of him, he is only aware for certain that don Nicolás does have a drink now and then, but not continuously as is said, nor with such excess; for though he does scold some Sons, and whip others, he has done this because he has found them drunk, living in sin, and incorrigible, and for having lacked respect for him—just as the present witness has done many times during his term as governor.

The fact that the exgovernor chose to defend don Nicolás at all suggests that he was a member of the same faction. Yet the tepidness of his defense seems to indicate that the governor's faction was comparatively weak—a fact that soon became all too apparent to don Nicolás himself.

At this point in the case the collected evidence was sent for review before the *asesor* (legal advisor) of San Luis Potosí, who found that the charges against the governor were serious and should be addressed immediately "to prevent the ruin that can result among such folk, who ordinarily act without the necessary reflection." On the other hand, he found the "method" of the case inadequate, and not at all a sufficient base for passing judgment, and he came up with a thorough schedule for conducting a proper trial, beginning by formally jailing the governor and sequestering all his property. This property amounted to nine cows and calves, three mules, twenty-five sheep and goats, three religious paintings (Guadalupe, St. Vincent Ferrer, and St. Joseph), a bench, and a table; it was not the riches of an urban elite but the goods of a prosperous enough villager.

In the end the case did not come to trial. Within a week of the sequestration of his property don Nicolás wrote, in his own hand, a petition setting forth an agreement which he had reached with the defensor. Reflecting on the charges "which the común of the pueblo has placed against me, which according to reports are justified" (as he conceded without quite confessing), and on the fact "that I cannot easily manage to undo and destroy the information that the común has given," don Nicolás agreed to retire entirely from public life. "The Sons of the pueblo cannot, for any occurrence, call me for anything: but that I will only live like a private Son of the pueblo." In return the defensor agreed to drop the entire case against him. Later the defensor added another condition, that don Nicolás's sequestered goods should be auctioned off in order to pay back the sixty pesos of missing royal tribute. The officials in San Luis accepted this bargain, and the case ended with a promise from don Nicolás to obey the terms of the agreement "promptly and blindly" and with his thanks to his judge "for the love and charity with which he has looked on him." Two months later don Juan de los Santos, the former governor who headed the petitioners, appeared once more as governor of Mexquitic.

What questions and what concerns were most important to each of the actors in these cases? For the defensor, judging from the questions he chose to put to don Nicolás and from the differences in presentation between his first petition and that of the widows, the key complaints were those of misgovernment and cruelty. His formulation of the suit places him in the long colonial line of paternalist defenders of the Indians. The asesor who reviewed the merits of the case may have had the same in mind when he declared these "excesses" worthy of a trial.

The defensor's interest, expressed only at the end of the case, in recovering the missing royal tribute was perhaps a matter of playing to the San Luis officials who decided the case. Perhaps he judged them to be mainly concerned with maintaining the flow of funds into the royal treasury, and with don Nicolás's reaffirmation of his personal subordination in the scheme of colonial government. In any case, such an interest was by no means incompatible with a paternalist defense. On the contrary, concern with *vasallaje* (with its double meaning of "tribute" and "subordination") was a major factor in paternalist rule over the Indians, attested to by the frequency with which those who denounced oppressive conditions pointed to the possibility that the Crown might lose revenue.

It is all but impossible to discern the intentions of María de Jesús, the plaintiff in the first suit, for her complaint was couched entirely in the terms put forward by the defensor. I would speculate, though, that where the defensor emphasized the arrogance of the governor in usurping the power of "the superior judge" to impose harsh punishments on his subjects, María may have been more concerned with her and her husband's own dignity, as validated by their valor in defending their land, the land of Mexquitic, from the men of Tlaxcalilla (an element of the case that the defensor does little more than mention). Certainly the widows in the second case, presented in their own purported words, showed such a sense of personal dignity and importance in standing up to both the governor and the hacienda administrators who would have them expelled from their land. Rather than speak of their own poverty, humility, and "wretchedness" (a stock colonial image of the Indian) in an appeal to the paternalist impulses of San Luis officials, they emphasized the governor's arrogance and malfeasance.

The plaintiffs in the third suit, local notables who claimed to represent all the Indians of Mexquitic, were, like the defensor, interested in prosecuting the governor for his malfeasance and cruelty, but their statements suggest that their key concern was the governor's disregard of their own authority as pueblo elders. Most important, they saw all of their complaints—the governor's drunkenness, abuse of "sons of the Pueblo," disrespect for pueblo elders, mishandling of community funds, and poor defense of pueblo lands—as different sides of a single problem. For them the heart of this problem was not, as one might expect, the conflict over resources and real estate (in 1764, and for almost another generation, there was still enough land to go around in the Mexquitic region, though the supply was beginning to diminish). It was the governor's high-handed manner.

What is most interesting in this dance of motives and motifs is the inescapable impression that the essence of the villagers' complaints never really registered on the colonial officials. There was an unbridgeable gap here. The petitioners from Mexquitic were concerned about the governor's encroachment on their own authority, autonomy, and even dignity. If San Luis officials had ever recognized such concerns, within the structure of colonial rule they could only have considered them symptoms of undue pride among their Indian subjects, not legitimate grounds for petition. At the same time, the petitioners adopted an idiom designed to get across their grievances to colonial officials in the most forceful way possible, by playing on the image of fathers and sons. Through this image they put themselves in a properly subordinate position, yet one from which they could press their legitimate demands on their superiors.

FIVE # People and Priest

In 1776 a group of people who described themselves as "the old Indian *republicanos* of the pueblo of Mexquitic" sent a petition to the alcalde mayor of San Luis in which they bitterly criticized their governor. Beyond detailing the governor's misdemeanors, such as confiscating property to pay off his own debts, embezzling fiesta money, and threatening anyone who dared denounce him, the former officials accused him of cruelty, haughtiness, making decisions in secret, and breaking with local custom. The principal break with custom, the elders complained, was the way he had been elected—in the priest's house, using a "raffle that they [the governor and the priest, presumably] said was for the election, and which they did not understand nor do we understand how it was done nor how the priest and the governor devised it." Seeing how the governor "gets along so familiarly" with the priest, however, "and having seen in the priest his desire that the governor be elected this year, we did not dare say anything." Moreover, they alleged, the governor was careful to cultivate the good will of the "neighboring *hacienderos*" (hacienda owners), treating them well and selling them animals at low prices, and thus winning them to his side and even getting letters of support from them.[1]

In this petition all the elements were brought together for a scenario that was to repeat itself for the remainder of the century. The pueblo, in the words of the alcalde mayor, was "divided in factions [*bandos*], without concert or subordination."[2] The governor's faction, however, was allied with both the priest and the local hacendados. In other words, the indigenous elite was divided, and the social forces that monopolized power and authority in colonial Mexquitic—the indigenous civil government of the pueblo, the landed interests of hacendados and ranchers in the jurisdiction, and the ecclesiastics of the parish—were more or less united.[3] In the 1764 case discussed in the previous chapter, the elite plaintiffs alluded to collusion between local landed interests and the governor, pointing to the potential for alliance between two of these dominant forces, though that alliance (if real) was a minor factor in their complaint, and in any event their victory in the case put an end to it. It was only after the parish was secularized in 1769 that the third actor, the priest, emerged as a political presence and the potential for imbalance in the local power equation became at times a reality.

For nearly two centuries Mexquitic knew continuity under the Franciscans. Two friars occupied the friary at all times, and their linked stays bound the history of the parish in an unbroken chain stretching back to its foundation. The friars tended to identify their interests with those of the parish friary, the Franciscan order, and the long-term survival of Franciscan ascendancy in the north. To be sure, there were individual differences among friars. Cases of licentious and self-interested friars abound in Inquisition records (none of them from Mexquitic, however), while at the other extreme there were those such as Fray Blas Correa in 1640, who stood out for his zeal in defending the rights of Mexquitic against neighboring haciendas. But the general tendency of the institution of the friary was to emphasize corporate stability over the vagaries of individual temperament. Parish priests, by contrast, each came and went with their own retinues of family and servants and with their own personal histories, connections, and fortunes. Their ties to the parish's past was minimal, and their interest in its future was tenuous and never institutionalized. The goals of priests tended to be personal, to secure a larger parish with greater income from ecclesiastical fees, for example, or a sinecure in a larger city.

As a large parish located conveniently near the comforts of San Luis, Mexquitic was itself a desirable curacy, and its priests turned their ambitions less toward gaining a better parish and more toward building up their own estates or securing control over village politics. They pursued these goals, moreover, in their own personal styles and using their own networks. The rule of the priests in Mexquitic, then, was much more idiosyncratic than that of the Franciscans, and the novel demands, expectations, and alliances of a new priest could cause considerable friction in the pueblo.[4]

"FATAL AND PERNICIOUS CONSEQUENCES"

The eighteenth-century conflicts between priest and pueblo in Mexquitic began with don Gerónimo Sandí, the third to occupy the curacy (1776–1787). Sandí's intervention in pueblo politics apparently grew from a crusading sense of morality. Soon after he had entered Mexquitic he began noticing things he did not like. Above all, he found that it did not conform to his idea of what a pueblo should be, namely a single Spanish-style urban center arranged neatly around the parish church. The Franciscans who witnessed the blossoming and spread of ranchos in Mexquitic for 178 years had never shown displeasure with the resulting dispersal of households, and San Luis officials who inspected the pueblo had been satisfied as well, finding its Indians "subdued and urbane." It was true that colonial law stipulated that Indians should live in their pueblos rather than in scattered ranchos, but the legal pueblo of Mexquitic comprised its entire three leagues of territory. Writing in 1778, Sandí describes his efforts from the moment he had entered the pueblo: "I have tried by all possible means to remedy the fatal and pernicious consequences that . . . result, as I have found, from the dispersion in which the families who make up [Mexquitic] live in their ranchos."[5]

The pernicious consequences of not living in the center of the pueblo were, as Sandí saw it, the people's "general ignorance about even the most basic mysteries of our Holy Faith" and their tendency to form illicit and even incestuous sexual unions. He was unmoved by the practical problem of how his parishioners, numbering nearly eight thousand, could make a living if forced to live in the central community with its limited supply of arable land. In fact, he rejected "the frivolous pretext that they need to live out there in order to guard and care for their cattle." Attending Mass was the important thing; they could walk to their fields if they had to. He reported spending much time and energy in a fruitless effort to coerce people to abandon their ranchos, move nearer to the parish church, and attend Mass and catechism regularly.

Sandí blamed his lack of success in these unprecedented endeavors on the governor of Mexquitic, Urbano Sánchez, whom he drove from office in 1778 and continued to persecute over the next few years. The alcalde mayor agreed that the dispersion of ranchos in Mexquitic contradicted the draconian spirit of the decrees aimed at suppressing the regional rebellion of 1767 (see chapter 3), and he approved of these moves. He forwarded the Sandí cases to Mexico City with a request for more extensive punishments in Mexquitic and the imposition of a Spanish *teniente* on the pueblo. The royal attorney charged with protecting the rights of Indians (*fiscal protector*) rejected those recommendations with a benevolent paternalism that could only have reinforced the image of the people of Mexquitic held by the Spanish elite in San Luis, referring not to the privileges granted to the Tlaxcalan founders of the pueblo but "to the poverty, unhappiness, stupidity, and special ignorance" of Indians in general.[6] The degradation of the image of the people of Mexquitic in the official ideology formed a key part of the wider context for the conflicts between the priest Sandí and the pueblo.

In 1779, not content with having filed suits against the exgovernor and most of the officers of his república, Sandí set out to arrest a niece and a sister-in-law of Urbano Sánchez as "accomplices in [Sánchez's] excesses" and for their alleged "disrespect for his [i.e., Sandí's] person and character."[7] Sánchez had gone into hiding, but according to Sandí's outraged testimony to the alcalde mayor his relatives continued to flaunt their disrespect, calling the priest "tú" and pretending they did not know or care who he was. Sandí responded to this insolence with violence. At one point "it was necessary to give her a slap," he reported, and later "it was necessary to threaten them, borrowing a saber from one of the servants who accompanied [me]."

Even as the deposed governor's relatives were being marched under guard to San Luis, they continued to slight the priest's authority (*mando*) with insolent phrases, which Sandí took pains to report verbatim to the alcalde mayor. "The priest has no business coming here to bother us; the priest doesn't have authority over married women." "What was the priest doing in his rancho? He was annulling his marriage, his and his children's." "Now you'll see, little priest, I don't owe you a thing." "Why should they [i.e., the relatives] go to the city? The priest isn't their judge, the priest only has authority in his Church, 'cause not even the señor Alcalde Mayor has authority over them and they don't owe him or the priest a thing."

Most insolent of all, "in another multitude of taunts they expressed 'that although the priest said they didn't know Christian doctrine, they knew it as well as their priest did, and that, as for a Pater Noster and an Ave Maria, any *padre* could say that without any help from the priest, and that others better than the priest had taught them.' " The word *padre* comes across ambiguously here. It means, first, that any male head of household could say the prayers for his family, and in this sense it is consistent with the sense of male outrage (seconded, in this case, by the women of the affected families) at the priest's assumption of authority over the father's domain.[8] At the same time it refers back to the *padres,* the Franciscan friars who had recently left the parish. By referring to both types of "fathers" at once, the word "padre" becomes a way of linguistically including the departed friars in the family of Mexquitic and excluding Sandí, who was addressed less respectfully in the reported speech as *cura* (parish priest) or *curita* (little priest). The "others" who had taught the prayers in Mexquitic before the priest arrived were, of course, the friars, who had never taken it upon themselves to meddle so deeply in the private lives of their parishioners, nor in the public conduct of their governors.

The alcalde mayor approved of Sandí's punishment of this insubordination and, as mentioned in chapter 3, additionally ordered two cavalry companies to march through Mexquitic as a warning. But even this show of force, the alcalde mayor found, "was not enough to set an example for them. . . . Since their main object is to live outside the limits of their pueblo, they have retired to where they think themselves farthest from hearing Mass, from Christian catechism, and from the other offices that credit them with being true and obedient natives."[9] In other words, living off in their rustic ranchos, the Tlaxcalans had not only become mere "Indians," they were just a hairsbreadth from becoming wildmen—like the Chichimecas their ancestors had been sent to civilize.

Sandí was soon able to rid the pueblo of the governor who was not to his taste and influence the election of a new one. This alliance formed the political backdrop to a violent incident that occurred in 1780, when the men of a rancho in Mexquitic severely beat a high-handed Spanish intruder. The men expressed confidence that "their governor" would take their side and perhaps even jail the stranger. Instead, the governor sided with the Spaniard and blamed his beating by the Indians on "the bad administration of justice of Urbano Sánchez."[10] A factional fight among the Mexquitic elite became joined with a struggle between two opposing ideologies, one upholding the people of Mexquitic as noble settlers with the right and duty to defend their land and privileges and the other holding all "Indians" as innately inferior and needing to be kept in their place. The faction that remained in control of the governorship, in the end, espoused the point of view and supported the interests of the local colonial power structure.

Florescano and Gil Sánchez have written of the links between the "vertical stratification" of colonial society by race and the formation of "equally rigid" social and economic strata within the racial groups: "Through these internal systems of stratification the colonial elite could co-opt and absorb individuals and groups of the lower strata who adopted their values and aspirations, without thereby destroying the bases of the profound stratification that articulated the system."[11] The present case seems to illustrate this tendency to perfection. Sandí, a new priest who was socially, economically, and ideologically allied with the provincial elite, was able to co-opt one section of the Indian elite and leave them in control of the pueblo government.

It is important to recognize that there was nothing inevitable in the form these alliances took. In other pueblos, and at other times in Mexquitic itself, both economic and ideological divisions existed among the various Spanish elites. Priest and landowners joined forces against the provincial government, or landowners united against government and priest. Political conflicts between priests and Spanish corregidores in Indian towns were as common and as bitter as those between priests and parishioners.[12] And, as in Mexquitic, there could also be deep divisions among the Indian elite, which regardless of their origins became characterized in this case as pro- and anti-priest.

It is on an intimate level such as this that we can best see how general trends are articulated in practice. The present case suggests that the colonial power structure tended to co-opt the colonized elite during times of change, when elite ideology was being transformed. Earlier in the century there had been a general agreement among the ruling provincial elite, the Franciscans, and the pueblo elite on a favorable view of the Tlaxcalans. By the late colonial period—when elite opinion had changed, a new priest with new views of Indian society had come to town, and new hacienda owners had entered the scene (see chapter 7)—a new faction of the Indian elite had come into favor. More to the point, deciding which faction of the Tlaxcalan principales held power, formerly a minor concern to anyone outside of that intimate circle, had become a matter of interest to powerful outsiders. This seemingly mechanical series of changes gave rise to a series of wrenching conflicts that peaked in 1810.

Given the new harmony among the bearers of power in Mexquitic, though, it is perhaps not surprising that for the moment no further conflicts were recorded in the pueblo. Sandí resurfaces in the provincial documentary record only in 1785, shortly before he left Mexquitic. Taking an apparently sincere interest in the welfare of the "poor people" of the pueblo during one of the worst famines in Mexican history, he pulled strings with the alcalde mayor to ensure that they got a share of what corn was available in the province.[13] But in a second letter on the same topic Sandí made it clear that his basic opinion of the people was unchanged.

They were facing hunger because of their "gross way of thinking" and their "laxity or laziness," for they had land to sow, but they left it fallow.[14] The basic argument of this letter figured prominently in later land conflicts—that the sons of the pueblo had plenty of land, but they were too lazy, ignorant, and disorderly to use it productively.

Sandí went into semiretirement soon after he penned these letters, his place at the altar taken by a series of assistant priests. In 1788 one of his assistants, the San Luis–born Bachiller José Ignacio Lozano, was promoted to *cura propio* of Mexquitic, the fourth to hold that secularized post. There he remained for another forty-five years, until his death from Asiatic cholera on July 25, 1833. His exceptionally long tenure spanned the end of the colonial period, the Wars of Independence, and the first decade of independent Mexico. Over the course of those years he became arguably the most powerful and influential priest in the parish's history, counting among his friends and compadres numerous high officials in the cabildo of San Luis, the priest of the city, the owners of the haciendas surrounding Mexquitic, and every high-ranking Spaniard commissioned to oversee the pueblo elections. He also amassed a small fortune, for he was able to donate 6,000 pesos in 1825 toward the foundation of the Colegio Guadalupano Josefino, forerunner of the Autonomous University of San Luis Potosí, and at his death his estate was still worth over 40,000 pesos, more than half in the form of outstanding loans to the owner of La Parada.[15]

In the last decade of the eighteenth century Lozano prided himself on stimulating the economy of Mexquitic, yet he also stood accused of usurping its common lands, exploiting its cofradías, and interfering in its politics. He railed against Hidalgo when the insurgency broke out, tided over the uprising that swept Mexquitic from November 1810 until March 1811, denounced his enemies as seditious Indians, and continued to sign his name with the royalist coda "Cura por S.M. (Q.D.G.)" ("Parish priest by the grace of His Majesty, may God preserve him") until October 1822, more than a year after Mexico won its independence.[16] The political and economic relations that tended to set priest against people in Mexquitic were clearly outlined in Lozano's long, complex tenure as parish priest during the crucial juncture of late-colonial and insurgent Mexico. His life and lawsuits are worth examining in some depth.

"INDUSTRIOUS, HARDWORKING, AND INGENIOUS INDIANS"

The legal imbroglios surrounding Lozano began in 1797 over a matter apparently far removed from Sandí's meddling but moralistic concern for his parishioners' way of life. The previous year Ventura Cleto, an Indian of Mexquitic, had bought and cleared a large field near Corte, and in association with his neighbors had dug a two-kilometer irrigation canal from the Río de la Parada. But then, his neighbors alleged, Ventura had claimed that he had done almost all the work on the canal and had taken it and the vital irrigation water as his own. The prime mover of this usurpation, they claimed, was not Ventura but the priest, who was using the illiterate Indian as a front. Lozano had set the scheme in motion by loaning over 1,000 pesos to Ventura for clearing the field and financing the canal; the priest then joined forces with the owner of La Parada to have the Indian build a stone dam on the Río de la Parada that diverted its water into the new canal. As a final touch, Lozano had forced the association of neighbors to accept insufficient payments for the work they had put into the project, using his influence and authority as priest to intimidate them. The neighbors sued Ventura over the confiscated canal, the inhabitants of the valley around Corte sued Lozano for cutting off their water supply, and three women sued both Lozano and Ventura for the return of the land cleared by Ventura, claiming it was theirs by legitimate inheritance. Their petitions were supported by the governor, "fulfilling his obligation as a true Father of the Fatherland" (*Padre de la Patria*), who forwarded them to the intendant of San Luis Potosí. The priest later accused this governor and his república of drunkenness and disturbing the peace of the pueblo.[17]

The lawyer for Ventura's opponents invoked, in support of their suit, the standard image of the Indian as an ignorant, irrational, poverty-stricken, and (to put the best face on it) suffering minor. The double-edged nature of this image was manifest in the double role that the lawyer gave it. He made fun of Ventura, "an Indian who even lacks the common sense of reason [*las luces naturales de la razon*]," for presenting as his own a petition full of erudite references to classical and legal sources with which he could not possibly have been familiar (f. 24). Yet he appealed to the status of his own clients as wards of the state—in other words, as people legally categorized as lacking "the use of reason."[18] He maintained that "it is never licit for any motive" for parish priests to make such contracts "in the fields of their parishioners, to whom their authority and respect (as in the present case) may do harm, and especially when [the parishioners] are Indians, whom the laws so favor."[19]

The lawyer for Ventura picked up on the double use that his opponent made of this image of the Indian and responded to it with heavy irony. "Why, if they are all Indians, does their party have a right to restitution, and not mine?" he demanded rhetorically. Like "the contrary party," he went on, Ventura "is an Indian and an impoverished person," but he has something else, "which, according to their defense lawyer, they do not share," namely "his terrible rusticity, incapable of recognizing what is bad for him, since as their lawyer assures in his brief no. 4, 'he even lacks common sense.' "

> So that if he does not have a right to restitution for being Indian and impoverished, as he has this predicate in common with the others; at least he should be more favored for his incomparable rusticity among the Rational beings, which is the special predicate that he is given; and if [their lawyer] confesses to me that he has no right to restitution in either case, for they are all privileged, then he will also confess that, in asserting these things, he only wanted to soil [*emporcar*] one more piece of paper.[20]

After mocking the other lawyer's use of the veteran image of the miserable Indian, Ventura's lawyer called up an entirely different image of the Indian as a potentially industrious laborer:

> He notes that the Laws favor the Indians and asserts that it is not licit for the parish priest to loan them money to finance [*habilitar*] their croplands: so that, in his mind, a priest can loan money to a store owner, to a private individual, to an agriculturalist [*campista*] so that they can finance their fields, but not to an Indian who is his own parishioner, because financing it so that it becomes useful is no favor, although for anyone else it is. More clearly: To favor the Indians, the laws ordain that they be compelled not to be lazy, to cultivate their fields, and to have oxen. . . . Law 21, title 1, book 6 of the *Recopilación* . . . charges the priests to try to persuade the Indians in the cultivation of their land.
>
> This, I think, must be effectively understood so that the industrious, hardworking, and ingenious Indians are not prohibited from being financed by their priests; and in truth this is the best way to persuade them, since words would have little effect without help, and without deeds. (f. 31)

Thus Ventura's lawyer revealed that beneath Lozano's apparently materialistic pursuit of private gain at the expense of the common Indians of the parish lay a deep concern with uplifting them toward a better and more productive way of life. Though this argument would be easy to dismiss as a mere rhetorical flourish, I also see in it a new moment in the history of images of the Indian in Mexquitic. The image of the industrious Indian, which Ventura's lawyer introduced here, developed out of the image appealed to by the opposition's lawyer of the Indian as a suffering, irrational minor, which Lozano's predecessor had so often called upon. The priest Sandí consistently referred to his parishioners as "poor wretches" (*pobrecitos, miserables, infelices*), and in the same vein he asserted that the famine of 1785 resulted from their ignorance and idleness.

Lozano emphasized instead, much in the Enlightenment spirit of the "Bourbon Reforms" then sweeping Spain and its empire, that paternalist leadership, exercised by himself and his landowning friends, could lead the Indians into redeeming industriousness. In contrast to Sandí, Lozano reserved the terminology of "wretchedness" to refer specifically to his political enemies and applied its mirror image of "industry" to his allies, who he asserted formed the majority in the pueblo. He had not taken water from the people of Mexquitic, he declared, but rather Ventura Cleto had dug a canal to irrigate his own land with his own hard work, "and everyone would attain irrigation if they applied themselves to the work of digging canals." [21]

The theme of the Indian's potential for industrious labor, when rightly prompted by the higher authorities, came to be a staple in Lozano's rhetoric and lawsuits over the next fifteen years. When the conflicts swirling around the priest, the haciendas, and the local officials momentarily ebbed, Lozano and other colonial authorities took time to note that the working poor (always the majority in the pueblo, and so far as we can tell uninvolved in the cases against the priest) continued to fend off hunger through their own diligent work. They would compare this "new industriousness" with the wastefulness of pursuing lawsuits against themselves and generously give themselves the credit for producing the "change" they perceived in the pueblo. Thus Lozano's friend, the San Luis regidor don Francisco Justo García, reported on Mexquitic in 1804 after serving for three years as elections commissioner:

> Three years ago this pueblo was a swarm of drones, by no means industrious, given to idleness, without civilization, and without the resolve to undertake anything that would be useful to them. Today it is a swarm of bees who know how to turn the most negligible stuff into sweet and abundant honey: 150 offices in which they make cloth, 400 individuals employed in them, in the spinning

wheels, in spinning rope, in farming, in shoemaking, in forges and in carpentry, in the scrublands taking juice from the plants, making the countryside grow fertile, busy in their fields, and in many other things in which they are employed—without a doubt all this proves that their spirit is capable of learning whatever they are taught and they wish to learn. I do not know if I should flatter myself that I am the one who, through my influences, has attained what Your Honor [the intendant of San Luis] has so often ordered and so often urged.[22]

Lozano, who also flattered himself that he had made the people more industrious, congratulated García on his "vivid and sweet words" to the leaders of Mexquitic, "exhorting them . . . that they not be idle, and thus call the others to work and to industry; that they learn to cultivate the land, and speak Castilian better."[23] But the emphasis that García and Lozano placed on increased commercial industry in Mexquitic was indeed little but self-flattery. Economic activity in the pueblo was largely non-subsistence from at least the early eighteenth century, and probably from its foundation—not at all surprising, given the proximity of markets in the nearby mines and the city of San Luis, both prodigious consumers of the wood, charcoal, hay, pulque, prickly pears, and *lechuguilla* rope produced in that semiarid countryside. There is no independent evidence that the priest really fomented weaving and spinning, as he claimed. The large number of looms in Mexquitic in the early 1800s probably owed less to the efforts of Lozano or García than to the fact that textile industries throughout New Spain expanded "when warfare and blockade disrupted transatlantic trade, particularly between 1795 and 1808."[24]

García's language was instructive. The Indians he first found—in their natural state, presumably—were "drones," while those he found after three years as commissioner in Mexquitic were industrious "bees," who turned the flowers of the desert into products useful to the colony. In "proving" that Indians could learn "whatever they are taught and they wish to learn," García implied that they needed the guidance of a member of the Spanish elite to advance and thus were not capable of acting rationally on their own. In this way Lozano and his allies painted their intervention in the economic life of Mexquitic as an activist form of neo-paternalism and a fitting response to the kind of standard, "pro-Indian" paternalism that their opponents continued to invoke. When Lozano was accused in 1804 of punishing his enemies by forcing them to stand naked in front of the church, he retorted that the former governor whom he had driven from office might try to alleviate their poverty with the same brand of paternal interest: "In order that they not be naked, which is how most of them go around normally, [exgovernor] José Manuel Ventura can endeavor to clothe them and to make them more civilized (*aser que entren en mas policia*)." One of Lozano's witnesses, a ropemaker from Mexquitic, elaborated: "What usually happens is that since those who rebel against fulfilling their duties to the Church are the same natives who are given over to laziness and the vices which that gives rise to, they usually for the same reason have very little clothing to wear." [25]

As Lozano saw it, most of the people of Mexquitic had already been made industrious, "coming into this city daily to sell," while his opponents drew their strength exclusively from the shrinking ranks of the wretched. "For who would doubt," he concluded in a stinging remark, "that in so populous a Pueblo, which has more than ten thousand Indians of all classes, there would be at least seven hundred perverse abandoned men of evil customs and worse hearts, who for that reason, or just to cause damage, or . . . for some reward, would offer to testify to anything." All the false accusations against him, in Lozano's view, could be traced back to the year 1797, when don José Manuel Ventura was governor and "the peace began to be disturbed in this Pueblo. . . . This dismal event had no other origin than that this Governor and all the Individuals in his República, to the scandal of the entire Pueblo, lived Drunk every single day." Lozano reproached them, as was his duty, but "accustomed to live in liberty, and without subordination," they were offended, and Manuel Ventura formed an alliance of his kin, in-laws, and spiritual kin—"the most rotten part of this Pueblo, incestuous people, professional drunks. . . . To this confused agglomeration they have appropriated the name of *común*." In fact, Lozano wrote, the real *común* had nothing to do with Ventura's band, and their allegations against him were utterly baseless. [26]

"RESTLESS AND TURBULENT INDIANS"

Within a year of the allegations that Lozano had a hand in usurping pueblo land and water, he was accused of abusing the cofradías and Indian labor. Both controversies soon became deeply entangled in factional pueblo politics, for the leaders opposed to Lozano claimed that every year "they elect, under the priest's supervision, individuals from his faction," who would not pursue claims against him or his friends, the hacendados, in anything but a perfunctory and half-hearted way. [27] The case went on from year to year, election to election, official to official, with several opposition leaders and their lawyers ending up in jail along the way, until it was ultimately resolved against those opposing the priest—who promptly appealed this definitive verdict.

Given the factionalism that was so apparent in Mexquitic in the late colonial period, it is not surprising that the facts in these cases should prove slippery. What can be determined with some certainty often seems shallow and inconsequential when set next to the claims of "bestial sins" and "diabolic spirit" that the two sides threw at each other. As Tutino remarks on the cases involving the priest Lozano, "the truth cannot be ascertained in testimony filled with such invective." [28] But each set of antagonists also viewed and therefore presented events according to their own ideologies when they inscribed their versions of the events. Some of the contested meanings through which the priest, his allies, and their opponents expressed themselves can be heard in the distortions and rhetoric of their slanted depositions.

A basic representation in the Lozano cases was that of factionalism itself. One might think that the polarization of the pueblo into factions, which so many provincial authorities noted and bemoaned, would have filled them with the same doubts about the validity of any testimony from Mexquitic that we feel today. Indeed one official, the first intendant of San Luis Potosí, Bruno Díaz de Salcedo, did express such doubts in a penetrating analysis of the early phase of the case, but after his death in 1799 these misgivings were not raised again by judges, magistrates, or assessors. A key to their method of weighing the acrimonious testimony in a case such as this is the conception of factions (*bandos* or *partidos*) that comes across in the suits and the verdicts. A constant refrain throughout the case is the characterization of one faction as *la parte sana*, "the healthy part" of the pueblo, and the other as *los díscolos* or *los revoltosos*, the "unruly" or "rebellious" ones. In other words, the pueblo was not merely divided into two groups with different agendas and opposing interests, but into good and bad, "healthy" and "unruly" parts. The question was not to discover the truth in the contradictory evidence the two sides provided, but to discover in their evidence the true moral character of each side. Faced with, and perhaps sharing, this conception of factions, each side in the case was apparently less concerned with presenting direct testimony in their respective petitions than with constructing a rhetorical narrative that firmly placed the petitioners within the "healthy" group of villagers and their opponents among the "rebellious ones."

This essential strategy weighed heavily against the fortunes of the opponents of Lozano, for they were in the unlucky position of having to argue that the parish priest, the governor, and the local large landowners were not only squeezing the pueblo economically but were in fact the inciters of sedition in Mexquitic. As it turned out, this proposition did not sit well with the colonial officials to whom it was addressed. In December 1804, the self-styled "común" of Mexquitic complained, in a petition filled with classical allusions and written in erudite though occasionally ungrammatical language, about all aspects of Lozano's tenure in the parish. In order to keep the governor under control, they claimed, Lozano imposed candidates who were "inept, or young, or naturally stupid." He had usurped pueblo land and water rights. It was, they wrote, "a great hardship, and close to cruelty, that when the water that is born in the same land in which we are born is distributed, we should remain like thirsting Tantaluses, with all the water taken away before our eyes to foreign fields; for though in reality they are not foreign but our very own, they can be thought of as foreign, since we do not enjoy their use." Though they "provid[ed] our parish priest with firewood, charcoal, and hay . . . as well as mayordomos, servants, and cooks," they continued, "the priest does not fulfill all the duties connected with his office, as he does not preach sermons every Sunday of the year but only during Lent." They attributed all these failings to Lozano's "implacable hatred" and to "his perverse designs that conspire to no other end than that of ruining us and destroying us." "Oh times, oh customs!" they concluded, "that in a Country situated in the center of Christianity such a perverse Practice should be permitted and tolerated."[29]

This attempt to paint Lozano as a perverse enemy of Christianity did not move the royal attorney (*fiscal protector*) who heard the case. Two years later opposition leaders fared no better when they argued in even stronger terms that local officials were ineffective in pursuing lawsuits against the surrounding haciendas because they were selected "from those simple souls who cannot distinguish good from evil." This was, they maintained, because of "the influences of one lone man who abhors peace, who has become by the same token a most suspect, unruly rebel, irreproachable, with no fear of God, of the world, or of his superiors. Let us say it more clearly: a man of diabolic spirit is the cause of all these problems. And let us see who: the Priest."[30] Despite their efforts to portray Lozano as an "unruly rebel," it was the opposition leaders themselves who were thrown in prison.

The main rhetorical strategy of petitioners on both sides in the Lozano cases was to present, as a kind of subtext or undercurrent to their ostensible arguments, a series of oppositions contrasting their own moral character to that of the opposing party. Examples of such oppositions abound in the documents, giving the impression of a dualistic worldview that cries out for a structuralist interpretation. A typical example is the 1807 petition filed by the governor, the eight officials of his república, seven former governors, forty former officers, and sixty-four other citizens.[31] It is remarkable only for the sheer amount of vituperation that its authors managed to cram into six handwritten pages. The immediate purpose of the petition was to counter a request by opponents of the priest (eight former officials and ten electors) to have the colonial government intervene in the long-standing suit between Mexquitic and La Parada, but this purpose was overwhelmed from the first lines by a barrage of invective and counteraccusations. When these apparently tangential accusations are closely examined, however, they reveal the system of oppositions that underlay the petitioners' political thought.

The governor and his allies contrasted their own peace-loving nature with the "malevolence" of the opponents of Lozano. Personalizing their attack, they singled out one opposition leader, Basilio Robles, as having a "brooding spirit that does not tire in its search for the destruction of the peace, harmony, tranquility, and quiet that we, being solicitous of the mutual good of this común, are eager to maintain." Basilio, they continued, had kept the "individuals of that común . . . deluded with his fatal persuasions, . . . sacrificing [them] to his passions and interests." The common people, "these unhappy wretches who are ignorant of their true good," by contrast, did not know their own interests, but being easily dominated by unchecked passions "have united with the said Basilio Robles." They were "credulous," easily influenced subjects who had been captivated by the "deceptions" of those "tyrants," though their true well-being was the concern of the república and not Basilio.

In structuralist terms, the común formed the neutral center point of a tripartite division, with Basilio and the governor forming opposing poles: their evil, our good; their "brooding spirit" and our "quiet, calm, and naturally peaceful character"; the moral abandon of "these restless men" who have "forgotten the sentiments of Catholicism," and the "religiosity and piety" of us who live "by the maxims of Religion" and "give the priest the obedience he is due." They similarly contrasted "the malevolence of [Basilio,] this man filled with audacity, imprudence, and boldness," with "the honor, reputation, and conduct of our beloved Priest, Bachiller don José Ignacio Lozano, whose . . . particular operations and distinguished birth make him deserving and worthy of the office that he fulfills with such prudence, maturity, and ability." Basilio's "principal objective: the satisfaction of his appetites and passions," the república wrote, contrasted with Lozano's "zeal of a Shepherd who solicitously keeps watch over the happiness of his Flock." Finally, the "distinguished birth" of Lozano contrasted with the "low birth" of Basilio. "Yes, sir," the petitioners concluded, addressing the viceroy directly, "Basilio Robles is not a noble Indian, nor will he ever be recognized as such in our pueblo."

The governor and república portrayed factionalism as an unholy war waged by passion-bound men against the pious peace promoted by the local officials. The contested terrain in this war was the simple souls of the común, those ignorant commoners so liable to be swayed by passion, not reason. The royal attorney in Mexico City agreed wholeheartedly with this presentation, noting that "the pueblo of Mexquitic is now divided into factions, the healthy part being that of the present administration and república, which follows their parish priest, a virtuous and orderly subject, and the contrary party, opposed to the priest, is composed of . . . restless and turbulent Indians." He concluded that the intendant of San Luis "should look on the unruly Indians with the equity and compassion they deserve for their ignorance and poverty." The intendant found it within the bounds of his compassion to have Basilio Robles and a companion jailed for several months, without trial or charges against them, in the San Luis prison.

"AND THE PUEBLO WILL HAVE RESPECT"

Emphasis on the subjugation and obedience of the subjects of the Crown was a staple of colonial documents, and these cases were no exception. Images of wretched or industrious Indians, of rebellious or submissive Indians, formed the idioms in which they were heard and judged. Lozano and his allies repeatedly blamed the profusion of suits against themselves on the unruliness of their enemies, who were "accustomed to living with liberty and without subordination," in Lozano's words. In the view of one lawyer for the governor, "those unruly Indians and malcontents . . . who because of their licentiousness wish to live without subjection, despotically, and at their own discretion, have hated the priest . . . for no other reason than that he took them to task for their bad habits." The governor himself seconded this opinion: "Far from giving due obedience to the present Governor and Parish Priest, they are revealing themselves with the utmost haughtiness and pride, this giving birth to the lamentable situation to which we find our Pueblo reduced, and to the frequency of homicides, drunkenness, incest, bestial sins, with quarrels, rifts, and disagreements."[32]

Similar questions of respect and authority had been at the heart of the cases involving Lozano's predecessor, Sandí. Sandí accused and even assaulted the former governor and his family for their disrespect toward himself in his priestly role. His opponents, for their part, criticized and disdained the priest for his radical departure in behavior from "others better than him." Each side conducted a kind of monologue, reacting to perceived offenses by the other against their own notions of proper relations between priest and people, but the political force that in the end settled the case lay with Sandí.

Lozano became entangled in much more complex cases, in which the theme of the proper reciprocal relations of priest and parishioner was enmeshed with long-running political conflicts and land and water disputes. But these complications served to emphasize, rather than conceal, the factors of political and economic power that propelled the priest-and-people controversy. The opposition initiated the lawsuits, attacking Lozano for his alleged breaches of law, custom, and propriety, but because of Lozano's political influence they were promptly pushed into a defensive position. The issue of the priest's behavior toward his parishioners was successfully shunted aside, and his opponents were forced to argue on the priest's own ground. In the colonial courts, the only relevant question was whether the people, the Indians of Mexquitic, were behaving properly toward their priest, and that behavior was defined in the vocabulary of subjugation.

In 1798 Intendant Bruno Díaz de Salcedo had raised quite a different image when he described the opponents of Lozano languishing in the prison of San Luis. In his analysis of the case, which was already quite involuted, the intendant wrote to the viceroy that "these wretches, worthy of all compassion, suffer much more because the Indians of Mexquitic, descendents of the noble loyal Tlaxcalans, have always imitated their ancestral compatriots in their fidelity."[33] Here, curiously interwoven with the themes of wretchedness and paternalistic compassion, is the last reference I have found by a Spanish colonial official to the noble Tlaxcalan status of the pueblo and to its fidelity (which is a much nobler attribute than submissiveness, even if it describes the same actions). The pueblo elites on both sides of the Lozano affair, however, continued to invoke the image of the noble Tlaxcalans, which otherwise was strikingly absent from the repertoire of the cases.

In 1807 the opponents of the priest and the governor argued that they had a special claim to the ear of the viceregal court because "from the time of their ancestors, the founders of the pueblo of Mexquitic, they have been exemplars of loyalty and fidelity to Our Catholic Monarchs who have governed us." The governor responded, in the counterpetition analyzed above, by playing on the concept of nobility that for him was implicit in his opponents' claim, contrasting the "distinguished birth" of Lozano with the "low birth" of one of the opposition leaders, who he maintained was "not a noble Indian, nor will he ever be recognized as such in our pueblo." When this counterpetition landed the opposition leaders in jail, they continued along the same line, but they transposed the vocabulary of fidelity into that of obedience. They wrote that they had been jailed as "unruly and rebellious" only because "we are defending what, since the earliest infancy of our Conquest, our King (May God Keep Him) granted us, . . . like obedient sons, without insubordination."[34]

The authors of these petitions of course attempted to frame their insistence on the nobility, the privileges, and the loyalty of the Tlaxcalans in language appealing to the colonial authorities. But their continual references to the authority of the king who established the pueblo did not disguise key differences between their idiom of Tlaxcalan nobility and the generic Indian images invoked by Spanish lawyers and officials. When the royal attorney recommended "compassion" for the "unruly Indians," he based his judgment on an image that effectively denied them the status of actors in their own right. They deserved "equity," he argued in effect, not because they were pursuing just aims but because their acts were the phantasmal products of ignorance and poverty. The leaders of Mexquitic, by contrast, invoked a positive image of the colonized as defenders of the rights granted by the king. Theirs was also a specific image, rooted in the same local pride that priests and officials so often saw as unruly insubordination, which set the Tlaxcalans of their pueblo apart from the Indians of other towns. Governor Rafael Melecio Sandate concluded a petition to the intendant with an appeal that moved swiftly away from the standard image of the impoverished Indian toward a call for the dignity of his office and his town: "For although I am a Poor man, I am Governor, and the Pueblo will have Respect, for that is what I expect from your Justice."[35]

It is a commonplace that contemporary images of Indians have colonial origins. What these cases suggest to me is that we may look specifically to colonial interchanges such as that between the lawyers for and against the opponents of Lozano to discover how elite colonial images became part of the vocabulary of Indian people such as those in Mexquitic. We can see in them that the image of the noble Tlaxcalan had already been erased from the colonizers' lexicon by the end of the colonial era. The people of

eighteenth-century Mexquitic would certainly have known of the attitudes of Spaniards toward Indians from their commercial dealings in the
city of San Luis, but it was lawsuits such as these that brought them into
direct contact with elite ideology about the Indian and compelled them
to make use of those elite images in order simply to have their cases heard.

"VERY DIFFICULT OR ALMOST IMPOSSIBLE TO PROVE"

I first encountered the formidable figure of Lozano during my initial trip
to San Luis in 1980, on an afternoon spent at the recently opened state
archive in search of a likely subject for a project combining anthropology
and social history. A document that I found that afternoon, criticizing the
priest for his exploitation of the cofradías and the Indians of the pueblo,
helped convince me to focus my research on Mexquitic.

Perhaps this is the time to acknowledge that my research was based at
first on an image I had constructed of the Mexican peasant, based on my
reading of what I considered (and still consider) to be among the best
ethnographies on Mexico, Paul Friedrich's *Agrarian Revolt in a Mexican
Village* (1970) and Arturo Warman's . . . *Y venimos a contradecir* (1976). My
understanding of Mexican agrarian history, drawn from a reading of Tannenbaum (1929), Simpson (1937), Wolf (1959), and Womack (1969),
completed the picture. It was a heroic image of epic struggle, pitting the
class of landowning, power-wielding villains against the virtuous, hardworking, and ultimately triumphant villagers whose lands they had
usurped. Simplistic, of course, a comic-book vision of reality when baldly
stated and placed against the depth and subtleties of everyday life (or of
the works that gave rise to the image). But it was this image, still unstated,
that underlay my proposals, held my imagination, and propelled me into
fieldwork and into the archives of San Luis, where I fully expected to find
just these characters.

"Humanity trembles to see the sufferings of innocence," the petition
began, "and the blood freezes in one's veins when one notes with horror
that the rights, and the justice, of the poor are almost always disregarded."
It continued, ominously, "The idea is that the just and the miserable
should perish, and that those who have more power should triumph."
This was the right case: in Lozano I had clearly found my villain. More
searching soon found an accomplice in his compadre Coronel Angel
Prieto de la Maza, the owner of La Parada from 1783 until his death in the
1810s, with his hardened let-them-eat-cake attitude toward the landless
peasants of Mexquitic.

The petition was written in 1798, in the form of a letter to the viceroy of New Spain, by a friar (Franciscan, I like to imagine) who identified himself only by his assumed religious name, Alegría (Joy) (a full translation appears in appendix E). Rereading it now I sense a peculiar double imagery, like watching an optical illusion in which background and foreground alternate. It is easy to read the petition in the heroic peasant mode, with Alegría giving voice to pugnacious villagers who stood up for their rights against overwhelming oppression. But it is clear to me now that the imagery that Alegría himself used, through which he sought to appeal to the conscience of the viceroy, was not heroic at all. He portrayed the Indian—not peasant, Indian—as a wretched, suffering minor and eternal ward of the state. He repeatedly used the word *razón,* "reason" or in this context "rightness, right," playing against the negative aspects of this image. Colonial Indians were defined as the opposite of *gente de razón,* "people who can reason," but in Mexquitic, he argued, all the *razón* was with the Indian people. There the Indians had both right and reason on their side. *Razón* was the ally of truth and justice and the enemy of "the tyranny and slavery" imposed on Mexquitic by the priest, with his ability (as *gente de razón*) to influence the court and seduce a faction of villagers to his side.

After I found more documents on the Lozano cases, and read and reread them, the contradictions and complexities in those cases also became apparent to me. My research has not entirely vindicated Lozano, who did not hesitate to use his considerable power to personal advantage. But the texts cannot be read as just a case of "priest versus people," as I read them that first afternoon, through the filter of "villain versus heroic victims." Lozano's first years in the parish went as smoothly as Sandí's last, judging from the silence of the judicial record. The series of scandals and conflicts that erupted at the end of the century, however, raged with such divisiveness that it was, in the words of the first intendant of San Luis Potosí, "very difficult or almost impossible to prove" the suspicions they raised.[36]

Though the opponents of Lozano consistently claimed to represent *el común,* all the people of Mexquitic, I have found that they were as much a faction of the elite as the local officials who supported the priest. They flourished their titles as principales and former office-holders, and (increasingly) their literacy, as much as the other side did. Admittedly, Lozano's opponents were drawn from a sector of the elite who were gradually displaced from power during his tenure, to a large extent as a result of his machinations. But the fact that these elites could no longer send their servants and day laborers to water their fields, and that they were no longer assured of alternating in the local government, did not make their claim to represent the común any less tenuous than that of the governor and his república.

Rather than trying to ascertain the slippery facts of these cases, in these pages I have taken the course of reading them for what they can tell us about the cultural models of relations with authority current in Mexquitic at the end of the colonial period and of evolving images of the Indian. Yet in spite of the difficulty of detecting truths amid the rhetoric in the lawsuits that swirled around Lozano for fifteen years in the middle of his tenure, by looking at the secular progression of the cases in the context of a broad corpus of documents about Mexquitic we can discern some important trends with reasonable certainty.[37]

Mexquitic underwent profound changes during the near half-century that José Ignacio Lozano served as priest. Some of these changes he celebrated, others he deplored; he took pains to deny some he had initiated, while he took credit for others that he only witnessed or exploited after the fact. But he was present through them all. John Tutino, who has analyzed the Lozano cases, notes that the priest saw profits to be made in Mexquitic, "a community with substantial resources that were underutilized."[38] Among the great variety of charges of opportunism leveled at Lozano by his opponents, however, the activities we can state with some certainty that he actually carried out were limited to dominating land and water resources in and around Corte, supporting the wealthy local landowners and merchants in their often antagonistic relations with the pueblo, and, whether or not these were innovations on his part, taking advantage of the cofradías and of his privileges as a cleric. Lozano's own claims of fomenting "industry" were, as we have seen, probably inflated, for the people of Mexquitic had been selling the products of the countryside in San Luis for generations, while the fate of weaving and other craft industries depended (as they still depend) more on the vicissitudes of international trade than on the support of paternalistic superiors.[39]

During Lozano's tenure the economic prospects of pueblo residents grew increasingly tenuous, but mainly for reasons that had little to do with Lozano or his purported innovations. The principal cause of economic change was long-term, sustained population growth, to a point where the people of Mexquitic could perhaps no longer support themselves on the products of the unirrigated countryside.[40] The resulting shortage of irrigated land grew critical at the same time that neighboring hacendados, backed by Lozano (and, if we believe their opponents, his allies among the pueblo elite), succeeded in gaining control of the water supply while maintaining their hold on the few bits of arable land in Mexquitic that might have allowed a switch toward subsistence farming on a larger scale. The opposition focused on Lozano as the symbolic instigator of the transformations they were living through, in part because of his role in supporting the hacendados against the pueblo and in part because of his relatively minor but politically sensitive intervention in community lands, water rights, and politics.

The first and most enduring accusations against Lozano were that he had rented out community fields to outsiders and that he meddled in the selection of pueblo officials. These two charges were intimately connected. The community fields, lying in the valley of the Río de la Parada and known as the hacienda of Mexquitic, had in fact been rented out annually by the pueblo itself for at least a century and a half as a way of raising money for tribute, fiestas, and other public expenses. The rental process, however, had always been controlled by the governor and was one of the bases of his power and authority. Lozano was apparently the first priest who tried to gain personal control over the rentals, and by giving them to his own allies and proxies he became deeply involved not only in the local economy but in pueblo factionalism. Controlling community lands without controlling the governorship would have been impossible. The consequent persistence of a single pueblo faction in power for roughly the last thirty years of Lozano's tenure significantly distorted local politics.[41] This was the political setting for the transformation of community land into the nucleus of the private hacienda of Corte, which grew throughout the nineteenth century at the expense of former pueblo land and was eventually annexed to La Parada.

This innovation was countered by an equally important divergence from tradition. This was the demand by some pueblo leaders to cease renting the community fields to outsiders altogether and to revoke the perpetual lease of adjacent land to La Parada, in an attempt to ease the growing land shortage. This move was both moral and necessary in their view but it was hardly a customary right, as they claimed, for though the land belonged to the pueblo, the people of the pueblo had never worked it themselves. By representing their attempted repossession as a restitution of lost customary privileges, the leaders were neither making a mistake nor rewriting history; they were employing the language of the colonial administrators, who as they knew valued custom far above innovation.[42]

The growth of the pueblo and the tightening of its land supply in the 1780s and 1790s coincided both with elite usurpation of water in a key agricultural area of the pueblo, Corte, and with the entrenchment of a tightly restricted official elite in power. Lozano abetted both of these processes at the very least. For twenty years under Lozano, pressure from land-starved residents and power-starved former elites built up against an immobile upper crust. After decades of seeing every attempt at change through the administrative channels of the colony thwarted, in the words of Tutino, "the villagers of Mexquitic awaited an opportunity to rebel." [43] This they found with the arrival of the Hidalgo rebellion in November 1810. Rising up, they quickly occupied the two most hated symbols of their oppression—the hacienda of La Parada, which they parcelled out and planted in corn for their own use, and Lozano's office, which they sacked, forcing the priest to take refuge in the hacienda of Peñasco.[44] But four months later the royalist militia of La Parada expelled the insurgents, and after two years Lozano returned to a pueblo swept clean of opposition, which he ruled for another two decades.

THE PRIEST AND RELIGION TODAY

Early in my field research, after returning from a trip to the national archive in Mexico City where I had found documents about the conflicts between the people and the priest around the year 1810, I talked with Ramón about what I had read. As I described the scene to Ramón—how the people rose in favor of Hidalgo, the priest's violent opposition—Ramón smiled as if he knew all about it.

"Yes, the priests have never liked Hidalgo. You'll notice that they never have a good word to say for him. All the other public figures, especially politicians, make speeches in favor of Hidalgo, but the priests will never preach a sermon about him."

"Why not, wasn't Hidalgo himself a priest?"

"Yes, but he understood the problems of the people, the trouble they had making a living—the priests then were like employees, they were paid by the hacendados. When the poor people confessed to them, if they told him, say, that they wanted to rob the hacienda, he would go report to the hacendado, and the poor person would probably end up shot.

"And that's just how things are now," Ramón continued with a leap of thought, "after all the struggles and the revolutions of the people to make their lives better, the government now is just as bad as it was then." Ramón complained at length of how every national government, "that almost-Spanish Mafia," had robbed the country during the administrations of "those Spaniards" Echeverría (1970–1976) and López Portillo (1976–1982). One of his many side-remarks was probably meant to be prophetic. If the Spaniards had only learned to listen to the Indians and take their problems and sufferings into account, he declared, the kings would still be ruling here today.[45]

Ramón read the Lozano case not through colonial images of the Indian, but through post-Revolutionary populist images of the elite. The priest was a lackey of the hacendados; hacendados were Spaniards (and vice-versa). He then gave these images a contemporary twist by equating the Indians of colonial Mexico with both the impoverished workers of the haciendas and the people of Mexico today. He equated the "Spaniards" who controlled the haciendas and the colonial government with the "near-Spaniards," the light-skinned rulers in Mexico City, and implicitly equated the priests, as lackeys, with contemporary government bureaucrats. It was not that Ramón's comments on Lozano derived from his own political experience in contemporary Mexico; rather, he viewed both my story of Lozano and his own impressions of modern politics in terms of Mexican Revolutionary imagery, which he interpreted in his own way.

The view of pre-Revolutionary priests as hacienda employees, ready to betray the secret of confession at a moment's notice, is a staple of the modern political vocabulary in Mexquitic. Whether the image is based on actual experience with the priests of La Parada or (as I suspect) on the lessons taught in the classrooms of Mexquitic after the Revolution, the Protestants of the municipality are concentrated in the communities immediately surrounding La Parada, and they themselves cite the priests' alleged abuse of the confession as a sign of the hypocrisy of Catholicism and the superiority of Protestantism. The same conclusion was not drawn by most people in the municipality, whose relation with the hacienda was less intense. There the dominant tenor of religious life is that of "pious anticlericalism," criticizing the life-style of the priest while upholding the values of popular Catholicism.[46]

These conflicting evaluations of priests, Catholicism, the Evangelical movement, and the role of religion came out in a conversation with Rosendo, Ofelia, and their daughter. Rosendo, an older man who has spent most of his life handcrafting leather and tending his flocks of sheep and goats, is the son of a *peón* who was expelled from La Parada in the 1920s as a trouble-making "hijo del pueblo"; Ofelia has lived all her life in the town, and their daughter was visiting from her new home in San Luis.

"Over there, the hacienda of La Parada obliged the workers, at least once a month they had to go to confession," Rosendo said in his leathery voice. "The padre would grill them, 'Come on, my little son, tell me what you've stolen from the hacienda. How many goats have you eaten? Come on now, to save your soul—otherwise you're damned.' No, they had the people all tied up. Then the managers would tell the shepherd, 'Look here, you ate this many goats.'

" 'Hey, now, that old son-of-a . . . ,' the shepherd would say, 'how'd that blasted guy find out.' Well, of course," Rosendo laughed, "the padre would go and he'd . . ." Rosendo's voice broke off, choked by laughter, but his daughter commented in amused tones, "Because that was best for the little padre."

The conversation turned toward a condemnation of the sacrileges committed by the people of Mexquitic living nearest La Parada during the violent overthrow of the hacienda regime. Ofelia took up the tale: "All those people destroyed the whole hacienda. All the ejidatarios— well, now there aren't any of them, either, they've all died, too. The saints, they took all the saints out of the hacienda chapel, everything."

"There was a schoolteacher named María Martínez," Rosendo re-called. "She was here as a teacher. I was in her class in 1928—she taught me. And afterward she went to Porvenir and there she joined up with a man and they went and stripped the saints and she put on the dress. . . .

"No," Ofelia corrected him, "the one who put on the dress was her mother-in-law, doña Ventura, Juan's mama."

"Are those the people they say are Protestants?" I asked.

"Right, that's who they were," said Ofelia. "And Juan used the robes of the padre, the ones for saying Mass, he used them for trappings for his saddle horses. But those two didn't last! A thunderstorm came and the late Juan was carried off by a swollen creek, just imagine."

Their daughter, playing the role of Greek chorus, remarked matter-of-factly: "A punishment from God."

"This Juan, he was crossing the creek when the water carried him off, horse and all," Ofelia went on. "And his mama, doña Ventura, also died. They didn't last. Because these people did a lot of destruction in La Parada."

The daughter passed stern judgment: "Ambitious people." [47]

When we returned to Mexquitic in the fall of 1984 after a few months' absence, we discovered a huge truck pulled up in front of the priest's house. A crew of boys and young men were happily unloading heavy sacks and boxes of food from the truck and piling them inside the house. While we were gone, we were told, the priest and his brothers had joined a Catholic initiative to provide basic foodstuffs to the poor at low prices.

The boys unloading the truck were each to be paid from the cargo with a two-kilo tub of *cajeta,* a thick caramel syrup made of milk and sugar. Inside the vestibule of the priest's house the *cera escamada,* ornate figures of molded wax that are offered to the church during the annual fiesta, had been removed. In their place stood mountains of rice, corn, and powdered milk in sacks clearly marked in English and Spanish: "A gift of the people of the United States of America. Not to be sold or traded."

The food was being sold, though, at absurdly low prices. The priest's younger brother, in charge of accounting in the operation, maintained that they were not actually selling the food, merely charging a fee to cover transportation costs. No one we talked with showed interest in such explanations. From their point of view, this was simply another store, and since it had the lowest prices around it did not lack for customers. At first the only ones who complained were the other store owners, who feared they would lose business. The "padre's store," however, quickly turned into a kind of patronage system. A small group of local women were put in charge of deciding who the deserving "poor" were, and to no one's surprise most of their own relatives, including many of the store owners, ended up on the list. Padre José Luis injected his primary religious concern, too, by barring unmarried mothers from participating, even though they probably make up a majority of the truly needy in the town.

Altogether the priest was doing a booming business. By June 1985, he announced in a sermon, he had sold more than five tons of food—half a million pesos' worth, at his going rate. Townspeople who attended Mass regularly told us that he often spoke of his food distribution service in his sermons. The main criticism we heard of the priest was not that he sold food that was meant as a free gift, but that he was neglecting the spiritual with his emphasis on the importance of economics and politics. A sermon is for explaining the Gospel; if José Luis wants to talk about the economy he should have gone into politics, they would say. In the same sermons he would denounce "folkloric Mexico," the fiestas and fireworks that are the hallmarks of public religion in Mexquitic. His criticisms, however, only provoked the young men in the town into a defiant insistence on raising enough money for an impressive display of fireworks and brass bands.

By the time of our return trip in 1987, José Luis and his family had turned Mexquitic into the regional distribution hub of the food enterprise. The entire lower floor of the priest's house had become a great warehouse; in every corner and courtyard of the former friary, sacks of grain were heaped three or four meters high. Huge tractor trailers were unloaded daily in front of the church, and smaller trucks and pickups pulled in daily to move the food out again to the communities. The distribution system in the town had become more baroque, too. Padre José Luis was promoting a parish savings cooperative that he had initiated by selling food only to people who had an account, but few trusted this novel system (which was administered by the priest's brother) with their money.[48] Some people discovered that, faced with such obstacles from the priest and his family, it was easier to get their rations from a neighboring community, where the local woman in charge of distribution was only too happy to sell them food in return for a small gratuity.

The food distribution program had an equivocal effect on Padre José Luis's relation with the people of Mexquitic. People jumped at the opportunity of cheap food with the same spirit they show in happily ransacking the trailer trucks that occasionally overturn on the hairpin curve in the highway next to the town—a spirit in rejoicing in an unexpected bonanza from a mischievous fate, which might suddenly give them a two-year's supply of Nescafe or Lux soap. In this case, the priest's reputation was perhaps the truck that overturned. I did not get the impression that anyone felt grateful to José Luis for having brought in the food, just a slight distaste for his neglect of the Gospels and a slight sense of opprobrium for the rumored hint of corruption that surrounded the operation. To my eyes, immersed as I was in local documents of the eighteenth century, the padre seemed to be replaying the drama of José Ignacio Lozano in a modern idiom.

Priests have not been entangled in lawsuits with the people of Mexquitic since the days of Lozano. It is not so much that tensions between the two have reduced, as that the steady decline in the real power of the priesthood has lessened the practical importance of those tensions. But the priest is still a key figure in their town, and his role calls out for interpretation. In stories and rumors that people freely circulate about their priests past and present, a consensus emerges of the ideal place of the priest in society.

The priest's proper place, as I hear their stories, is in the church. In the religious realm, he should not meddle in fiestas and other aspects of traditional religion, as some recent priests are criticized for doing. The current priest, Padre José Luis, has drawn some criticism on this score, both for his opposition to the use of elaborate fireworks displays on the fiesta and for his campaign against the fairly common practice of couples living together without benefit of marriage. Though the latter is arguably within the legitimate domain of Church concern, he seriously inconvenienced some when he refused to baptize the children of unmarried couples. Later, after a steady stream of parishioners bypassed his intrusive new rule (and higher clerical fees) by going to San Luis for baptisms, he began holding free group-wedding ceremonies of eighty or more couples at communities around the municipality as a novel means of eliminating this social scourge. His innovations are controversial, accepted by some, laughed at by others, and viewed as an unwelcome sign of politics in place of religion by many more. For the most part, however, people are able to keep interfering priests such as José Luis in their place simply by not involving them in the religious aspects of everyday life.

Further, the priest should concentrate on the spiritual, not the economic. Better yet, he should separate the two realms, keeping his religious role within the church while helping people economically outside it. Padre Marcelino is well thought of for his unimposing devotion to his religious role in the 1970s, but Padre Esparragosa is recalled with true fondness for organizing informal schools to teach music and weaving to the children of the town in the 1930s and early 1940s. His efforts, curiously reminiscent of those which Lozano attributed to himself, passed on potentially useful skills that people such as Ramón still use to help eke out a living. But the little-remembered Padre Cecilio, who was priest in the late 1920s (during the closing of the churches under Calles), was recalled with positive disdain by Rosendo and Ofelia as "a very poor, very stingy padre." He would, they laughed, eat the chicharrones off the scale faster than they could be weighed. His most telling trait was that "he didn't employ a maid." That is, he did not provide even the minimal economic input that someone of his station could be expected to give the town.

In short, the priest should keep his paternal intervention in town life to a beneficent minimum and otherwise respect his parishioners' ability to manage their religious and economic lives without him. The key point, and in pointed contrast to what we can learn from colonial court cases, is that people are primarily concerned with defining the priest's obligations toward them, rather than their own proper attitude toward the priest.

Today the priest occupies a paradoxical position in Mexquitic society. On the one hand, his is a powerful presence. As the only representative of the Catholic Church hierarchy in the municipality he has behind him the weight and authority of that body (admittedly greater under the colonial regime than it is today, but still nothing to ignore). He has a monopoly on the privileges of the priesthood in the town, from deciding when and how to hold Masses and baptisms to collecting the fees for his religious services. He also has an automatic place among the local elite and, one would think, an indispensable place in the religious lives of the people of Mexquitic.[49]

Yet, despite this presence, he is absent from the most basic religious ceremonies and the most wrenching religious controversies in people's lives, except in a minor, almost faceless capacity. For more than two centuries the people of Mexquitic, as Indians under colonial rule, were officially prohibited from assuming the priesthood themselves. For the past two centuries they have outnumbered their priests by more than ten thousand to one. By now they have invented rites and learned to lead their Catholic life without intervention from above, treating the priest more as a ritual prop than a spiritual leader.

As with many aspects of religious life, this absence of the priest is most evident at funerals. On the morning of January 5, 1984, as I waited in the vestibule of the priest's house for permission to consult the archive, Pitacio arrived to ask the priest to bless the corpse of his cousin. This old man, he explained, had been baptized and raised a Catholic, but had been taken in late in his life by one of the two Protestant households in town. Later that day the priest stood on the steps of the church, a purple smock covering his white robes, watching as a jovial group of young men from the town took a coffin down from the back of a pickup truck. The truck was being driven by strangers, evidently Protestants from San Luis. Neither they nor the members of old José's latest household, who sat in the back of the truck, got down to see the priest sprinkle the casket with holy water, nor to watch the young men carry it into the church, nor to listen to the short Mass said in the memory of José.

Afterward a procession of sorts headed for the cemetery, two kilometers away. As we waited in front of the cemetery door for the *melino* (gravedigger) to arrive with the key, the procession broke up into four groups: the women from Mexquitic; the older men; the young men who had carried the coffin—and who were apparently there to have a good time; and the Protestants. These were a young preacher in a black leather jacket and shining shoes who asked me earnestly if I was not from the Summer Institute of Linguistics, six other young men and women from San Luis, two middle-aged women from Ohio, and the members of José's household.

When the melino (who doubled as the town drunk) finally arrived, he and Pitacio began a loud argument over where the grave should be dug and followed this with a loud joking session. The jokes, as in *Hamlet,* appear to be a staple of funerals in Mexquitic, relieving somewhat the oppressive wait as the grave is being dug. But in this case it seemed to me that Pitacio and the melino were also using their verbal sparring to claim the center of attention for themselves as representatives of the town, unlike the Protestant outsiders who lined the gravesite. They were implying by their loudness that they had every right to be there, whether or not old José had belonged to their household. But during a lull in the joking the young preacher took over—if there had been a microphone, I thought, he would have grabbed it—and began a long sermon about the Christian burial they were about to give their friend José, who had died a Christian, and who had picked the right path, one of only two paths that are offered us: to heaven, *la gloria,* or to hell. He then announced that they, the Christians, would sing a hymn. Throughout the ensuing Protestant harmony the Mexquitic contingent remained pointedly silent.

The preacher again took up sermonizing about heaven, hell, and going to see the Lord, and just as the sermon and the hymns were beginning to seem as interminable as the digging the melino paused, stood up in the grave and asked, "But what does this *gloria* that you keep talking about look like?"

The interruption was greeted with general relief, and with laughter from the young men, who had at last gotten what they came for. The preacher, though taken aback, did his best to explain his conception of heaven.

"Well, I've been in *la gloria* already, and it's not at all like that," the melino answered.

"What do you mean?"

"Yes, I've been in *la gloria,* but there you have, on one side, God sitting, and on the other side is the Devil. And God has a long beard, down to here, just like in the painting."

"But what is the Devil doing there?" the preacher asked, looking for a way to turn this mad interruption back to his advantage.

"To decide what to do with you. And you're right when you say that there is only one path: it's straight into the ground, and from that there's no coming back."

"But you say you've been in *la gloria* yourself!"

"Yes, but they didn't want me yet, they threw me out."

"Ah, you mean you dreamed you were in heaven."

"What do you mean, 'dreamed.' I was really there! Only they didn't want me yet and they threw me out. But when it's your time, there's no way out."

The preacher, disconcerted, tried briefly to speak on the theme of visiting heaven but soon gave up and called for another hymn, which was sung with great determination. Still, the melino continued to rise from his digging as he remembered such details as, "There was this big hallway there, and you could see Christ in the door," and, "There was a huge cauldron there in the middle of the floor."

"What was that for?"

"To stew the sinners in!" [50]

The melino's trip to heaven was well known in the town—hence the presence of the young men, who knew what to look forward to. The sense of oppression that had perceptibly settled on everyone from Mexquitic with the beginning of the sermon had now dissipated, and in the silence after the hymn Luisa Hernández, who is also known as a habitual drinker, began muttering and then saying quite audibly, "Hypocrites! Here they come to talk and sing. They know that this is the end, you die, you get buried, and that's it. Hypocrites!" An amused young man tried to calm her, but she was visibly upset by what she regarded as an attempt to take advantage of the death of a poor old man in order to preach to people against their will and refused to be silenced. As the final hymn, "When Jesus Christ Comes," began, she began shouting, "Hypocrites! When is he coming? Never! You die and that's it!" Soon the grave was filled in, the night grew darker, and everyone broke away and headed for home.

The next day, Ramón (who had not attended, but was told about the funeral) compared the scene there, with two religions fighting over a body, "one pulling this way and the other pulling that," to the confusing noises that come from a radio "when it pulls in two stations at once." But neither he nor I took note at the time of the absence of the priest from this highly charged and symbolic conflict between evangelizing Protestantism and traditional Catholicism. The Mexquitic contingent at the funeral, representing the Catholic faith, took all their cues from their own understandings of the religion, which at times could stand quite at odds with priestly teachings. This was no more remarkable than the general absence of priests, apart from the perfunctory church blessing of the body, from funerals that are instead led by a *rezandero,* a lay specialist in religious rituals, chants, and dirges.

On April 21, 1985, it was a young daughter of the rezandero himself who, sadly, had just died after a short illness. We arrived at six in the evening at the rezandero Cosme's house in El Llano, two kilometers outside the town, to attend the wake. The child's small body was already completely covered with the flowers "offered" by the other mourners. In the case of *angelitos,* children who have died before they have married or known sin, the wake is preceded by a "coronation" in which the child's godparents dress the angelito as a saint and crown it with woven palm leaves. As we waited for the godparents to arrive, women in an improvised shelter on one side of the house prepared food and tortillas for those who would wait through the night, and on the other side of the house men readied another shelter to hold the coffin for the ceremonies. In the courtyard a son of Cosme periodically set off fireworks.[51]

Finally, around eight, Cosme set off for town to bring the godparents. Soon afterward Cosme's brother Tano, who is also a rezandero, arrived and began to lead the mourners in hymns of praise to the Virgin of Guadalupe, while they carried the angelito and an image of the Virgin in a short procession from the house to the shelter. The hymns continued for some time before a few women told Tano that the godparents were about to arrive. They apparently expected Tano to go out to "meet" the godparents, but he only replied: "I wasn't told. Did they bring a representative?" They replied that Cosme was walking with them and was singing. Still Tano did not leave the shelter.

In the end, a group of women, who had somehow acquired one of the rezanderos' handwritten books of hymns, went out to join Cosme and respond to his litany. Singing, they slowly entered the shelter where the body lay. The godmother was not accompanied by her husband, a member of the town's political elite who "couldn't make it." Her oldest son had acquiesced in taking the place of the missing godfather. The two of them, chewing gum as they would throughout the evening, set about removing the flowers from the body of the angelito.

Here Tano interrupted her and asked, "Did you bring a representative?" She apparently did not understand the question and continued to remove the flowers while trying to ignore this strange man. It soon became painfully obvious that this woman, who had never before had to "crown" one of her godchildren, had no idea what a "representative" was and little more idea than we did how to go about doing a coronation. Nor had she bothered to ask, not being an anthropologist of her own community. When Tano found himself forced in the end to raise his voice and say, "Stop, please, don't you see I am talking to you? I asked if you had a representative," the godmother could only reply, "What do you want me to do?" and admit, at last, that she had not brought one. Then Tano told her that he was the "rezandero of the house," but that he could act as her representative if she wished. Prodded by the women around her, the godmother at last managed to ask him with more or less the proper formality to be her representative, and the ceremony proceeded. Tano now told the godmother and her son what was needed of them at every step of the way, while leading the hymns at the same time.

But around midnight, when the ceremony was formally over and everyone was prepared to leave the shelter, Tano suddenly launched into a fierce speech. He said he was sorry he had not gone to receive the godparents but that he had not been told whether or not they had brought a representative. He then spoke of how shameful a group of Catholics they all were. "You pretend to be Catholics but you are not. Catholics kneel before a corpse. I am not a Catholic, but look at you, who are, and you don't know anything. You think you only have to go to Mass and you're saved. If you go straight out to drink liquor, or if you see your neighbor and don't even say hello, it doesn't matter, you go and confess to the priest, and he tells you, Yes, my sons, go out and drink, do whatever you want." He declared that he was no longer a Catholic because he was disgusted by the laxity of Catholics who don't even care enough about their religion to learn its proper rituals; even so, he knew more about Catholic rituals than any one of them.

Lupe, who stood next to us, whispered that Tano had once decided to become a Protestant, making his point by throwing an image of Guadalupe on the ground and burning it. But "God punished him." The next day, his fifteen-year-old daughter died, and after that he returned to Catholicism. Now, from what he said, it seemed he was back with the Protestants, but he continued to carry out these Catholic burials while criticizing those who attended them.

The next day the funeral proceeded without interruptions. A procession carrying a small coffin and accompanied by a brass band wended its way from El Llano to the church, where the priest briefly blessed it and said Mass; then on to the cemetery, where Cosme himself led the mourners in hymns and prayers, with his powerful, haunting voice, somewhere between a song and a shout, while the melino dug the grave and joked.

Priestly influence is equally difficult to discern in the stories that are told to impart morality to children and a sense of meaning to the world. One day, after yet another morning weeding her small parcel of land, Esperanza told us a story of the origin of weeds that contains a moral lesson on the kind of industriousness that Lozano had so often praised.

"They say there was a man who had an hacienda. So he sowed his hacienda using his animals, sowed it all. And his corn grew. There goes his corn, up and up. He just sowed it and that was it. So what did the man have to do? He didn't have anything else to keep him busy. No children, no nothing. So they say that by and by, he went to his field. He wavered, he walked around it, but no, his corn, his beans keep growing on up. So he walked back to his house and just crossed his arms because who did he have to talk to? Just the wife there, no son, no nothing. By and by, till he got bored and went to his field. And then they say that he said, 'Ay, what will I do? There's nothing to keep me busy. I just wish a lot of work would come my way, for me to work. To not be idle. I'll ask God to give me work, so that I won't think evil thoughts.' That's all he said. 'Yes, I want work. Something to entertain me, to keep me busy.' And after a while the man left.

"The next day he gets up and goes to his hacienda to see. He just starts to enter his hacienda and check the corn: choked with weeds! 'God help me, what's all this? What's happened to my hacienda? All green, all.' That was it. 'This isn't beans. This isn't corn. What this is is grass, weeds, yes, because it grew by itself.' And he said, 'Blessed be God, just look, now I have plenty of work! Great! Now I won't have to be thinking evil thoughts. Now I sure have work.' Ha! He gets to work, weeding and weeding, pulling and pulling. What a field of weeds. And when he looked back, 'Yeah, now you can see the corn and beans. No, but I'm tired already from all this bending and stooping.' On he goes, working and working, pulling and pulling till just the corn was left. By the time he was halfway through weeding his hacienda of land, the man started to complain. 'Ay, there's no strength left. Ay, I can't get rid of these weeds.' The next day the weeds had all grown back. Ha! After that he cursed what he had done. As soon as he finished over here, left it clean, he turned around and looked it was all choked with weeds again. So he never finished. 'Ay, no!' 'Well, then, you asked for work.' He had looked for work.

"They say that that's why there are weeds. When you sow, at first the corn comes up real pretty. But right away the weeds start, and if you leave it alone the weeds grow faster than the corn and beans. The weeds grow tall, and the beans and corn stay short. That's why they say that if that man hadn't asked for work, it wouldn't have been like this. But on the other hand, what would the animals have eaten? Because that is the animals' food. Who knows how they would be fed otherwise? It must have come from on high, that's what I think." [52]

The key actions of this retelling of the Adam and Eve story—the prayer, the intercession of God, the curses—are Catholic, even orthodox, but they take place in an ethical matrix that thoroughly integrates Chris-

tian and non-Christian attitudes. As Esperanza tells the story, the unnamed man was forever condemned, like Adam, to earn his bread by the
sweat of his brow as a result of his own actions. Where Adam's action was
a mortal sin, though, this man's was a pious prayer. The work he called on
himself becomes an eternal curse, but as Esperanza notes the weeds that
God sent him turned out to be a blessing in disguise. The trickster nature
of God in this story does not, I think, derive from European Catholic
concepts of God the Father. The notion that paradise before the advent
of weeds and work was a place of boring idleness, too, strikes me as quite
distinct from European images of Eden. The depiction of work as a potential diversion that becomes an eternal curse, on the other hand, is not
unique to this story, but it was unlikely to have been taught to the Indians
by the colonizers who came to put them to work.

I read this story as a product of a composite Mesoamerican-Spanish
world, displaying the kind of understanding that might have come from
an early "moral dialogue" between friars and the people of central Mexico.[53] The dialogues that produced such mestizo understandings of Catholicism ceased long ago, even before Mexquitic was founded. Matters
of faith, and even many matters of ritual for people such as those of Mexquitic, belong to a terrain into which priests rarely venture.

SIX   # Modern Politics: Mexquitic and the Nation

Right now . . . the politics in the municipality is: that within a year people's spirits will be red hot. You already know how passionate politics gets in Mexquitic.
—LETTER FROM A FRIEND BEFORE THE
1988 ELECTION

The emotions aroused by politics in Mexquitic today appear paradoxical in the eyes of an outsider. Within the Mexican political system, the victory of the ruling party, the Partido Revolucionario Institucional, or PRI, is a foregone conclusion in the vast majority of races. In municipalities such as Mexquitic, where PRI candidates are anointed through a closed selection process before running virtually unopposed, the ruling party has never lost an election, and no opposition party has ever garnered more than 20 percent of the vote.

But for a select few, the cultural descendants of the colonial notables who controlled pueblo politics in the eighteenth century and of the indigenous nobility who ruled preconquest Tlaxcalan communities before them, politics is both a passionate participant sport and a way of life. As in the colonial era, political activity remains a necessary adjunct to economic status. During the colonial period, control of the governorship meant control over the distribution of pueblo resources (especially land), the power of arbitration over personal conflicts within the pueblo, and a prominent place in the network connecting the pueblo with powerful outsiders in the broader society of colonial Mexico. Today the duties and powers of the municipal presidency are much the same or even greater, especially since the federal government began financing municipalities in the 1970s. The political system in Mexico since the Revolution is a spoils system writ large, and for many municipalities politics is the only industry in town.[1]

The precise nature of the historical connection between the colonial and the modern elites of Mexquitic is an important question, and its answer, for now, remains locked up in the voluminous but uncataloged and poorly preserved documents of the nineteenth century.[2] What I have seen inclines me to think that there was great continuity across the two divides of modern Mexican history, the wars of Independence and the 1910 Revolution, but this is merely a hypothesis. The point that I emphasize in this chapter, then, is not direct continuity but the more basic fact of the persistence of a controlling elite, rift by factionalism, who have been able under a somewhat different electoral system to enter the closed world of politics and turn it to their advantage.

This chapter is based primarily on oral history interviews in the town of Mexquitic rather than on provincial archival sources. It thus treats the ways in which people within Mexquitic understand the political process, rather than the interplay between local and regional elites. This results, strikingly, in the near absence of the question of Indian identity, a key concern of regional and national elites that is neatly elided from the internal discourse of politics in Mexquitic. The emphasis instead is on the localism of politics in Mexquitic. The political regime of the municipality is deeply bound up in both regional and national politics, but it is not determined by those larger forces in any direct, mechanical, or predictable way. Though in many ways subordinate to national events, twentieth-century politics in Mexquitic has its own internal dynamics.

DON LUPE

One Saturday late in August 1987, a few days after we arrived in Mexquitic for a brief return visit, Bernarda stopped to greet us as we stood in the tiny park that faces the *presidencia municipal,* the local government offices. After saying hello, Bernarda lowered her voice to tell us that don Lupe, the former municipal president, had died. Though Lupe was only in his forties, the news did not really surprise us—after all, about a dozen townspeople had died since we left Mexquitic in August 1985, and everyone we talked with had been cataloging the deaths to us since we re-

turned. What did surprise us was that no one had mentioned this particular death before. "When did he die?" we asked, innocently.

"Just a few hours ago," Bernarda told us.

"But how, what did he die of?"

"He was killed, shot dead."

Now this was shocking. Someone we knew had been killed, in what
we assumed to be a political murder, the first in Mexquitic since the last
reverberation of Revolutionary violence in 1930. We recalled the graffiti
that had appeared all over town the night before New Year's 1983, when
don Lupe, J. Guadalupe Cortina, was inaugurated. The graffiti, roughly
scrawled across houses and walls, had called for "Death to Cortina." We
also remembered the many warnings of violence we were given before we
began our fieldwork here—first from anxious relatives with vague premonitions and ingrained prejudices about Mexican "bandidos," then
from equally anxious friends in the city of San Luis, with equally ingrained prejudices about the murderous nature of the people of Mexquitic. I will return to the graffiti and the theme of violence later; meanwhile,
this murder turned out to have a slightly more prosaic cause, an argument
over irrigation water.

The next day an enterprising young boy came to Mexquitic hawking
copies of *El Momento de San Luis,* which carried the banner headline,
"Former Mayor Shot to Death." The story related that Lupe had been
irrigating his fields at two in the morning in his home rancho of Maravillas
in the eastern part of Mexquitic, when two men from the rancho arrived
and asked him why he was not allowing them to use the water. Lupe, who
had become the head of the local irrigation commission after his term as
president ended, responded with insults and curses, according to witnesses
cited by the newspaper, and then started toward one of the men as if to
attack him. This man turned and said, "Let's go," but his companion instead pulled out a .38 revolver and began firing. Some witnesses said the
other man fired shots as well, emptying the .38 into don Lupe. "Both men
then fled, aided by the shadows of the night." One was captured the next
day; the other was still in hiding when we left Mexico a month later. The
newspaper account concluded:

> The deceased had many enemies. On not a few occasions they
> publicly accused him of prepotency and arbitrariness. . . . He also
> had many enemies from his activities as a police agent [*polijudicial,*
> his employment several years before becoming president]; never-

theless, those who killed him are people from the countryside as he was, and the causes [of the murder] have been completely brought to light: for refusing to give them water for their crops.[3]

The gaps in this sparse account were soon filled out by rumor and the reworking of memory. In concocting these rumors, many of them scurrilous and unfounded, people filled out the relatively small base of known facts by intercalating other events, envisioning them through more or less shared conceptions of how the political process works. What emerges from the rumored stories about don Lupe, then, is a series of images or imaginings of the meaning of local politics. Lupe and his assailants, it was said, had never gotten along. They had been feuding for years. The one who had done the shooting, someone said, had been paid to do it by the other, who hated Lupe. Lupe, others elaborated, was hated by everyone in Maravillas; he had done nothing for his rancho when he was president, and now he was charging stiff fees for the right to use the irrigation water, which by law should be free. One woman told us that Lupe had made such a fortune from his abuses of public office that his widow, incensed by the murder, was offering a reward of a million pesos to the person who captured the missing killer alive or dead, preferably the latter.

Two or three weeks after the event I joined a conversation in the plaza in front of the presidencia between "El Capulín," who is active in local politics, and a man from Maravillas who was in town that day for business at the presidencia. As they talked they drew a very different portrait of Lupe and his demise. Lupe had done well for himself as president, El Capulín noted, but the president who succeeded him in office had not let him keep the red truck, nor the yellow truck, nor the van that he had bought for the municipality during his tenure. He only got away with the pickup, he said, and even that had recently broken down. The man from Maravillas told of Lupe's difficulties in supporting two houses. Lupe, he mentioned, had taken up with "another woman" while president, dividing his time between her and his own family. In fact, the man hinted, it was the economic difficulties he had been going through lately that had led him to charge, illegally, for the use of irrigation water. And then, they both remembered, Lupe had not been himself lately, ever since he left the presidency. For instance, at a recent municipal council meeting Lupe had refused an invitation to enter the council room and take part, as he should have, being a former president. Instead, he stood sullenly outside the door for the duration of the meeting. Yes, they sighed in agreement, he had known. He already knew what was coming to him. And look, José added.

There's the red truck that got us started on this conversation. Lupe is gone, and the truck is still here.

In this brief conversation, Lupe's death—a sudden, shocking, senseless event—was interpreted and placed in the context of the recent course of Lupe's life. As it was told, Lupe himself was transformed into an almost tragic figure. He had overreached himself as president, and in the economic eclipse that inevitably followed he had foreseen his own end. Two years earlier, when Lupe was president, people in the town had also viewed him as having overreached himself but hardly as having the kind of stature that might one day make a tragic figure of him. He was a *pulquero* (pulque seller), a *ranchero,* the *perro jolín* (bobtailed dog), as the youth had dubbed him. "Don't you see," Ramón told us, "we all know him, he's from Maravillas. They all live from maguey there—tapping maguey, selling pulque, and he's no different. He used to ride his motorcycle to San Luis every day, like all the men from Maravillas, carrying his two barrels of pulque strapped on behind to sell there. And now look at him: he's buying up dozens of hectares in Maravillas and he's building a house in a colonia of San Luis that they say is worth five million. And what has he done for Mexquitic? For here, for the town, nothing."

Many of these stories revolve around the tensions between the municipality as a whole and the municipal seat, which I will simply call "the town" (following current usage, and at the risk of confusion with the quite different colonial arrangement). The municipality, rather like a county in the United States, contains nearly 100 communities (commonly called ranchos), many of them diminutive but several of them actually larger than the town. The communities can achieve a kind of symbolic independence through being granted a local official (*juez auxiliar*) empowered to resolve minor conflicts that spring up within their borders, but most power in the municipality resides in the president, his council of eight *regidores,* his municipal treasurer and secretary, and his minuscule police force of two or three *comandantes.* The entire municipality is governed by the municipal president, whose office is located in the center of the town, across a small plaza from the colonial church. This fact tends to emphasize the sometimes strained relations between the municipal government and the townspeople, who tend to assume that their central position in the municipality entitles them to a privileged position in its politics and in the distribution of its resources.

Don Lupe became president in the uncontested but tense election of 1982, in which unmarked and defaced ballots outnumbered legitimate votes in the town. The municipal election held at the same time in the city of San Luis was one of the first in recent Mexican history in which an opposition candidate won the mayoralty of a major state capital and was officially recognized as the winner.[4] Townspeople, adopting the rhetoric of San Luis opposition leaders, complained with a certain unanimity that don Lupe had won through electoral fraud and claimed that the numbers of votes for the ruling party were inflated. Among the many rumors that swirled around municipal politics in this embittered atmosphere, one of the most insistent aimed at explaining how a pulque farmer from Maravillas had become president. It was the job, we were told, of the PRI party chief in San Luis to name the official candidates for municipal elections around the state, and he customarily gave the nod to the highest bidder. Mexquitic, in turn, was said to be controlled politically by a *cacique,* or political boss, who had made a regular scam of the president's office, offering large amounts of money to put up relatives or friends and then milking the municipal treasury for all it was worth. It was widely reported in Mexquitic that the cacique had paid two million pesos to secure the candidacy for don Lupe, his compadre. Bernarda, one of the few townspeople willing to give the cacique the benefit of the doubt, had a slightly more charitable view of his role. Who knows how he does it, she said, maybe he does pay, but maybe he just asks his friend the party chief to do him the favor.

In talking about the election, politically active townspeople focused on the role of the cacique, the alleged payoffs to party officials, and the status of don Lupe, whom they viewed as an outsider—from a rancho rather than from the town—who would allow the town to continue sliding into ruin, and as a near-illiterate whose candidacy was an embarrassment in a municipality where so many more educated people might have been chosen. Loyal PRI supporters and municipal presidency cronies, on the other hand, spoke bitterly of the complaining townspeople as reactionary and antidemocratic (that is, anti-PRI). In the midst of these accusations and counteraccusations, the graffiti appeared.

The slogan painted in crude black letters across our own house that New Year's Day read:

MESQUITIC: RREPUdIA: A: CORTINA
KASIqUeS SeRRANOS

"Mexquitic repudiates Cortina; *serrano* political bosses." There is a play on the meaning of *serrano* here: literally it means "from the mountains," that is, "hillbilly"; but, much more immediately in Mexquitic, it is the last name of the cacique himself, don Aristeo Serrano from Corte Primero, who had controlled municipal politics there since 1965.

CABBAGES AND KINGS

A short, stout man with a serious face hidden behind thick horn-rimmed glasses, don Aristeo seems an unlikely actor for the role of cacique. At a banquet held by the priest of Mexquitic, who enjoyed inviting to Sunday dinner all those he considered his influential friends, we once pointed out don Aristeo to a reporter from a San Luis newspaper (society page), noting that he was the most powerful person in the municipality. She couldn't suppress a squeal of laughter at the idea of don Aristeo as powerful or perhaps at the idea that there could be anything worth calling "power" in this dusty, godforsaken town. But despite his appearance don Aristeo was a rich man, a millionaire in pesos, at a time when a million pesos was still a substantial amount of money.

The other men that don Aristeo was said to have placed in the presidency also tended to be well-off. For instance, don Nico, whose term was nearing its end when we arrived in Mexquitic late in 1982, had not been educated past the third grade, but like don Aristeo he was a wealthy garlic farmer from the rancho of Corte Primero. Many farmers from Corte, on the alluvial plain of the Río de la Parada that the priest Lozano was accused of usurping two centuries earlier, had become wealthy in the 1960s and 1970s when the digging of deeper wells and the growth of the urban market of San Luis made intensive truck farming both possible and very profitable; they later expanded their market operations to Guadalajara and Monterrey as well. (When the water table fell and the wells began to dry up in the late 1980s, a number of these entrepreneurs dropped farming and went full-time into long-distance marketing of vegetables and fruits.) By the end of his term don Nico was said to own several houses in San Luis, which he rented out, two large hauling trucks, and of course a brand-new pickup truck.

Our compadres Claudio and Ramona commented to us, early in 1983, on the penchant that "people in the ranchos" had for displaying their wealth through objects such as new pickups. Go to the ranchos, they told us, and you will find families living in single-room houses with dirt floors, no running water, no hygiene, and a dozen half-naked children. And it is not for lack of money that they do not improve their houses (for our compadres, both schoolteachers, had proudly remade their own). Even when they are rich, they told us, those people prefer to show off their wealth with new trucks, or if they are from poorer ranchos, with new motorcycles or new bicycles, while continuing to live in the same impoverished way. Don Nico was a prime example—just look at how he had arrived in Mexquitic as president "vestido de manta," dressed like an Indian. At the end of his term, when we knew him, Claudio and Ramona complained that he continued to wear the cheap clothes of the ranchero, such as the worn pink polyester shirt that he did not change for the entire month of December.

In giving this description of don Nico, Claudio and Ramona were lamenting the fact that the job of president routinely went to the uneducated but rich farmers who pay off, and often are related to, don Aristeo. They wished instead to see the position go to one of the many well-educated teachers or other professionals from the town. During don Aristeo's twenty-year hold on municipal politics in Mexquitic, from his own first election as president in 1965 to the end of don Lupe's term in 1985, the people of the town of Mexquitic yearned to return one of their own to power. More precisely, a sizable faction of the town elite did; other townspeople, who saw that their own fortunes were only tangentially related to those of the elite, viewed this political struggle more dispassionately.

Much of what I have been able to discover about the political history of twentieth-century Mexquitic comes from interviews with Rosendo, who has a remarkable memory for facts, events, and dates. Though Rosendo is closely related to several of the elite families of Mexquitic, he does not see himself as one of the elite: "Before, all the earlier presidents were from right here, all these prominent men. . . . They are the most distinguished ones. Like, not me here, because here I'm however the government wants me to be!" After carefully relating the names and terms of office of every municipal president since 1920, Rosendo concluded by saying, "Really, the truth is that I'm not involved in politics. Whoever the president is, it doesn't interest me." His claim of disinterest, however, cannot erase the centrality of the political games of the elite, which forms the conceptual framework of recent local history. Though uninvolved in politics, Rosendo cannot help recalling his family history in terms of the political history of the municipality.

We heard a similar contradictory claim of detachment from Atilio, who recalled the late 1940s when, as a child of nine years, he worked as a goatherd for the richest man in the town, at a pay of three pesos a month plus the castoff clothes of the man's sons. At that time, he recalled, the presidency was controlled by the "rich men" of the town of Mexquitic, such as don Raúl, Pedro N. Vásquez, and don Pedro Quistián, who were all deeply involved in local politics, and also don Juan Martínez with his inherited wealth. Don Pedro Quistián, who was never president, nevertheless was constantly in the presidencia, municipal secretary one term and treasurer the next, but the real power was held by don Raúl and Pedro Vásquez, who "played ball with the presidency. Don Raúl went out and don Pedro Vásquez came in; he left and the other came back in." For his own part, Atilio realized by the age of ten or twelve that there was no opportunity for him in Mexquitic. If he continued to live there, he would spend the rest of his life as a goatherd. He ran off to San Luis (as the sons of the very poor often do), where he lived in the street and worked at odd jobs. Gradually he built up enough work experience to become an independent construction contractor, building schools for the federal government. Thus Atilio escaped the lack of opportunity and the claustrophobic control of the local rich on the presidency, only to end up with a government job and a way of life that is completely dependent on the vagaries of national politics.

Taking as a starting point the view that the local politics of Mexquitic has long been controlled by an elite (the "prominent men," the "rich"), the history of the presidency in Mexquitic since the 1920s can be seen as a larger version of the "ball game" that Atilio described. Over the years, the presidency has been passed back and forth not just between the rich men of the town but between the elites of the town and those of the rancho of Corte. From the late 1920s through the 1930s, the presidency was controlled by Corte; in the 1940s and 1950s, by the town of Mexquitic; in the 1960s and up until 1985, by Corte; and since 1986, by the town once more. Altogether, sixteen of the twenty-six elected presidents since 1921 have come from these two communities (which hold no more than a tenth of the municipal population between them), and half the remaining presidents came from nearby ranchos. But the history of contemporary politics in Mexquitic goes beyond a simple struggle for control between the elites of two communities. For two decades the elite of Corte dominated municipal politics through the direct, personal control of the cacique. In the earlier period when Corte dominated the municipality (1928–1938), it was also controlled by a cacique, Pilar García, who happened to be an uncle of don Aristeo. To understand the course of the presidency in Mexquitic, then, let us turn to an overview of the historical development of local caciquism, drawing out the connections between local and state-level caciques.

CACIQUES AND AGRARISTAS

Pilar García's rule was short-lived and born in violence. He entered the presidency in 1930, after the previous president (also from Corte) was killed on his orders. From that point until his overthrow in 1938 "he named whoever he wanted to, and that person was president," as Rosendo put it. But the antecedents of the violence that inaugurated his rule go back to the beginnings of the Mexican Revolution in Mexquitic, when Pilar García's older brother, Pedro, was the most prominent of the local revolutionary leaders.

Pedro García was elected in 1912 as the first "post-Porfirian" president of Mexquitic, since the fall of Mexican dictator Porfirio Díaz a year earlier was slow to register on the municipal level. His rule lasted only one year, the span of a presidential term then, and he was succeeded by another "Porfirian" president in 1913. That same year Madero, who had led the movement against Díaz, was assassinated, the national government fell into the hands of a military dictator, and the most violent epoch of the Revolution began. Pedro García was one of the first local leaders to rise up in arms. According to don Raúl, Pedro García fought on the side of Venustiano Carranza in the Revolution. According to Rosendo, whose account perhaps reflects more closely the confused nature of those years, Pedro García "was a soldier, for the government, and he was a rebel, a revolutionary. Sometimes he was with the government and sometimes against it, and so on."

In the town of Mexquitic Pedro García is mainly remembered for three violent incidents he is said to have committed or instigated. First was the murder of the former municipal president Nemecio Vásquez in 1913. Later in the same year came the murder in one day of three employees of the presidencia, including Lorenzo Flores (a nephew of Nemecio Vásquez and the father of don Raúl), in a struggle not for political power but for the attentions of the new primary schoolteacher—a "question of skirts," as don Raúl put it. And finally, in 1914, the somewhat gratuitous burning of the municipal archives, which have never since been kept in any order.[5] Pedro García never returned to rule Mexquitic as president or as cacique, however, for he was killed (perhaps later that year) at Concepción del Oro, where he had led his contingent of rebels into battle. According to

Rosendo, he had killed a federal soldier in the battle, stripped him, and then put on the soldier's uniform; his own men then shot him, thinking he was a *federal*.

The next period in the political history of Mexquitic that lives in local memory saw the rise of the "agraristas," the local militias formed to fight for agrarian reform—or so they represented themselves; I suspect they were originally just the remnants of Pedro García's rebels. The influence of the agraristas grew with the rising fortunes of their regional leader, the revolutionary general Saturnino Cedillo, who began his career as a cacique in northeast San Luis Potosí. General Cedillo rose to national prominence as a result of coinciding state and national struggles for political control in the early 1920s, a time when Mexican society was still so fragmented by the Revolution that state governments operated as quasi-independent fiefdoms and elections were conducted as much by military force as by votes. The national struggle concerned President Alvaro Obregón's desire to handpick General Plutarco Elías Calles as his successor in 1923, against the wishes of several revolutionary generals, who felt themselves more deserving of the office. The disaffected generals selected as their candidate Adolfo De la Huerta, who ran under the banner of the Partido Nacional Cooperativista, which dominated the national Congress under the leadership of Jorge Prieto Laurens of San Luis Potosí. Later in the year, when the election results were predictably announced in favor of the official candidate, De la Huerta lent his name to the military revolt in which over half of the national army rose up against the government. Some months earlier, a struggle for the governorship of San Luis Potosí had pitted the Cooperativist leader Prieto against the radical populist Aurelio Manrique. It had also set the regional military caciques, who were the real power in most of the state, against one another. Cedillo, with a solid base in the northeast and with agrarista contingents around the state in municipalities such as Mexquitic, weighed in on the side of Manrique, while the Santos clan, who controlled the semitropical Huasteca in the east, sided with Prieto. Prieto counted also on the armed members of his own party, as well as on the sympathy of conservative hacendados and, it seems, of the commanders of the army garrisons stationed in San Luis.[6]

The gubernatorial campaign in San Luis Potosí had been filled with violence. In Mexquitic, Bernarda recalled how soldiers from the military garrison quartered in an old *mesón* next to her house came in the middle of the night to drag her father, one of the first agraristas in town, from bed and search his house for pro-Manrique propaganda. Fortunately they found nothing and her father was spared the promised beating, but elsewhere in the state several people were killed during the campaign. The election that followed was a "farce," according to Ankerson, who quotes the American consular report: "The chief activity of the election seems to have consisted in sending several automobiles loaded with club bearers and gunmen to each election booth, running the election judges away, and capturing the ballot box."[7]

Both candidates for governor declared victory and proceeded to set up rival administrations, Prieto in the capital city and Manrique in Cedillo's rural stronghold, while their militias continued to battle for dominance. (By this time the Santos clan had switched its allegiance from Prieto to Cedillo's man—wisely, as it turned out.) President Obregón, who at this time was trying to dissuade De la Huerta from running for office, declared his neutrality on the outcome of the state race by announcing that both administrations were invalid, though in so doing he only further antagonized Prieto and his backers. For a time it seemed that Prieto would eventually be recognized as governor. Militarily, the army garrison in San Luis had begun to reinforce Prieto after Manrique decreed a radical agrarian reform program, which was aimed primarily at Prieto backers such as the owner of La Parada. Politically, Prieto controlled the state congress, and Obregón still wished to neutralize the opposition to Calles.[8]

In the end, however, Prieto's continued support of De la Huerta on the national level undid his position in the state. As the national campaign got under way, Obregón ordered the San Luis army garrison back to barracks, thus freeing Cedillo's agrarista militias to begin a rapid conquest of the municipal administrations in the state. When the De la Huerta revolt broke out in December 1923, most of the soldiers quartered in San Luis left to quell it. Cedillo then took command of the garrison, and under his protection Manrique entered the city to take possession of the governor's office. Following the collapse of the rebellion in April 1924, Cedillo's position in the state, and therefore that of his clients, was guaranteed. He had opposed the faction that had risen up against Calles, and his help in suppressing the rebels was now needed. Within a month he raised 1,500 mounted troops, mainly from among his agraristas. Among these were the agraristas of Mexquitic, led by Pedro Hernández of Corte Primero, who were set to benefit from the expropriation of the hacienda of La Parada that Manrique had recently decreed.[9]

Within months of the end of the rebellion, Cedillo rewarded his agraristas from Mexquitic with a provisional grant of ejidos from the haciendas of La Parada and San José del Corte. The ejidos were under the control of a "committee" in Corte Primero, and the ranchos granted land at this time were Corte and its immediate neighbors, all bordering the haciendas. This control over the ejidos probably gave the Corte Primero leadership their base for assuming control over the entire municipality a few years later. The treatment of the agraristas in San Luis contrasted sharply with what occurred in other states where agrarista contingents had also been used against the rebels. Elsewhere, the agraristas, who usually had been promised land before the fighting but given none afterward, began to use their arms to take over haciendas themselves. This development disturbed the government, and the federal army, many of whose officers had become hacienda owners during the Revolution, began a sometimes violent program of disarming the agraristas. The difference in San Luis was Cedillo. The central government recognized his utility as a regional cacique, and he in turn recognized that his power in the state derived from his command of the regional agrarista militia, which he resolved to reinforce for political reasons as well as, Ankerson demonstrates, out of a genuine commitment to agrarianism.[10]

As Cedillo strengthened his base in the state over the next two years, the new governor Manrique undermined his own, in part by passing widely unpopular and rather puritanical legislation, such as prohibiting bullfights and the sale of alcohol, and in part by making himself obnoxious to both Cedillo and President Calles. Where Cedillo's strategic agrarian reforms gave him a strongly committed following throughout the mostly rural state, Manrique was more concerned with urban problems and with bringing socialism to industrial workers, a small minority concentrated in the state capital. Cedillo and his followers in the state congress ousted Manrique shortly before his term ended in 1925 and selected a Cedillista as interim governor to pave the way for Cedillo's own election as governor in 1927.[11] Soon after Cedillo's election, the leader of his agraristas in Mexquitic, Pedro Hernández, described by Rosendo as Cedillo's "darling" (*consentido*), was elected president of the municipality.

Not long into Cedillo's term, the federal government again called on him and his militias to suppress another revolution: the Cristero rebellion, which had been waged since 1926 by opponents of the extreme anticlerical measures imposed by the Calles administration. The center of the rebellion was in the Bajío and the Altos de Jalisco just south and west of San Luis Potosí. If the Cristeros found almost no support in San Luis, it was in large part because of Cedillo's policies. On the one hand, by carving up the generally unpopular large haciendas into provisional ejidos for his agraristas, he had defused the economic and agrarian tensions that helped fan the Cristero revolt. On the other, by toning down or judiciously ignoring anticlerical decrees, he gave the conservative Catholic contingent in the state little cause to rebel.

In Mexquitic, don Raúl recalled, "there was not much restriction" in the practice of religion. The church remained open in the hands of a neighborhood committee (*junta vecinal*), and the priest continued to celebrate Masses and baptisms, though not in the church—"in private houses, but discreetly." This was, according to don Raúl, a major reason why the people of Mexquitic did not respond to the Cristero movement; equally important, in his view, was the lack of what he regarded as fanaticism among the Catholics of the municipality, in comparison to those of Jalisco or Guanajuato. In those states, for example, "if some couple goes there who are not married by the Church, to work or live there," the people will disapprove of them. "Why? Because they almost approach fanaticism." [12]

Thus when Cedillo was asked to raise 8,000 troops to combat the *Cristeros* early in 1929, the agraristas of Mexquitic responded. Most of them came from the ranchos that had provisionally received ejidos in 1924, but others, such as the dozen or so that went from the town of Mexquitic, fought on the promise of ejidos to come. They amassed in Mexquitic on March 3, Rosendo told us, and with Pedro Hernández at their head marched to San Luis to join Cedillo's forces. Unlike Cedillo, however, who personally led his troops into battle despite serving as governor, Pedro Hernández cited his duties as president and returned to Mexquitic. Most of the Mexquitic contingent was caught in the siege of Tepatitlán (an affair which looms somewhat larger in local accounts of the war than it does in published histories), yet when the war ended and the agrarista militia disbanded in June, "only eight soldiers were dead." [13]

THE RULE OF PILAR GARCÍA

The militias, still armed, returned home, "and they came back, and then the rumor came out that they were going to do the definitive possession." Three months later the agraristas of Mexquitic were rewarded with what they had fought for: the final distribution of ejido parcels from the haciendas of La Parada and San José del Corte.

But soon afterward the armed struggle for power that had been playing itself out on the national and state scenes was repeated on a municipal scale. While Cedillo's "darling," Pedro Hernández, had sat out the Cristero rebellion in the presidency, Pilar García, youngest brother of the late revolutionary Pedro García, led the Mexquitic agraristas into battle. After the definitive distribution of the ejidos, the local agraristas, now renamed the "rural defenses" (*defensas rurales*), remained under Pilar García's command. Before the end of the year, one of Pilar García's gunmen had assassinated the municipal president, allegedly at the orders of the budding cacique. As in the case of Cedillo himself, military force translated into political power. In December Pilar had himself elected president of Mexquitic. In Rosendo's words: "In 1930 Pilar García got hold of the presidency and he didn't let go of it till '38 and the Cedillo business. He named whoever he wanted and that person was president."

One of the reigning motifs in Mexican politics is "anti-reelectionism," the principle that a president or governor cannot succeed himself in the same office. This was the slogan with which Madero assaulted the dictatorship of Porfirio Díaz and his endless series of presidential terms, and following the Revolution the principle was promptly codified and made law everywhere in Mexico. Even under colonial law, the governors of Indian towns could not legally succeed themselves. In Mexquitic the same principle (whether as law or as custom, I do not know) continued to be observed throughout the nineteenth century. But where there is a prohibition, there is a way around it—in this case, by what Atilio above called "playing ball with the presidency," alternating terms between two or more people. When someone is able to play this game with the office of president, it is taken as a sign that he is not just president but has a deeper control over the very process of becoming president.

Pilar García was president in 1930–1931, and after taking his obligatory term off he returned to office in 1934–1935. Just before the end of that term, however, he handed over the presidency to another of his men and entered the state legislature as a representative for the region. What might have been his third turn in office, beginning in 1938, thus went instead to his henchman Pablo Valderas—the gunman who had reputedly assassinated the former president Pedro Hernández and two dozen other people in Mexquitic over the course of Pilar García's cacique rule.

But by 1938 the edifice of power and power vacuums that made the García regime possible was on the verge of collapse. In 1924 the federal government had needed Cedillo and his militia—even if it had not, keeping him happy and neutral was easier than risking yet another rebellion, perhaps not easily quashed. Cedillo, in turn, needed local caciques such as García to provide him with the statewide militia that was his power base. A decade later, Cedillo had consolidated his personal, agrarian- and military-based rule in San Luis, but in so doing he had kept his dominion out of step with the rest of the country. Over the 1920s and 1930s Mexican national politics had been painstakingly consolidated under the centralized control of the presidency and of the ruling party (the predecessor of today's PRI), founded by Calles in 1929. Playing down the personalistic and military aspects of political power that were so evident in the violent phase of the Revolution, and still so prominent in Cedillo's San Luis Potosí, was a key element in this consolidation of national power. Machine politics was replacing military caciquismo.

The triumph of the new machine politics was realized under the presidency of Lázaro Cárdenas, elected in 1934 to succeed the third of a series of Calles's political puppets. Cárdenas moved decisively to eliminate Calles's cacique-style influence on the national government; in order to do this he gave great impetus to processes that had already been under way during the Calles years. He strengthened the ruling party and its alliances with the officially recognized labor union and the national organization of rural workers—one of the continuing bases for the PRI machine. And he continued the policy begun by Calles of rotating army commanders around the country, to prevent any of them from establishing the kind of personal political connections that could pose a military threat to the federal government. By the mid-1930s there was no foreseeable source of a military challenge to Cárdenas of the type that brought Cedillo to national attention in 1924 and 1929—none, that is, except for Cedillo himself. By the late 1930s a direct conflict between Cedillo and Cárdenas seemed inevitable. Early in his term, in 1935, Cárdenas attempted to tame Cedillo and bring him into the machine system, by making him secretary of Agriculture and then taking away any real authority from that position. Over the next two years the ideological differences between the two men, combined with Cedillo's determination not to let go of his power base in San Luis, led to an increasing rift. In August 1937 Cárdenas "accepted" a resignation that Cedillo had not yet offered—a clear sign to the politically aware that Cedillo was on the way out.

The same year saw increasing labor unrest in the city of San Luis, where the national labor union, allied with the ruling party, was attempting to take control of the local "Cedillista" unions. This led in 1937 to the first real electoral contests in the state since the 1923 election in which Cedillo had supported Manrique for governor. Ironically, it was now Manrique, back in San Luis for the first time since Cedillo ousted him in 1926, who was leading his old constituents, the industrial workers, against the Cedillo regime. One of the accusations Manrique raised against Cedillo was that the large dam built in Mexquitic in 1922–1924 for the purpose of supplying the capital with drinking water had been illegally purchased by

Cedillo and his old friend and associate, General Francisco Carrera Torres, who was diverting the water from the city and using it to irrigate his hacienda, Peñasco.[14]

Given Cedillo's control over San Luis, the local elections went overwhelmingly to his picked candidates, but the fact that they were contested and that the national party machine supported some of his opponents was read as one more indication that Cárdenas was prepared to get rid of the old cacique one way or another. In 1937 an anonymous opponent of Pilar García in Mexquitic took advantage of the apparently inevitable break by denouncing the local cacique and his ties to Cedillo:

> This García has armed people—killers who commit murder and do not even cross the threshold of a jail—political power, and, finally, he is one of those who swear up and down that the day [Cedillo] embarks on armed struggle he will be able, in the twinkling of an eye, to organize 2,000 peasants or more to go to the battlefields and defend his shameless acts. . . . The arms that the Republic has placed in the hands of the peasants are for the caciques, who, using them wrongfully, have violated the prescriptions of the Constitution and established a reign of terror.[15]

The reference to "armed struggle" in this denunciation refers to the well-founded fear that Cedillo, with his private army of 15,000 agraristas, was plotting a rebellion. The plan, in summary, was a replay of the De la Huerta plot, which Cedillo himself had helped put down in 1924. The opposition, seeing Cedillo as its champion, would put him forward as their presidential candidate in 1940; then, given the electoral fraud that would inevitably result, Cedillo and his sympathizers in the army and other state governments would rebel. Cárdenas could foresee such a course of action only too well and responded by hounding Cedillo into premature open rebellion.

The anticipated revolt came in May, and Pilar García did support it. In his capacity as president of the state legislature he signed a decree on May 15 withdrawing recognition from the Cárdenas regime and naming Cedillo commander in chief of the "Constitutional Army."[16] Unfortunately for Cedillo, there was no such army; on May 25, when Pilar García was gathering his militia in Mexquitic and preparing to join up with Cedillo (who was back in his original stronghold in northeast San Luis), the town of Mexquitic was already occupied by 1,000 federal soldiers, and another 500 were searching for him in his own rancho, Corte Primero.

Pilar García narrowly escaped arrest (his chauffeur hid him under his seat and drove him out of Mexquitic straight past the soldiers), and the Mexquitic agraristas disbanded. The same scene was played out all over the state, so that of the vaunted 15,000 agraristas, only 1,500 managed to join the revolt. By September, less than 150 rebels remained, and the government soon declared the rebellion over, though the army continued to search for Cedillo's hideout. Early in 1939 Cedillo was ambushed and killed.

There is a striking interplay of congruences and incongruities between the various levels of this political history. I have highlighted three of these levels—national, state, and municipal—but of course one could discern an endless range of levels, macro and micro, from regional and international to rancho and household. Within this interplay, there is a counterpoint between historical inevitability—the apparent determination of "micro" factors by their "macro" contexts—and the quirks and inconsistencies of local, even personal histories.

The dominant political form in both the municipality of Mexquitic and the state of San Luis in this period was a militarized caciquism. Cedillo's paramilitary rule, by armed force and intimidation, was precisely imitated by his client Pilar García. This parallel was of course no coincidence—Cedillo backed the local caciques loyal to him—but neither was it an inevitable configuration. It emerged in part from the way Cedillo constructed his power, based in large part on local militias with loyalties to a local cacique who in turn was loyal to himself (but also on militias without local caciques); and in part from the parallel but separate history of Mexquitic itself, which led from land and power struggles in the nineteenth century to the emergence of Pedro García as a revolutionary leader in the early twentieth, and finally to Pilar García's cacique rule. The same kinds of parallels and connections can be made between the emergence of Cedillo's state-level cacique rule in the 1920s and the national history of the first two decades of the Revolution. Just as Cedillo built a private army largely from the militias of local caciques, so the revolutionary armies of Villa, Carranza, and Obregón were in good measure pyramidal coalitions of state and regional caciques such as Cedillo. And in the early years, Cedillo's paramilitary regime in San Luis was both a mirror of and a constituent part of the national regimes of the revolutionary generals Obregón and Calles.

But by the 1930s, with the carefully maneuvered transition from paramilitary cacique rule to well-oiled machine politics on the national level, the most crucial incongruity in this political history emerged, as Cedillo (and with him Pilar García) ignored the national trend and continued in the strong-arm tradition. When Cedillo eventually came into direct conflict with the federal government, this divergence was resolved in favor of the political machine, and both the state of San Luis and the municipality of Mexquitic were brought into the system. Yet it would be a mistake to think that because such a resolution was all but inevitable—given the nature of the conflict and the greater power of the federal forces—the conflict itself was also inevitable. It was, in the end, Cedillo's personal history that led him to continue in the mold of the military *caudillo* at a time when that role was clearly becoming out of place in Mexican politics. Another cacique could well have followed the lead of the national leaders Calles and Cárdenas, reformulated his personal base, and integrated himself into the emerging national machine. That is in fact what was done by Cedillo's successor in San Luis—his old rival and sometime ally, Gonzalo N. Santos, who was to dominate state politics for the next quarter-century.

This counterpoint of political currents was more than a temporary artifact of the turbulence of the Revolution. We can trace it at least as far back as the nineteenth-century roots of the recent political violence, militarism, and cacique rule. The Bustamante affair of 1869–1870 is a notable example of layered continuities and divergences between local and national trends. Juan Bustamante was a Potosino hacendado, the organizer of a private militia, a colonel of the Liberal national guard, and the Juarista military commander of San Luis Potosí, of which he was nominally governor during that bizarre interlude in Mexican history, the French invasion and the Empire of Maximilian. He was apparently a kind of Cedillo figure, "lacking administrative experience and even postelementary education, accustomed to ruling militarily during times of disorder, with no law but his own will." [17]

After the triumph of Juárez and the Liberals in 1867 Bustamante continued as governor in San Luis, but rival Liberal groups succeeded in driving him from office two years later. At this time pro-Bustamante militias in various parts of the state began an uncoordinated series of uprisings, including a brief one in Mexquitic. The Mexquitic revolt, in which a large number of armed men from the rancho of Jaral attacked the presidency, left three of the defenders dead and others wounded, but it was put down by the local authorities in less than two hours. Some of the other local insurrections were also quickly put down, but elsewhere, as in neighboring Ahualulco, the Bustamante party continued in power, though their gubernatorial aspirations were shunted aside when Bustamante gave up the fight and retired to Saltillo.[18]

Students of nineteenth-century Mexican history are familiar enough with the *pronunciamiento,* the declaration by some general or other that the present government is invalid and that he and his army will personally set things right by might of arms. The Bustamante affair, like the later Cedillo case, shows that such pronunciamientos also took place on the state and local level. Unlike Cedillo, Bustamante carried out his state-level coup at a time of relative quiet on the national scene, yet he provoked no intervention to speak of from the national government. The manifest divergence of trends on the different levels of political life at such a time resulted from a sense of local and regional autonomy, and in turn has helped to perpetuate that regionalism despite a nominally centralized national political system.

THE VIOLENT TENOR OF LIFE

Violence was a pervasive aspect of daily life at all levels in the era of military cacique rule, from the household to the nation.[19] The form that private disputes took mirrored the local political regime, in which Pilar García relied on his gunmen to maintain his supremacy. Already in 1913 the revolutionary Pedro García and his men used quasi-political violence to resolve a private dispute, when they followed their assassination of a former president with the murder of three rivals for the attentions of the schoolteacher. After the anti-Cristero campaign in 1926, this type of violence became rampant in Mexquitic, as Rosendo recalled with the sense of humor that strikes the outsider as slightly morbid:

> Here all the people were armed at that time. They came to be
> armed in the campaign. And every so often they themselves would
> be killing each other, one group against another. There were lots
> of murders, really. Taking revenge for offenses. And out with the
> rifle and "wham." [Rosendo laughed.] Eh. Things got ugly, really.

The worst of the violence ended with the disarming of Cedillo's agraristas after the failed revolt in 1938. They were disarmed easily, as Rosendo and Raúl told us. The federal government announced that the *defensas rurales* were to receive modernized weapons and ordered them to report to the municipal seat. There the rifles were carefully registered, the agraristas were assembled, and they were told they could return home; that was the end of the *defensas*. Rosendo said that many people had just become "agraristas" at that time, buying rifles from the deserters of Cedillo's army (and sometimes selling animals to do so). He himself had acquired a rifle in this way, but since all the weapons were clearly marked "Government Property," he explained, there was little he could do but surrender it.

Even after the agraristas were disarmed, the echoes of violence continued to reverberate in Mexquitic for decades. Still today the violence is present, if only as a frequent topic of conversation—and every few years a shocking incident like the murder of don Lupe can make real again the threat of violent vengeance, bringing back what is remembered as a former everyday presence. The theme of violence in the past of Mexquitic comes out readily in talk about the municipality. When we were new in town, doña Paula would reassure us about its peacefulness by bragging that, despite all the people who come to the fiesta in Mexquitic, it has never yet occasioned a single murder. We were also told more than once (and with some exaggeration, one hopes) that in the past if someone held a party for a wedding or a baptism and no one was killed, "it was like there was no party."

In this kind of talk, the violence is always situated, either in space (not here, but over there) or in time (not now, but back then). This is a familiar enough process: the cannibals are always the members of the next tribe over. And we certainly see enough of it in ourselves; as I noted above, we were warned by anxious relatives before we first left for Mexico to watch for the "bandidos," a warning that draws its force as much from the racist stereotype of the violent "Latino" as from atavistic memories of the bands of highway robbers that obsessed nineteenth-century travelers in Mexico or of the murders of North Americans by "seditious bandits" in northern Mexico during the 1910s.[20] The same can be said for the warnings about the criminal nature of the people of Mexquitic that we received from our friends in the city of San Luis, though in their case the implicit racism drew on the atavistic memory of the Indian origins of Mexquitic.

Soon after we arrived in Mexquitic this process of localizing the violence continued, as we learned that the "killers" were not the peaceful inhabitants of the town, but the citizens of certain ranchos, notably the Cortes and Ojo Zarco. Interestingly, the racial basis of the accusations of violence implicit in the warnings of family and friends here became explicit—"the people are killers" in those ranchos, "they have killer blood."[21] This conception of violence as being in the "blood" of a "people" is important—though it may seem ironic, at least to an outsider, that townspeople would speak of the murderousness of people with whom they are closely related as a kind of hereditary trait. After all, historical justifications for placing the violence in particular ranchos can be found. There is also a close tie between the political-economic train of events that led these ranchos into violence and the implicit conception of the rancho as a kind of family.

Looking at the localizing of violence with a historical eye, we can see a number of connections between time, place, and violence. Given the roots of Pilar García and the agraristas in Corte Primero, it is no surprise that Corte is singled out as one of the ranchos of *matones,* killers. An even more direct connection between the ranchos of the Cortes and Ojo Zarco and violence derives from the conflicts surrounding the regional implementation of agrarian reform in 1924–1928. The agraristas of Ojo Zarco, as supporters of Cedillo, were provisionally granted an ejido in the midst of the neighboring hacienda of Peñasco (municipality of San Luis Potosí) in 1924. This immediately led them into conflict with the hacienda tenants, whose fields they had to cross to reach their new ejido.

Later, when the tenants had been granted their own fields as ejido land, they complained that from the beginning the ejidatarios of Ojo Zarco had "proceeded to set fire to our houses and steal our animals, corn, and everything they could lay their hands on, breaking down doors, beating and squeezing families, and even forcing the comrades [i.e., the ejidatarios of Peñasco] to bring their carts full of corn to Ojo Zarco." This accusation was made after an apparent battle between the two ejidos in July 1940 that left the comisariado and two others from Ojo Zarco dead from machete and bullet wounds, and six others gravely wounded. The crowd of ejidatarios from Peñasco who had surrounded and all but massacred the nine men from Ojo Zarco claimed that the latter had fired first and also that the cattle they were leading through Peñasco fields were in fact stolen.[22]

The murderous reputation of the people of the two Cortes, Corte Primero and Corte Segundo, is based on a similar feud—with each other. As Ramón and Flor explained it to us, in the 1920s the ejidatarios of Corte Segundo loaned a part of their ejido to those of Corte Primero. Years later, in the 1940s, the children of the original ejidatarios had forgotten about the reasons for the original loan, and each ejido began to claim the land in question as their own. Each side had numerous documents to back their own claims (as is typical in such cases), and the litigation over the disputed land has dragged on for decades.[23] In the meantime the people of the Cortes took matters into their own hands. According to Ramón, it was not safe for someone from one Corte to pass through the fields of the other. If people from both Cortes were at a party, someone was bound to be found dead in the morning (*amanecer muerto*), and girls from one Corte were never allowed to marry into the other. This intense feuding has abated only in recent years, not because the ejido dispute has been resolved but because it has become almost irrelevant due to a decade-long drought, which has left the contested fields untillable.

Though these feuds are apparently of recent origin, they fit into the pattern of intervillage conflict which Dennis (1987) has described for Oaxaca, where some of the local wars have been fought on and off for centuries. In fact, there is something primordial about even these contemporary conflicts, as they are described by people in Mexquitic, something of Cain and Abel, or of Jacob and Esau, something of the sun and the moon, which were described to us during the solar eclipse of 1984 as two brothers fighting "to see which one is the stronger." Entire communities are imagined as metaphorical families, for new ranchos are said to be created when their parent communities "give birth" to them. A household or group of related households will break away from the parent community, and the rancho they form will often continue to be called by the name of the founding family (Los Coronados, Los Urbina) even though other families moved in afterward. When two closely related ranchos such as the Cortes quarrel, then, it is like two brothers fighting.

Ramón and Flor described the struggle between the Cortes while telling us the story of a fight between two brothers from a rancho near Mexquitic over a garden plot that they had inherited in the town. That long and bitter fight, whose history is familiar to everyone in Mexquitic, ended a few years ago with the murder of one of the brothers and the flight of the other, his presumed killer, away from San Luis (some say, to the United States). The fratricidal brother is said to return sometimes from his hideout for a nocturnal visit to his wife, who now has ended up with the garden; we used to see her arrive three times a week in her white pickup to tend the flowers and vegetables. The juxtaposition of this tale with that of the Cortes, which shares the themes of violence and struggle for land, served to underline a theme of fratricidal struggle. It was as if to say that the two Cortes, which once were one, were playing the roles of two brothers fighting viciously over their inheritance.

Rosendo too illustrated his story about a feud between two families, the Garcías and the Romos of Corte Primero, by referring to intercommunity fights. "Those Romos had a grudge against the Garcías," he told me. "The boys still get into fights now and then. Aristeo took a few shots at Cundo Romo." I asked if that was because of politics, and he answered:

> Who knows but them? One bunch had more money than the other or whatever. It's just like here in the hacienda of La Parada. It was all one hacienda, the people, you know. But here on this side of the river, in Ranchería de Guadalupe, it was called "this side," and over there it was "the other side." It was all one, but they couldn't stand the sight of each other! If there was a dance on this side of the river, those from over there didn't come. And if there was one over there, these from here would go, but it would be to beat up on them, eh.

This notion of the community as a kind of extended family seems to underlie another connection between place and violence—the former tradition in certain ranchos of resisting the intrusion of outsiders into their territory. We see something of this resistance in the intercommunity feuds, as when the tenants of Peñasco would not allow the cattle of Ojo Zarco to cross their fields, but in some ranchos resistance was generalized and directed against all outsiders. Tacho and Lalo, each in their seventies, spoke of this tradition one day in a conversation with Lucio, a young man from the nearby rancho of Moras, where Tacho was born. Tacho recalled how safe the rancho used to be; even if you left your jacket out in your field with money in the pocket, it would still be there, untouched, when you returned. Everyone habitually left all their farm tools out in the fields, and if you were out there working and you needed a tool, you could simply borrow your neighbor's without any worry. No one ever had to go around asking for a borrowed tool to be returned.

Tacho asked Lucio if it could still be like that. No, not at all, was the reply. On the other hand, Tacho went on, the people of Moras did not like strangers. If a stranger passed through the rancho they would drag him off to the presidencia in Mexquitic or perhaps just beat him up on the spot. Once, he related, a gentleman came by, showing off his fancy clothes and pistols; the people of Moras knocked him off his horse, beat him up, and stripped him. But things are not like that anymore, Lucio affirmed. Nothing is safe now—they even steal flowers grown for the market straight from the fields—but no one beats up strangers, either.

Lalo set this propensity to react violently against outsiders within the context of the lawlessness of the 1920s and 1930s. In those days, he said, officials were only after money, not justice, and would let anyone off for a bribe no matter what their crime, so people would at times take the law into their own hands. Lalo and Tacho recalled two instances of this. Once two brothers with reputations as fighters were beaten to death by a large crowd after they killed two other men. And another time, Lalo related, a man from the rancho of Ojo de Pinto was caught by another crowd after killing a man, beaten unconscious, tied up, and dragged the eight kilometers to the presidencia in Mexquitic. Tacho remembered the story well, for this man had caused Tacho's grandmother to die from sadness by breaking into her store and stealing her life savings. As the crowd drew near the town, Tacho said, the man began to come to, and one of the men carrying him picked up a large rock and smashed his skull. Thus the turbulence of the time led not only to the individual violence of the *matón* but to the violence of collective retribution.

"All this," said Lalo, "happened when I was a boy, around 1925. It has all changed now." Lucio, following the theme of the violence of the past, told of how his own grandfather had killed two men, cutting their heads off with an axe, and afterward had "become very Catholic," wearing an enormous crucifix and several large rosaries around his neck everywhere he went, as penance. Lucio asked, "Are there none of these murderous people (*gente matona*) left?" "No, no," Tacho and Lalo said, with a kind of nostalgia. "That is all gone and over." Thus the telling of these juxtaposed tales both contextualizes the violence and—recent incidents such as the murder of don Lupe aside—removes it to a distant, almost mythic past.

LOCAL POLITICS AND THE STATE

With the ousting of Cedillo and the disarming of the agraristas, the violence and militarism surrounding the Revolutionary period abated, and the municipality of Mexquitic and the state of San Luis were integrated into national machine politics. This integration did not, however, bring to an end the incongruities between local and national political history. Pilar García's cacique rule had been broken, just as Cedillo's hold over state politics had, yet this did not spell the end, even politically, of García himself. Unlike Cedillo, who as the main target of the federal government was tracked down relentlessly and finally killed, García was able to escape the initial roundup of Cedillo supporters and later was allowed to escape punishment for his actions as head of the Cedillista state congress.

After the end of the Cárdenas regime García returned to Mexquitic to exercise his diminished power in local politics. The immediate result of his return was a period of confusion, at a time of consolidation and conservatism in the national government. Locally, the 1941 election brought to power politicians from the town, who had been shut out for a decade by García's control of the presidency. But Pilar García was able to interfere even now, causing the president to go into hiding for a time by sending him a death threat, and then having him arrested (on what charges we were not told) and finally removed from office. The next elections, in 1944, were hotly contested, with speeches by the rival candidates ending in a hail of stonethrowing; to keep the peace, the state government eventually imposed its own candidate, a complete outsider to Mexquitic, as interim president. So it was not until 1947, almost a decade after the fall of Cedillo, that the town faction fully took control of the municipality with the election of don Raúl.

Don Raúl has strong family connections to the old town elite. A grandfather, a great-grandfather, and at least three uncles and great-uncles had served as municipal president since the mid-nineteenth century, including Patricio Jiménez, the leading politician of that era, who has now been apotheosized as a forerunner of agrarian reform in the municipality, as we shall see in the final chapter. Yet in Raúl's own life history these ties are not readily apparent; in fact, they seem to have been shattered by the murder of his father when he was a two-year-old child.

As Raúl relates his own story, his career followed the basic path of the typical "successful politician" of his generation—those born around 1910—which Camp has delineated (1988). Made an orphan early in life, Raúl was raised by his grandmother, who he remembers as having encouraged him to continue his education beyond the three years of primary school then available in Mexquitic. Unlike the politicians that Camp describes, who went on to earn doctorates and law degrees and to become active in national politics, Raúl's education ended with a three-year internship in San Luis, where he completed primary school, and his political career effectively ended with his second term as municipal president. But in Mexquitic, up to at least the 1950s, receiving even a third-grade education was an attainment reached mainly by the children of the elite, who cherished (and continue to cherish) the value of education. Indeed, it was Raúl's second cousin who donated the land on which the primary school in Mexquitic was built, and later generations in his family have become educated professionals. Seven of Raúl's ten children became teachers and one became an electrician, while only one continues to work the land as

Raúl did. Several of his grandchildren are now teachers, one is a medical doctor, another a pharmacologist, and another is studying architecture.

In talking with don Raúl himself, one feels that he got more education in his six years of schooling than one would have thought possible. He speaks with the formal vocabulary and elaborate syntax of Mexican politics, and he can deliver a spontaneous disquisition on the social functions of religion that sounds as if it were taken straight from Durkheim. The rise of Raúl and the others of his generation to political power in Mexquitic and San Luis thus signified a marked shift in political style, away from the gunslinging Revolutionary era of the Garcías and toward an institutionalized, formal, and discursive style that perhaps hearkens back to an earlier, pre-Revolutionary political form.

Many people in the town of Mexquitic recall the 1940s and 1950s— the period when don Raúl was twice elected president—as a time when presidents were chosen by the popular will, and not simply chosen from above and imposed on the electorate. In other words, as a time when there was no cacique rule. But a child, such as Atilio, who grew up in the 1940s could see through the emperor's clothes: the "rich men" of Mexquitic were "playing ball" with the presidency, with the tacit collusion of the townspeople who elected them. And, as some will point out, the period of the town's dominance in municipal politics coincided with the state cacique rule of Cedillo's former enemy, ally, and finally successor, Gonzalo N. Santos; it was perhaps more than a coincidence that Santos became a compadre of don Raúl.

The labyrinthine twists and turns of local, state, and national politics surrounding the rise and fall of Santos, whose political machine controlled the state of San Luis in the 1940s and 1950s, and the twin reform movements of Dr. Salvador Nava in the city of San Luis in the early 1960s and the early 1980s, will form a fitting coda for this chapter on the complex of interrelations and contradictions among the many levels of the political life.

Gonzalo N. Santos, like Cedillo before him, came to power in the state through the self-contradictory strategy of promising land reform while at the same time maintaining a firm regional base within the state through owning or controlling large tracts of land.[24] Unlike Cedillo, Santos built an efficient political machine to maintain his power. Ramón recalled with apparent fondness how well the Santos machine used to work in comparison with the flatfooted maneuvers of Governor Carlos Jonguitud

(1979–1985). The occasion for the comparison was a "spontaneous demonstration" in the state capital on January 13, 1984, arranged to demonstrate the support of the people of San Luis for Jonguitud and their repudiation of Nava, the newly elected "anti-democratic" (opposition) mayor of the city. As usual at such rallies, truckloads of ejidatarios from the capital region poured into the city to join the crowd. I rode in with one of the relatively few trucks coming from the town of Mexquitic, where relations with Jonguitud were tense because of the conflict over don Lupe. There were rumors that we would be given lunch at the end of the meeting, but that never materialized; only the owners of the pickups were given money to pay for the gasoline they used.

Since Jonguitud was the president of the national teachers' union (his power base), every schoolteacher in the state was also obliged to take the day off in order to be present. Ramón had gone along as a musician in the band playing for one of the groups of teachers. He told of how, before the demonstration began, all the teachers had been drawn into formation to be taught the chants and cheers that were to be shouted during their march. But first a party official told them, "Anyone who is not agreeable to doing this should step forward and state your objections." Of course, Ramón said, no one dared to do any such thing, just as later no one dared to be lax in shouting the cheers, for there were sure to be informers among them. Ramón said he felt sorry for the poor teachers, forced to go through with this farce; at least he was being paid for the day. "It's not like years ago, when everything was cheaper, and the party was in better control," he commented. "Like when Gonzalo N. Santos ruled here, for eighteen years, first as governor and then as the one who chose the governors. Even though there weren't many means of communication in the state, no trucks or buses, he would always guarantee a big crowd [at a political rally] by giving five pesos, which was a lot back then, to everyone who came on foot, and twenty-five to each one on horseback. In those days they never lost the municipality of San Luis to a Nava."

The truth is that the Santos regime came to an end precisely because they "lost" San Luis to Dr. Nava in 1961, when he was first elected as mayor on a wave of popular opposition to the continuing corruption of state politics under the cacique.[25] A curious counterpoint has been played out in the politics of Mexquitic and San Luis since then. Nava's first election in the city of San Luis led the national party leadership to dismantle the Santos cacique regime in the state, which was blamed for the loss of this major election. In Mexquitic this shift in state politics eventually resulted in the loss of power for the elite of the town, who were apparently connected to Santos (don Raúl's compadre) and the return to power of the elite of Corte Primero, under the cacique leadership of don Aristeo. From the point of view of the townspeople, at least, this meant that the triumph of a democratic reform movement in San Luis, which brought a corrupt state cacique regime to an end, led in Mexquitic to the demise of a regime perceived as democratic, and to the return to power of a political faction (that of don Aristeo, Pilar García's nephew) viewed as corrupt. The new local regime was also, ironically, one that paralleled the ousted state regime in many ways, especially in its calculated use of machine politics, in contrast to Pilar García's and Cedillo's use of paramilitary force.

The ironic twist in this counterpoint came in reaction to the second election of Nava to mayor of San Luis in 1982, once more as a reformist candidate. In order to "win back" the city in the 1985 election, the official party launched—and in the state of San Luis vigorously promoted—a program of "democratization of the PRI." For the first time, something like a primary or caucus was held in municipalities across the state to choose the candidates of the official party. This was considered too risky a method to use for selecting the candidate for governor, but Jonguitud (who had harbored presidential aspirations) was nevertheless unceremoniously ignored in the selection process. The results of "democratization," again according to popular perception in the town, were that the popularly elected Nava regime in San Luis was overthrown by widespread electoral fraud, while in Mexquitic the cacique rule of don Aristeo (who had come to power at the end of the earlier "Navista" period in San Luis) came at last to a close; the town faction, which years earlier was ousted as an indirect result of Nava's election, was now "democratically" returned to power.

Though the colonial image of the governor as a father to his pueblo, as discussed in chapter 4, is no longer used in Mexquitic, the ambivalence that underlies the image remains. Indeed, the father image itself continues to be used in other parts of Mexico, such as the village in Oaxaca studied by Dennis.[26] The political situation in Mexquitic is quite different in many ways from the close approximation of the closed, corporate community that comes through in Dennis's account of "intervillage conflict in Oaxaca." There is no attempt at government by consensus, or by town meetings, on the municipal level in Mexquitic (consensus politics is more real in community and especially ejido meetings). Even in the eighteenth century government was by consensus of the elders, the pueblo elite. Yet the notion of consensus and of the need for popular legitimation of the governing class remains and has even been strengthened by the rhetoric of the Revolution. In fact, the history of Mexican politics in the twentieth century, from the local to the national level, looks quite different if we view it from this perspective, seeing the need to build, and perhaps to enforce, consensus as one of the driving aims of the official party.

From such a perspective, the electoral irregularities and strong-arm pressure that the PRI is frequently accused of using to win elections appear in a different light—not necessarily a better light, but a different one. It is often assumed by outsiders that the ruling party resorts to fraud, as it is presumed to do, because it could not otherwise win elections, implying that the party is undemocratic in the sense of lacking deep and widespread support. But in much of the country the PRI has actually remained until recently "the party of the majorities" that it styles itself. In those regions, San Luis Potosí among them, the party could possibly win a majority of elections, whether municipal, state, or national, by landslides (in North American terms) without resorting to extra-electoral means. From the point of view of a politics of consensus, I would argue, the purpose of the strong-arm tactics of the PRI—which all add up to the strategy known in Mexico as *triunfalismo*—has been to maintain the image of the PRI as the party of consensus. Not just a majority, but an overwhelming majority of state governors, mayors, and congressional deputies must belong to the PRI, and the president of the republic must be elected by the same overwhelming acclaim. Opponents of the PRI, even in Mexquitic, acknowledge the support that the PRI has in parts of rural Mexico at the same time that they disparage its supporters. The party has always found it easy to exploit the gullibility of the country folk, they say. My own point of departure, however, is not to assume the ignorance and gullibility of the people of rural Mexico but to assume that on the contrary they are voting for what they perceive to be their interest. At times they do so cynically, calculating that the party will win no matter what and that they might as well have the party on their side, but at other times they support the PRI because its rhetoric, if nothing else, favors popular causes.

I do not know, or dare to predict, where the PRI or the country is now heading. In the past, the PRI response to an election such as that of 1988, in which the center-left Frente Democrática Nacional (originally a breakaway PRI faction) was believed by many to have been deprived of the national presidency only by fraud, would have been predictable: a massive attempt to co-opt the FDN back into the party (or failing that, to eliminate it), perhaps by moving official party rhetoric slightly back to the left. Instead, President Salinas de Gortari acted as if winning with barely 50 percent of the popular vote (according to official returns) was quite enough.[27] In 1994 the PRI electoral strategy seemed to be aimed at producing the even slimmer majority achieved by the official candidate, through giving semi-official support to the eight opposition parties and thus diluting their votes. Whether this signals a breakdown in the PRI machine, a miscalculation on the part of the party leadership and perhaps the beginning of a new phase of adjustment and reorganization within national politics, or (as it appears) a calculated turn away from the tradition of consensus politics and toward a "modernized" or "Western-style" democratic model, remains to be seen. For the moment, technocrats, democrats and populists, and reformers of both left and right and machine politicians are contending at every level of political life, and the ultimate meaning of these struggles for Mexquitic is uncertain.

Today, in what is arguably the most volatile period in Mexican politics since the 1920s, the paradoxes and contradictions continue unabated on all levels of political life in Mexquitic. Voting abstention in Mexquitic, as in all of Mexico, is reaching post-Revolution highs as a large portion of the municipio finds the political system stagnant and elections meaningless. At the same time the rigid, closed electoral system of the past seventy years, in which electoral fraud (both real and alleged) was accepted so long as the results included at least the appearance of consensus and stability, has given way to a delicate balancing act and a self-consciously modernizing emphasis on the appearance of fairness and multiparty democracy. If the technocratic trends of national politics continue and penetrate to the municipal level, a political space may soon open up for groups such as the schoolteachers. Many of these professionals have long shown an active interest in local politics but have largely been left out of political circles since (as mentioned in chapter 2) they stand somewhat outside the class-like division of Mexquitic society into social strata, and thus apart from the elite stratum that has controlled municipal politics for so long. A larger question is whether the emerging political system will also, at last, prove democratic in the sense of giving a public voice to those long excluded from the game of political power—the small ejidatarios, farmers, day laborers, construction workers, and market women who work the land, make the food, and build the houses of Mexquitic.

SEVEN # Land, History, and Identity

Land has been at the heart of all the major economic, political, and cultural struggles that have divided Mexquitic over the centuries. The questions of who owns the land, who controls the resources to make it productive, and who benefits from the labor put into it have formed a constant background to the preceding chapters. These are first and most obviously questions of power, but they are at the same time cultural questions. The power to control resources cannot be separated from the power to define them.

This chapter opens with a brief sketch of four phases in the land tenure history of Mexquitic from its foundation to the agrarian reform of the 1920s. A first century of expansion, in which Central Mexican, Spanish, and Spanish-Mexican agriculture and livestock raising spread across the regional landscape and the land was carved into community and private domains, was followed by a period of boundary conflicts, which commenced in the 1720s. A third phase of heightened land disputes—between pueblos, between Mexquitic and surrounding haciendas, and among the people of the pueblo themselves—began around 1780 and intensified until 1810, when overt disputes were artificially cut short in the repressive aftermath of the Hidalgo uprising. A final phase of renewed hacienda expansion, at the expense of the pueblo, ran from the 1820s to the end of the century.

In reconstructing this history I have leaned heavily on legal documents, official sources produced by and for a colonial or state regime. But I have tried to listen past the built-in bias of these sources toward elite ideology, in order to hear hints of other stories with different, opposing ideologies. In the second half of the chapter I move from documented history to a mix of documented and oral history, exploring the tensions between legal bases for occupying land and the stories that people tell about themselves and their land, and the tensions between elite and alternative ideologies. I end with a series of local reflections, tentative, diffuse, and cast in mythic language, on the meaning of land for local identity.

EXPANSION AND EARLY CONFLICTS

The land tenure history of Mexquitic began with a century of expansion, as the rough hunting grounds of the Guachichiles were made to conform to the agricultural practices of the Tlaxcalans who came to "pacify" the land and of the Spaniards drawn north by the silver strike of 1592. From 1591 to 1700 the people of the pueblo formed ranchos throughout their three leagues of territory, and the surrounding sea of unclaimed land was taken over by Spanish commercial interests. The first de facto occupations of future haciendas and cattle ranches were quickly carried out by the more powerful of the miners, conquerors, and administrators of San Luis, such as Gabriel Ortiz de Fuenmayor, the first governor of the province, whose ranching and mining operations stretched westward to Sierra de Pinos and beyond. By 1605 Ortiz had legitimized his claim to part of this territory, the nucleus of the hacienda of La Parada bordering Mexquitic, by receiving a royal grant, or *merced*.

The importance of land and labor in seventeenth-century San Luis depended directly on their usefulness in providing for the mining economy. Scarce arable land was quickly identified, claimed, and cultivated, but equally scarce Indian workers were abused and mistreated. The harsh labor conditions of the mines and Spanish-run ore-processing plants and charcoal producers were arguably among the inducements for Mexquitic officials to stress their role as the civilizers of the Guachichiles in all their legal correspondence. By dwelling on their formal role as "soldiers" on the "Chichimeca frontier," a formulation they insisted on well into the eighteenth century, they kept their services to the Crown in official memory and shored up their declining position as "noble Tlaxcalans," exempt from the demands of tribute or servitude. At the same time the people of Mexquitic bent their own land to the economic uses of the mining economy, putting their products into the mines so that they could afford to keep their bodies out of them. The royal treasurer in San Luis noted and condemned this economic strategy in 1650:

The Indians of the district . . . receive no hardship but rather well-known advantages with the mines from trafficking in certain materials that they extract from the territories of their pueblos for the processing of silver, with which not only do they live lives of little affliction, but the opulence and ease of seeking their food makes those that live in the pueblos totally idle and lazy.[1]

The treasurer proposed to revoke the Tlaxcalans' exemption from paying tribute, reasoning that it would be easier to make mining work relatively attractive by adding economic burdens to life in the pueblos than by improving pay or work conditions in the mines. As it happened, the tribute exemption—one of the "perpetual" privileges granted the Tlaxcalans—was revoked many decades later, in 1712. In the meantime, the people of Mexquitic continued to supply the mine economy from the products of their land while maintaining a vigilant guard over that land, to prevent the miners from exploiting it directly.

The uses to which land could be put for the mining economy were many. Good farmland, of course, was useful under any economic regime, though in the San Luis mining area grain could easily be shipped in from the more fertile Bajío to the south. In practice, it appears, most farmland in pueblos like Mexquitic was dedicated to subsistence farming. But with the appearance of the mines, the scrublands that cover most of the area acquired new significance: they provided the great volumes of wood and charcoal consumed in the mines, as well as prickly pears, quiotes, and pulque, which were sold to the mine workers and in San Luis. The scrublands also provided grazing areas for the hundreds of mules of the mine-to-city trade, and for the cows, sheep, and goats whose hides and tallow were processed for the mines (meat was a mere by-product).[2] The relentless spread of ranching in the sixteenth century had intensified the Chichimeca War, between 1550 and 1590. In 1630, with the local ecology perhaps already degraded by forty years of ranching, sheep still far outnumbered people in Mexquitic—25,000 sheep to 400 people—and intruding herders continued to provoke skirmishes.

In 1622 the pueblos of Mexquitic and Tlaxcalilla joined to complain that, despite their recent service to the Crown in pacifying the region, "within a few years several Spaniards have taken away" the land they were granted, filling it with "cows, mules, mares, and horses" and thus forcing the people of the two pueblos to abandon agriculture and "buy corn at six pesos the fanega."[3] The asesor who read the complaint ruled that the people of Mexquitic and Tlaxcalilla could expel the intruders from their territories, and he even allowed them to hunt down intruding cattle with their bows and arrows.[4] This ruling temporarily settled matters in the pueblos, though the surrounding haciendas continued to have problems with the transhumant herds. In 1628 the Jesuits of the recently founded College of the Company of Jesus in San Luis, who had bought the hacienda of La Parada five years earlier from the widow of Ortiz, complained:

> Many herds of sheep and goats enter from the pueblo of Querétaro into said valley to graze, without owning land or estates, and to make fire, which they do armed and with premeditation, causing the herders and servants of said Hacienda to come to blows and the clash of arms.[5]

The large-scale transhumance implied by these petitions ultimately turned out to be a passing phenomenon in the occupation of the San Luis "frontier" by Spanish economic interests (though ecological damage caused by the roving herds may have been permanent). The greater threat to the lands of the Tlaxcalans in Mexquitic in the long run came from the same hacienda administrators who had been most successful in countering the invasion of the cattle, the Jesuits of La Parada.

In the struggle to carve properties and jurisdictions out of the land, to create and legitimate a social geography, and to define and defend boundaries in the early seventeenth century, the Jesuits of La Parada and the officials of Mexquitic (both governors and Franciscans) shared the advantage of corporate longevity. This allowed them to manage their lands with attention to their long-term corporate interest, and to maintain strategies over that long term. It also, crucially, endowed them with corporate memory. Individual hacendados might die childless, as did Gabriel Ortiz, the founder of La Parada, or they might leave their estates to children more interested in spending their inheritance than in increasing it. The Jesuits who bought La Parada, on the contrary, administered it as a long-term investment project in the confidence that it would continue to provide income for their college in San Luis for many decades to come. Their strategy was to expand the hacienda's size, its legal position, and its productivity, in roughly that order. The officials of Mexquitic apparently maintained a long-term strategy as well, for they went to the trouble and expense of defending their established boundaries long before pueblo population growth made the disputed land a factor in their survival. They were defending their patrimony, not fighting for their livelihood—as were the Jesuit administrators.

The corporate memory Mexquitic and La Parada each held was especially important in the long-term struggle for land rights because of the legal bases of land tenure under the colonial regime. Land tenure here was based on the legal fiction that the Guachichiles, as the "natural lords" of the land, had freely deeded it over to the Spanish monarch when they accepted his sovereignty; the king, in turn, was free to grant it (in royal *mercedes,* "mercies") to deserving subjects. This fiction was the legal basis for the territorial grants of both Mexquitic and La Parada.[6] The language of the land grants was exceedingly vague, however, referring for example to an *estancia* (usually a square league) of land in the vicinity of the Río de Mexquitic, with no further specifics. In effect, actual control and possession of land was primary; the merced was secondary, a legal weapon that could sometimes be used to good effect to support claims to disputed ground. With corporate memory came the ability to embellish the faint details of the mercedes, by evoking "custom" and "tradition" to legalize the occupation of boundaries that the grants left vague.

The Jesuit administrators of La Parada also had the advantage of organizing experience and ability. Very early on they spread out a wide net of economic activity in the Mexquitic area, taking de facto possession of virtually all land unclaimed by others through their activities of sheep and goat herding, mule raising, and firewood and charcoal operations. These operations finally brought La Parada head-to-head with the pueblo of Mexquitic, its only corporate neighbor and rival. By 1639, a decade and a half after they bought the estate, the Jesuits had organized charcoal-making and goat-herding encampments, run by their Indian servants, in the hills south of Mexquitic and had also retained possession of a goat ranch (Rancho de Cabras) that Ortiz had apparently carved out of Mexquitic territory bordering La Parada to the northwest.

Three individuals from San Luis had also intruded within the boundaries of the pueblo: Pedro Diez del Campo, the notary public of San Luis, who operated ranches to the east and north at Agua Señora, Ojo de Pinto, and Estanzuela, and the miners Francisco Diez del Campo and Alonso de Fraga, who raised mules for hauling charcoal in the west. But when the governor of Mexquitic, backed by the Franciscan prior, set out to defend the pueblo territory from these land invasions, the strongest opposition came from their corporate rival. This outcome seems as inevitable now as it did to the leaders of Mexquitic at the time, who in their suit called the Jesuits the transgressors who for their part appear to want nothing but to bother and disturb their parties, since when they judged that with the death of Grabiel [sic] Ortiz they would be able to quietly enjoy their land it turned out that the Fathers of the Company of Jesus had succeeded him through the purchase they say they have made from the widow of said of one *sitio de estancia*.[7]

As a result of the suit against La Parada and the other invading land-owners, in April 1640 officials from San Luis set out to measure the land that had been granted to the pueblo, apparently for the first time since its foundation half a century earlier. The measurement was conducted in the usual way, with a rope fifty *pasos de Salomón* (about seventy meters) long, its ends colored with red ochre "for greater clarity." One hundred and eighty lengths of the rope equaled the three leagues that Mexquitic had been granted in every direction from the door of the church. On the first leg of the measurement the "Fathers of the Hacienda" objected to the proceedings with an ingenuity and almost comic insistence that lends meaning to the word "jesuitical." At the halfway mark they reasoned "that, if the said Indians must be given a boundary" (they were not ready to concede even this point), "it should be there, . . . for his Majesty's merced should be understood as a league and a half in this direction and an equal amount in the other which together made up the three leagues." Undeterred, the measuring party continued to a fork in the path where a road leading directly toward the hacienda had been planted over with cactuses.

The Jesuits insisted, again without success, that the measurement should follow a new road they had made, snaking around to the south of the hacienda. When the old road brought the party across the Río de Mexquitic, the Jesuits notified them "that they were entering with said measurement into the jurisdiction of Guadalajara, whose boundary was said river," yet the officials continued on. Soon the reason for the Jesuits' objections became clear: the *casco* of the hacienda (its administrative center, houses, and barns) was itself located 600 *varas* (about 500 meters) inside the limits of Mexquitic. The San Luis official promptly gave legal possession of the *casco* to the governor of Mexquitic. On the following days, the party set out to measure and take possession of Mexquitic's territory in the other cardinal directions, without any further objections from the would-be landowners, who were promptly expelled.[8]

If the Jesuits were energetic, though unsuccessful, in their objections to the process of measuring the Mexquitic land grant, they were also eager to establish clear legal title to any land that was a possible source of dispute, even at the expense of coming to a compromise with their legal opponents. In this they differed from many other acquisitive large landowners; perhaps they were more conscious than some of the debilitating effect of endless, uncompromising litigation. In any case, they worked to bring the 1640 conflict between La Parada and Mexquitic to a rapid conclusion. The agreement they eventually hammered out left the Jesuits in the unqualified possession of the *casco* of their estate together with all land on the far side of the river. They also retained the land they had occupied on the Mexquitic side of the river, including Rancho de Cabras, in return for an annual payment of 75 pesos against a *censo* of 1,500 pesos on the land.[9] Just what the medieval word "censo" meant is not only a question for us, but a problem that would return to haunt the people of Mexquitic at a different point in their land tenure history, more than a century later.

At the same time, the pueblo arranged to auction off the small "hacienda" of Estanzuela that had been carved out of their territory to the east. This estate, which did not go to the man who had originally usurped it, brought in an annual censo payment of 25 pesos.[10] Four years later the pueblo also extracted an annual rental contract from the man who had been operating the so-called Hacienda of Mexquitic on pueblo land in the area of modern Corte. This rental (not a censo) brought yet another 25 pesos annually into the community chest.[11] The stated aim of the leaders of Mexquitic in acquiring this newfound income was "to convert the rent into medicines and comfort of the sick who are healed in the Hospital that has been founded in said pueblo, and in other unavoidable expenses which we make in public worship."[12]

The end of this first, expansive phase of land tenure and land conflicts, in which "free" land in the Mexquitic area was claimed and occupied and the claims then validated by royal merced, was marked by legal review of the titles of La Parada by a Jesuit lawyer around 1690. He was particularly concerned with the difficulties the hacienda had been having to the southeast with the ranchos of Cerro Prieto and Ojo Zarco. These ranchos were located on the Mexquitic side of the river, but beyond the pueblo's three-league boundary, and thus easily susceptible to the kind of land grabs that marked this first phase. La Parada apparently had taken de facto possession of the ranchos without securing formal mercedes. In 1684 a neighboring landowner had learned of their legal status and had them granted to himself.

The Jesuits waited prudently until the landowner died in 1688 before appealing the merced, claiming that the amount of land that their rivals

had been granted in their merced could be accommodated elsewhere, far-
ther from La Parada. In the end, the Jesuits were left with Ojo Zarco,
which came to form part of La Parada, while Cerro Prieto remained a
separate hacienda. The Jesuit who reviewed the documents concluded:
"Since the land of the College is surrounded on all sides by neighbors, on
no side can it be sure of its ownership, unless it has its titles at hand." [13] By
this time, one century after the foundation of Mexquitic, almost the entire area had been staked out by haciendas, smaller ranchos, or pueblos.
Legal title, and legal battles over possession, had correspondingly become
much more important.

The ultimate success of the Jesuits' manipulation of the merced system
can be measured by the fact that in 1767, at the time of their expulsion
from New Spain, the Jesuits actually held one and a half times as much
land in La Parada as they had been granted through mercedes. Their titles
comprised seventeen and a half *sitios de ganado mayor,* three *sitios de ganado
menor,* and fifty-two *caballerías,* a total of 35,306 hectares. But the legally
established boundaries of the hacienda, which can easily be followed on a
modern topographic map, surround an area of 50,900 hectares. When the
Jesuits had come to locate their land grants on the ground, they had clearly
placed them strategically.[14]

The settlement between Mexquitic and La Parada in 1640 marked the
beginning of a long period of calm in land relations in Mexquitic. For the
pueblo, the question in this first phase of land expansion and conflict had
been one of protecting a potentially useful patrimony. As lucrative as the
exploitation of the scrubland for firewood was in the early years, there was
more than enough land within the pueblo boundaries for the few hundred
citizens of Mexquitic to share it with their neighbors if they had wished,
or if they had been forced to share. Throwing out the invaders was a matter of saving resources for their descendants rather than of guarding them
for themselves.

It was only after many decades, in the 1720s, that land conflicts again
began to stir. This second phase of conflict involved a border conflict that
no one had apparently even noticed a century before. It turned out, upon
measurement, that the three-league boundaries of Mexquitic and of
Tlaxcalilla overlapped considerably.[15] The fact that this "back-burner" issue was now addressed indicates that the question was less one of protecting a potentially useful patrimony than of reclaiming land that was immediately needed for the people of the pueblo. Population pressure had
begun to be an issue. The transitional nature of this phase of conflict can

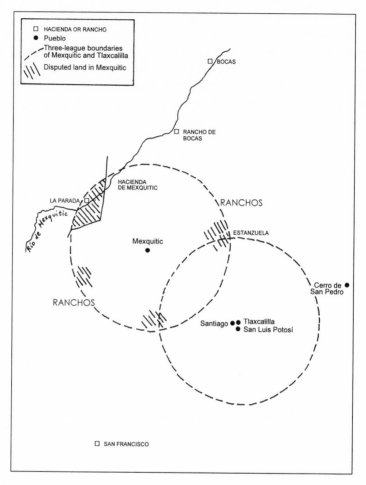

MAP 3.   The early phases of land tenure in the Mexquitic area: haciendas, pueblos, and the overlapping boundaries of Mexquitic and Tlaxcalilla

be gauged by the ways in which it was settled. In 1744, when Mexquitic had grown to perhaps 2,500 people, the dispute was settled amicably with a division of the disputed land between the two pueblos, and the tone was still one of protecting the pueblo patrimony. Twenty years later it proved that the people of Tlaxcalilla had failed to relocate from lands granted to Mexquitic, and the same settlement was acrimoniously reimposed in court. The emphasis was now on protecting the beleaguered citizens of Mexquitic, whose population had doubled, in the present.

Meanwhile the first recorded land suit inside the boundaries of Mexquitic had reached the San Luis courts in 1758. This conflict over inheritance between two brothers-in-law presaged a growing number of internal disputes in the 1780s and 1790s. The old days were coming to an end,
the days when, according to testimony in a land suit from 1798, "there
weren't as many sons [of the pueblo]" and "everyone took whatever fields
they felt like, and abandoned them when they felt like it and took other
ones, . . . and no one brought lawsuits about it and the government didn't
give land titles to anyone." [16] Land title was no longer just a matter for
haciendas and pueblos.

This second phase in Mexquitic land tenure history is also notable for
the apparent lack of conflict with La Parada. Despite the disappointment
of the leaders of Mexquitic in the 1620s, who had hoped that the death of
the first owner of La Parada would mean freedom from the nuisance of
the neighboring hacienda in the future, succeeding pueblo officials seem
to consider the boundary dispute permanently settled with the payment
of the annual censo (which was mysteriously reduced from 75 to 50 pesos
at some point in the eighteenth century). The administrators of La Parada,
for their part, evidently kept their part of the bargain, both letter and
spirit, and thus avoided further conflicts.

HEIGHTENED CONFLICT, RENEWED EXPANSION

On the night of June 24, 1767, the colonial militia, acting under sealed
orders from Carlos III of Spain, arrested every member of the Jesuit order
throughout New Spain. The king's reasoning remains somewhat mysterious, though most historians think he had determined that the Company
of Jesus, with its control of the educational system of the empire and its
fabled wealth, had come to present a challenge to his own preeminence.
However that may be, the arrested Jesuits were eventually expelled from
all Spanish possessions, their colleges closed, and their properties seized
by the Crown. Among the properties seized was La Parada.

For the next fifteen years the hacienda was run by government administrators while the Crown attempted to auction it off.[17] This was a period
of lax control over the hacienda, and the people of Mexquitic hoped,
much as their ancestors had after the death of Gabriel Ortiz, that this
would somehow mean the end of the hacienda and the return of land that
they now felt they needed for themselves. But La Parada was finally auctioned off in 1778. Its new owner, don Angel Prieto de la Maza, a Spanish

lieutenant colonel in the colonial militia married to the daughter of a rich San Luis miner, took yet another five years to raise the 36,482 pesos he had bid and take possession of the hacienda.[18]

In the 1780s a dramatically larger population in Mexquitic (now surpassing 8,000 people within the pueblo boundaries alone) led to land pressure and conflicts within the pueblo. From this time to the end of the century conflicts over land spread within the pueblo, between neighbors and within families.[19] The possession of La Parada by Prieto de la Maza in 1783 marked the end of a fifteen-year period in which the pueblo-hacienda relations that had been established and upheld for a century and a half were allowed to fall into disuse. This new, private, and (as it turned out) acquisitive hacendado could not comprehend that in the eyes of Mexquitic he had bought a censo, not a piece of land, and he soon gained the backing of a new, dynamic priest, Lozano, who was to become his close friend, political ally, and economic partner. These coinciding facts and trends together brought Mexquitic into a new and wrenching phase of land conflict. The legal battle between Mexquitic and La Parada began in 1789, with a petition from the governor of Mexquitic calling for the return to the pueblo of the land held in censo by the hacienda.

A censo, or "quitrent" (an equally medieval English term), was an "imposition made on real estate, with the obligations of paying an annuity and of not being able to alienate the property without first giving notice to the lord of the censo." [20] The key phrase here, "lord of the censo" (*señor del censo*), is what set the censo apart from more recent European and Euro-American concepts of property and payment such as rental and mortgage. A simple annual rental payment would have implied, in this case, that the land "really" belonged to Mexquitic and that La Parada was paying an annual fee for its use, while a fixed mortgage or equity payment would have implied that it was really La Parada's land and the annual payments were just the service on a debt. What is missing from these categories is the notion of a perpetual personal tie between the two parties involved. The censo was a property type deriving from "feudal" times in which land was "subject to a complex tissue of rights claimed by a whole hierarchy of interested parties," and "the individual family's rights of use over its own property were not unlimited and free, but tied into the tangled web of communal usufruct." [21] From the feudal perspective the censo was both an economic instrument and a recognition of a tie, and the payment was a monetary tribute to the seigniorial lord.

Looked at from a capitalist perspective a censo was both rent *and* mortgage, and the questions of ultimate ownership of the land and of the meaning of the payment shift unsettlingly. San Luis Potosí in 1640 was neither feudal nor capitalist. Though the ruling elite of the time had arguably more institutional memories of feudal structures than they had premonitions of industrial capitalism, there was still some uncertainty as to how to describe a censo (just as, in cases such as this, there was a typically American inversion of European norms when a farming town became the "feudal lord" over a large estate run by a religious order). By 1789 the original uncertainty had developed into full-blown incomprehension.

When witnesses were asked in 1640 whether it was in the best interest of Mexquitic to give out their lands in censo, they testified that "they will gain much utility from . . . *renting them,* because with that they *retain perpetuity* and benefit from their rents."[22] Here the annual payment is treated as a rent, while Mexquitic is said to keep "perpetuity" in the deal, which implies but is not the same thing as perpetual "ownership." The leaders of Mexquitic insisted on putting in the contract the conditions that the Jesuits had to maintain their property in good condition, implying a less than total freedom of ownership, that they had to keep their cattle out of Mexquitic, and that they had to notify Mexquitic before reselling their estate "so that [the new buyer] may be compelled to legally recognize this censo with us." The last clause was part of the standard definition of censo, yet they nevertheless felt it necessary to spell it out (and, in the end, it was ignored).

Under these conditions, they continued, "we of course waive and withdraw from the right, property, and lordship of said terrain . . . so that . . . they may possess it as their own."[23] Here it seems they are speaking in terms of an outright sale, with certain encumbering conditions, but again in the actual contract the "said natives" of Mexquitic "offer the *monte* [wilderness] that runs from the Rancho de Cabras to the estate of said College . . . with the qualification that said natives must be able to make use of said monte for cutting firewood, as they have done in the past and *because it is theirs, as it is.*"[24] In this formulation, they implicitly retained "ownership" of the disputed land. The prior of Mexquitic, to complete the picture of confusion, writes in the same document of Mexquitic's "dominion and possession" of the land, and refers to the payment in one sentence as "rent" and in another as "censo and tribute."[25] In his choice of words, the motifs of dominion and tribute dominate.

A century and a half later the feudal terms were gone. Instead, the legal arguments were given in terms of outright ownership, rents, and mortgage fees. The leaders of Mexquitic argued that they had been renting the land to La Parada; now that they needed it for their own people, they had the right to refuse to renew the rental agreement with the new purchaser of the hacienda and recall the land. The new owner, Prieto de la Maza, for his part insisted that the censo agreement was a purchase, and he treated the annual payment of 50 pesos (to which it had somehow been reduced) as a service on a mortgage debt of 1,000 pesos. His insistence reached the point of doctoring the documents. In the 1778 document detailing the extent and boundaries of the land that comprised La Parada, the Rancho de Cabras is referred to as "the fields rented out by the Pueblo"; in the copy preserved in the hacienda archive, "rented out by" has been crossed out and replaced with the words "bought from." [26]

The struggle over the meaning of the word "censo" was but one manifestation of the demise in colonial Spanish jurisprudence, and in popular and elite conceptions, of the "web of use-rights" that Behar has described. A sign of its demise that was more present in the everyday life of people in Mexquitic was the increasing privatization of pueblo land. Toward the end of the colonial period the local representatives of the colonial system insisted on the private nature of property within the pueblo. "All the Indians in those parts," the priest Lozano wrote in 1805, "have their pieces of land assigned to them, each one possesses his own: he supports himself from it, he receives its fruits: there are no common lands there." [27]

Still, there can be more than one image of "private" property, and that held by the colonial elite, such as Prieto de la Maza, was given meaning within a particular kind of moral economy that did not entirely coincide with that conceived of by the people of Mexquitic. Nor was the latter entirely limited to what Scott (1976) has called the "moral economy of the peasant." The notion of a right to subsistence was evident and central in the internal land suits of Mexquitic, as indeed it was in the colonial jurisprudence of New Spain. The right of Indian communities to possess enough land for their own survival was so well established that even Prieto de la Maza had to make his counterarguments within the frame of that basic assumption. But the moral economy enforced by the local political elite of Mexquitic, who had the power to distribute land to individual families and also to take it away, incorporated the tenets of Catholic morality as well. A man accused of incest or adultery could have his land taken away and handed over to a brother or cousin for ten or fifteen years. When I read such examples I am struck by the governor's repressive use of his powers to support the position of the clergy on public and private morality, but this was perhaps not what most struck people in Mexquitic at the time. It is possible that the enduring lesson they learned was less about the evil of adultery than of the good of redistributive justice, the principle that public officials had the right and the duty to redistribute land according to their notions of morality and justice. The notion of redistribution, linked perhaps to a different notion of justice, was to emerge as an explosive force in the agrarian revolution.

Prieto de la Maza, my exemplar of the colonial landed elite, had other ideas about justice. "Distributive justice is that through which something is apportioned to everyone according to his merits," he argued in his 1789 petition. The king had thus been right to distribute land to the founders of Mexquitic for the services they had performed, but, he argued, the great majority of those who now lived in Mexquitic were not descended from the original founders. "The families of Mexquitic have for some time been mixed with other castas, so that there is scarcely . . . anyone who might legitimately be Indian." They therefore had no rights to receive new land according to the claims of either "distributive, commutative, or legal justice," but instead "should be occupied in other tasks useful to the Republic and necessary to human usages." [28] In the tight syllogisms of Prieto's legal argument we see the conceptual matrix that undergirded the images of "industriousness" discussed in chapter 5, the complex interlinkage of notions of race and class (or, in Prieto's terms, descent and "industry"), justice, and land tenure.

The lawsuits between Mexquitic and La Parada followed in tandem, from 1797 on, with those involving Lozano. The same motifs discussed above, the images of the Indian, the representations of rebellion, appear here as well. Like the suits against Lozano, those against La Parada appeared to be grinding to a halt by 1809, twenty years after the case had begun. In that year don Juan Manuel Prieto de la Maza, nephew and heir of the first object of the suits, received a consultation on the progress of the suit from a lawyer who found, after reviewing the documents, that "the suit is in its last stages." After a slew of cases in which the lawyers and the connections of the Prieto de la Mazas beat down and overwhelmed the opposition from Mexquitic time and again, it is remarkable that the author of the consultation was only mildly optimistic about the outcome. La Parada, he wrote, had knocked down every basis for the suits brought by Mexquitic, save one: their right, as an Indian community, to subsistence. All depended on the inspection (*vista de ojos*) that was soon to take place.

If it proves that the Indians have enough terrain to cultivate in what they now possess, . . . they will probably be denied the restitution they request of the two *sitios* ceded and added to your hacienda. But on the other hand, if the said inspection should somehow make it seem that the Indians do not presently enjoy enough for their occupation and sustenance, that their properties are base [*serviles*] or of little use, then I hold it certain that they will attain their goal, and take the two sitios from La Parada.[29]

The supposed (and in a few cases real) bias of the colonial justice system toward the welfare of the "Indians" was the weak point of the defense of La Parada, as it had been from the beginning. In 1789, after the first petition from Mexquitic, don Angel Prieto de la Maza had responded to the notion that the pueblo was in urgent need of reclaiming their land with a mixture of contempt and fear:

If from, e.g., 14 families who began to settle the pueblo of Mexquitic there have been produced in 149 years so many that they no longer fit in the boundaries of three leagues that they occupy in every direction, with those there are now what number of people and families will they reach in another 149 years? . . . If the same conditions of people, the same variety of climates militate 149 years from now, then if for this precise reason they now are granted the land they have alienated and that belongs to La Parada, by then they should be able to take from all their neighbors whatever land they own, whether by sale, inheritance, donation, or any other title.[30]

The prospect that Prieto de la Maza presented here as a frightening reductio ad absurdum turned out instead to be unwittingly prescient. Mexquitic took over La Parada and their other hacienda neighbors in the agrarian reform 140 years later.[31]

In the meantime, the lawyer in the 1809 consultation offered both legal and extralegal advice on guiding the proposed inspection and winning the case. Should anything go wrong, he noted, Prieto de la Maza always had the recourse of pointing out that the legal representative for Mexquitic "is an Indian, and as such does not have standing [*persona*] to be at trial without a guardian for the purpose." But to be sure that nothing would go wrong "it is necessary . . . to keep the commissioned judge, the experts, etc., grateful," and to impress upon them during the inspection that if the Indians of Mexquitic "are not well-off it is because of their laziness, because they are occupied with making mescal, because their terrain is poorly distributed, . . . or because they like to wander in other parts." [32]

It is not quite clear whether the inspection was ever held or the lawsuit settled in the end. In any case, the events of 1810 rendered the subject moot. The Hidalgo revolt erupted in September, and on October 13 Lozano announced Hidalgo's excommunication and preached vehemently against the insurgency, but when the rebel forces took San Luis in November they were eagerly joined by a large faction from Mexquitic. With the priest and the hacienda administrators in flight or in hiding, they were at last able to put in practice the hope that their ancestors had long ago expressed after the death of Gabriel Ortiz by capturing La Parada. They held the hacienda for four months, until the royal forces retook the region on March 3, 1811. The administrator of the hacienda, a captain in the Provincial Dragoons of San Luis who like many hacendados and administrators had fought against the insurgency, testified three years later:

> The Indians of Mexquitic, although some of them behaved with honor and fidelity in the recent insurrection, most of them, in general, were criminal from the beginning, committing excesses . . . [such as] having appropriated the hacienda under my charge, in which the república was found, together with the greater part of la Indiada [the Indian rabble], harvesting and destroying its fields, of which they enjoyed more than half, . . . which disorder forced [General Calleja] to detach a division of troops . . . [in which I went as subaltern] to contain said excesses, and punish the ringleaders, as was done in spite of their scandalous audacity in calling out the pueblo by ringing the church bells to oppose the Royal Troops . . . ; with the leaders captured, ten of the most principal were sentenced to execution.[33]

The surviving faction in Mexquitic claimed, as they bid to have the colony reinstate the pueblo's privileges that had been taken away after the revolt, that all of the supporters of Hidalgo in Mexquitic, some two thousand of them, had gone off to war and never returned. Whether true or an exaggeration, it is certain that in the chilling reactionary climate that followed the defeat of Hidalgo, no leader from Mexquitic dared to oppose hacendado or priest in court, and this third phase of intense conflict came to an unforeseen end.

The de facto victory of La Parada over Mexquitic, represented by the suppression of the Hidalgo revolt, meant the elimination or silencing of the antihacienda faction of the Mexquitic elite after 1810. This victory was followed in 1821 by the *criollo* coup that toppled the royal regime. Mexican Independence was a complex event with complex consequences, but for present purposes the key point is that it left the landed powers in charge of the country, either directly or through the weakness of the central government. From the pueblos' point of view, the primary divergence of national from colonial rule was that, with regional elites in charge of the fate of Mexico, the central government was both unable and ideologically unwilling to continue the long-standing paternalist policies toward Indians. Among the first acts of independent Mexico was the abolition of the colonial *sistema de castas* and the legal distinction between the "races" that made such colonial paternalism possible in the first place. Indian tribute was abolished and along with it went the separate Indian system of justice.

One symptom of the redefinition of the colonial legacy by the postcolonial elite was the passage of a state law in 1827, Decree Number 1 of the First Constitutional Legislature of the State of San Luis Potosí, which declared: "Land belonging to the communities of the indigenous pueblos will remain the property of its present possessors, whatever the mode of its acquisition."[34] Pueblo land henceforth belonged, legally as well as practically, to the families that worked it rather than to the community. In one sense this early disentailment of community land in San Luis, like that in Spain (Herr 1974), merely put a legal stamp on a process of privatization that had been progressing in practice for decades. But it also provided a legal basis for going beyond that early stage. After the law was passed most of the remaining unclaimed land in the pueblo was divided up among its families—perhaps disproportionately among its most prominent families, though the evidence on this account is rather scant. Many properties of the defunct *cofradías,* which the municipal president supposedly passed on to the priest in 1836, were also claimed by individuals as their own at this time. Most important, if the land was legally owned by the individuals of Mexquitic it could also be sold by them, even to outsiders. To La Parada the law was a license for expansion and the sign that a new phase in the regional land tenure history had begun.

The Independence period coincided with another change of ownership for La Parada. Don Juan Manuel Prieto de la Maza died childless, like his uncle before him, in 1820. Two years later his widow's second husband, Pantaleón Ipiña, bought the hacienda from Prieto's heirs in Spain.

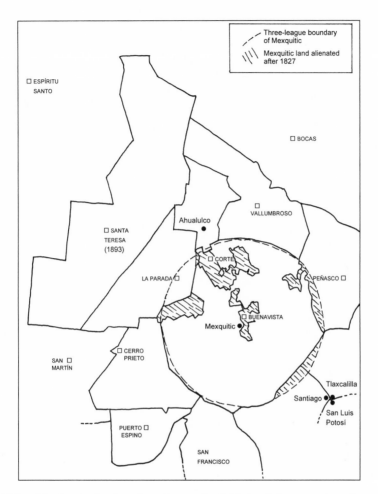

MAP 4.   The late hacienda regime: the terrain divided and the expansion of haciendas into Mexquitic (boundaries as of 1929)

Over the next five years Ipiña took out mortgages on La Parada totaling 60,000 pesos, or half the value of the entire estate. Despite this load of debt, Ipiña was quick to take advantage of the new state law that redefined "indigenous" lands as private. The hacienda archive records the purchases in 1828, a year after the law was passed, of two small fields in Mexquitic that bordered on La Parada. It was not until 1837, however, when the debts were paid off and the estate books were balanced, that land purchases took off. Over the following thirty-five years the owners of La Parada bought 197 parcels in Mexquitic and another forty-two in neighboring Ahualulco, extending the hacienda borders from the formerly disputed Rancho de Cabras deep into the bounds of the pueblo.[35]

At the same time, the new law legitimated the conversion of Corte from a community property rented out by the pueblo into a private hacienda. The effect of the land purchases by La Parada and the unrecorded purchases by Corte that probably occurred at the same time was to bring the entire valley of the Río de la Parada (once known as the Río de Mexquitic) almost entirely under hacienda control. It also meant that it was no longer possible to enter or leave Ahualulco without passing through hacienda lands, a graphic symbol to the people of that late-colonial pueblo of the extensive control of the new landlords. When one of the heirs of La Parada married the owner of Corte in 1869, they consolidated the local hacienda regime under a single family. To the east, the hacienda of Peñasco was also expanding into former Mexquitic land, and in the center of Mexquitic itself a local family began to consolidate its ownership of land in and around the small central valley, forming what became known as the rancho of Buenavista. Of the surrounding haciendas, only Cerro Prieto and Rancho de Bocas (later renamed Valleumbroso after a new owner's favorite summer resort in the Italian lake region) refrained from the expansion. The owners of the former were perhaps content with their mescal production, while the latter was occupied in ongoing conflicts with Ahualulco that paralleled the problems of Mexquitic half a century earlier (Sánchez Unzueta 1982).

For the people of Mexquitic, the nineteenth-century period of hacienda expansion meant a slow erosion of their economic and social prospects. The most fertile lands of the former pueblo were permanently removed from the circulation of fields among heirs and neighbors. Day labor on the haciendas became a necessity for many, perhaps most, families. Large numbers of families found it better to migrate, either temporarily or permanently, to the northern La Laguna region during the cotton boom of the 1870s and after than to scratch out a living from the meager hills of Mexquitic.[36] And perhaps many more harbored a smoldering anger against the haciendas that had forced them into these straits.

WALLS

By the end of the nineteenth century, the spatial division of the San Luis region into huge estates that engulfed the small fields of pueblos like Mexquitic, a division already long-complete at the close of the colonial era, had been given tangible representation on the ground in the form of huge enclosing walls. The walls encircled smaller estates, haciendas, and the ranches and *potreros* (grazing grounds) into which haciendas were subdivided. Called potreros after the fields they enclosed, the walls stood some two meters high and one meter wide, large enough to keep even untamed horses from jumping them. These imposing monuments still stand today, and their outlines can be clearly traced on aerial photographs and topographic maps.

The hacienda of La Parada was surrounded at its apogee by 150 kilometers of great stone walls, putting, it must have seemed, a definitive end to its long history of border disputes. In the colonial era the hacienda's borders had been maintained only by the equivocal evidence of boundary markers (*mojoneras* or *mohoneras*), piles of stone stuck together with lime and topped with a wooden cross, which inevitably crumbled into ruin within a few decades. Not only were the imaginary lines that connected the *mojoneras,* placed up to ten kilometers apart, unmarked and subject to dispute, but neighbors could claim that the *mojoneras* themselves were false, as the owner of a ranch bordering La Parada to the north did, though to no avail, during a boundary survey in 1778:

> They arrived at the plain of San Miguel de la Barranca, at the vestiges of a *mohonera,* where Martinez came out, raising objections, to state that he had enjoyed the use of that place for a dozen years, and that there was no *mohonera* there, that those were the ruins of an oven for extracting maguey juice.[37]

The walls literally fixed the hacienda boundaries in stone, ending such disputes through their unarguable presence. They gave both overwhelming physical evidence and a very fitting metonymical representation of the hegemonic power of the hacienda in this era. There is something uncanny in these immense monuments to ownership, in the way they follow their straight courses insistently, maniacally, across desert plains and fertile valleys, up steep mountain slopes and down barrancas, across creeks and roads. Don Rosendo told us of the construction of the twenty-five-kilometer-long wall that was built after 1893 to celebrate the division of La Parada between two heirs, adding a detail that does not figure in the hacienda records.

> One heir got the hacienda of La Parada, and the other got the hacienda of Santa Teresa over there. Up there in El Pelón, north of San Agustín, there is a stone wall from around San Martín all the

way to Ahualulco, straight as a wire. Yep, like a thread. Who knows how many engineers worked on it and they couldn't come up with a way to split the hacienda—the hacendado was offering who knows how much money for them to split it in half. Only one engineer could find a way to measure it, but he did it at night. Twelve o'clock midnight. That's what they say, who knows. The stone wall, I saw for myself—it's as straight as a string.[38]

The improbable detail of the midnight division of the hacienda provides an explanation and an interpretation of the improbable reality of the wall, straight as a string, that separates the estates of the two heirs. Midnight is, in Spanish as in English, the witching hour. In Mexquitic lore, midnight is one of the two times of day that the spirits in Purgatory are allowed to rest and wander a bit around the cemetery (the other, rather less ominous, time is twelve noon). It is the hour when children have seen *duendes,* the spirits of aborted fetuses and victims of infanticide, scurrying about the town bridge; it is the hour when *La Llorona,* wailing, once drove her black car through town. And, it goes without saying, midnight is the hour when witches summon the Devil to work for them. Rumoring that the dividing wall could only be built after a midnight consultation is a shorthand way of reinterpreting the wall, the physical symbol of the economic might of the haciendas, as an occult symbol of their diabolic power. Just as the stories that the people of Mexquitic tell about the founding of the town point to a tradition of interpreting their presence in that land as autochthonous and therefore legitimate, so this detail hints at an interpretive tradition that questions the sources of authority of the hacienda and denies the legitimacy of their power and of their presence.

Another story that directly confronts the question of the power of La Parada is that told about Patricio Jiménez.

PATRICIO JIMÉNEZ

Patricio Jiménez was born in Mexquitic in 1822, the fifth of the ten children of Urbano Jiménez and Eutimia Hernández. His family was well endowed with land by Mexquitic standards, as we know from the sales that they made to the hacienda of La Parada. Patricio's father was one of the very first to sell pueblo land to the hacienda in 1828, just a year after such sales were legalized. When La Parada began buying land on a large scale in 1837, Patricio's mother, by then widowed and remarried, was again among the first to sign a contract, selling a sizable field (about 64 hectares, by my estimate) for 250 pesos. Over the next thirty years she and two of her sons would sell another six plots, totaling about 15 hectares, for a total of 310 pesos.[39]

The sales to La Parada did not put an end to the family's landed holdings, it seems, for a granddaughter of Patricio Jiménez, Aurelia López, was the wealthiest landowner living in Mexquitic in the 1920s. The collection of fields that she and her husband Mauricio Dávalos (who was not originally from Mexquitic) owned in the heart of the municipality totaled about 1,000 hectares, most of it arid and hilly scrubland but including almost all of the small, irrigated central valley of the municipio. I do not know how much of this land, which came to be known in the Agrarian Reform records by the somewhat grandiose title of Hacienda de Buenavista, was part of the family patrimony and how much was purchased later. Don Raúl recalled, perhaps anachronistically, that Patricio Jiménez himself had lived in Las Trojas, "the granaries," as the ranch was known locally. The original partition of large estates in the agrarian reform of the 1920s passed this "hacienda" by—Mauricio Dávalos argued, with some exaggeration, that it measured only 24 hectares and was thus too small to be affected by the reform laws. It was only in 1940, after the son and heir of Dávalos had taken to threatening passersby with his pistols and after a political battle in Mexquitic, that two-thirds of the scrubland of the estate and all but a dozen hectares of its good farmland were expropriated and distributed in quarter-hectare plots to the ejidatarios of the town.

The family was not only landed, it was politically important in the municipality. Patricio himself was municipal president in 1869 and in 1871 was district representative in the state congress; the reports that he filed as president (now in the records of the Secretaría General de Gobierno of th̲   ̲how that he was not only literate but wrote
                              enth-century grace. Also in 1871, his
                              municipal president, followed the next
                              Flores. Over the next century, at least
                              clan, including don Raúl, would serve in

                              in Mexquitic today—including the de-
                              cling to their land, refusing to sell it even
                              pproaching miserliness. Patricio Jiménez
                              sition in local history as "the initiator of
                              c for defending his property against the in-
                              at most calls out for interpretation in the
                              is their sale of land to La Parada and its re-

lation with the family's political power. Two diametrically opposed interpretations suggest themselves. It could be that they sold their land in spite
of their political connections; in other words, that in the context of the
nineteenth-century political economy of Mexico the power of a local
elite was no match for that of an hacendado intent on territorial expansion, who forced them to sell. This would be in line with local interpretations of conflicts with the haciendas, as we will see. Or it could be that
the family used their political connections, especially the broad discretion
of the president in assigning title to community lands, to acquire fields
that they then sold to the hacienda for easy cash. This interpretation
would be more in line with a cynical analysis of the role of the local elite,
as well as with the future "hacienda"-owning role of the family.

Whatever the case, the crucial fact in the life history of Patricio Jiménez—what has made him the object of legend and official hagiography in
Mexquitic—is stated in his burial entry. "In San Miguel Mexquitic on
9 April 1872, I, Father Mariano Saldaña, interim priest of this parish, gave
church burial with high cross and processional candles to the body of don
Patricio Jiménez, adult Indian of 50 years of age, survived by widow Eleu-
teria Pérez, died of execution by gunfire." The events that led to his
death, and the identity of his murderers, will perhaps never be documented; my own efforts to discover clues in the unsorted avalanche of
nineteenth-century documents have so far been to no avail. But in Mexquitic the essential facts of the life and death of Patricio Jiménez are well
known.

Don Raúl told me the story of Patricio Jiménez in great detail, conscious of his dual role as descendent of the Jiménez family and as former
municipal president. In his telling, don Raúl linked the death of Patricio
Jiménez to two of the key motifs in the history of land tenure in Mexquitic—the land titles of the pueblo that granted the three-league boundary
and the walls of the haciendas.

"There existed until 1920 or 1925 a book called *Title of the Pueblo of
Mexquitic;* it was kept for some time in the presidential office," Raúl began in the characteristically formal speaking style he easily adopts on official occasions, to which my translation of his words cannot do justice.
"This title came into effect some fifty years after the foundation of Mexquitic. I suppose that this book was directly connected to the struggles
that the Spaniards had in these parts against the indigenous people—but
it was not easy to subdue them. It was to facilitate the submission of these
natives, because they, the Guachichiles, were tenacious, that they gave
them these titles. As a result the king of Spain endowed Mexquitic with a

territory of three leagues in radius from the church door. And in this expanse of land the Spaniards could own no property—it was exclusively for the natives.

"But the hacendados did not respect those boundaries; rather, they began to invade and despoil them." Raúl then gave a short explanation of the term *hacer el despojo,* "to despoil," frequently used in Mexican land tenure struggles to describe how the large estates swallowed up the small properties (*pequeñas propiedades,* a legal category) that surrounded them. "Within the small properties they would buy a bit here, a bit there, a bit over there, and so on, and when they had bought up several small properties they would draw an enclosing wall from one to another, and whatever properties remained inside the wall, those that belonged to people who did not want to sell, the hacendados would not allow them to enjoy the usufruct of them. Thus don Patricio Jiménez, having suffered the *despojo* of a small property of his by La Parada, undertook a petition to put into effect the conditions of the title. He formed a kind of committee of those who had been despoiled, and together with them initiated a judicial case before the judiciary of the state of San Luis. Naturally enough the authorities of San Luis were partial to the hacendados, they ruled in their favor. But Patricio Jiménez did not stop there; he solicited a revision before the national Supreme Court of Justice in Mexico. They ruled in favor of the petitions of Patricio Jiménez.

"When the hacendados realized this, they could find no other way of undoing the ruling than to disappear Patricio Jiménez. At that time there was still no strong government in Mexico. There was a Conservative Party that tried to continue giving the same privileges to those who had ruled during the colony, and against them there was a Liberal Party. In those times there were frequent outbreaks of violence; in that the hacendados took advantage of a military man who was here with the motive of a rebellion, or perhaps he was against the rebels—I am not exactly sure what he was up to; one of those officers.

"He left San Luis Potosí with a plan and with all the information he needed. When they got to Mexquitic, they summoned Patricio Jiménez. Patricio Jiménez responded to the summons. Patricio Jiménez was a politician, he had been municipal president, he had filled various positions in the municipality, and he had been a representative (I do not know whether federal or local); he was a respected man, and when that military officer summoned him he appeared.

"As soon as he appeared the military officer detained him. The next day they left, heading toward La Parada, taking Patricio Jiménez with them. When Patricio Jiménez saw they had arrived at a path that crossed La Parada, in the road from San Luis to Zacatecas, then Patricio Jiménez stopped and refused to continue walking, knowing what was going to happen to him: this has been passed down by tradition." On other occasions when telling the story, don Raúl adds at this point Patricio's reputed final words, "If you are going to kill me, may I die on my own land."

"And at that they murdered him, at the boundary between the hacienda and the small properties. There are still remains standing of the monument or memorial that they built on the spot to Patricio Jiménez. This is why Patricio Jiménez is considered one of the precursors of the agrarian cause in Mexquitic." [40]

In don Raúl's words, Patricio Jiménez becomes a personification of the titles of Mexquitic, doing battle against the evil forces of the hacienda, which becomes one with the surrounding walls that define and unjustly enlarge it. Through the retelling of his story Patricio Jiménez has entered a kind of second incarnation. His struggle, which was apparently to protect private property against the encroachments of large landed interests, has been transformed into an incipient struggle for agrarian reform. His death has been reinterpreted in the light of Revolutionary hagiography, and he himself has been transfigured into an early agrarian martyr. His status was given official recognition in 1988, when the memorial cross on the site of his death was rebuilt and rededicated by the ejidos of the municipality.

This mythification of Patricio Jiménez had already begun within a hundred years of his birth, as we can see from an early petition asking for land under the agrarian reform clause of the Constitution of 1917. This petition, which was presented by people from Corte Segundo in 1921, is interesting because it makes it quite clear that the act of interpreting and presenting history (especially in the case of land tenure history) is a specifically political act. Much as Raúl's related narrative of the life of Patricio Jiménez knit together the themes of the foundation of the pueblo and the walls of the hacienda, so this narrative weaves in yet a third theme, the struggle over water rights in Corte that was at the heart of the conflict with the priest Lozano:

A large part of the *despojos* of which we have been victims were registered posterior to the year 1872, in which by order of the regional latifundists the citizen Patricio Jiménez, former Municipal President of Mexquitic and energetic defender of the rights of same, was assassinated.

From that year on, the *despojos* came without interruption, at times with violence, menacing the people with imprisonment, or with conscription in the Army, if they did not sell their small properties, in which they had previously been corralled by putting up walls. . . .

The hacendados whom we have the misfortune to have as neighbors, not content with stripping us of our fields, have gone to the extreme of depriving us of the very water necessary to irrigate those properties that have escaped their greed.

In effect, the Hacienda of La Parada has appropriated the water proceeding from the spring called Carrizal, which is used by means of a canal that even today still conserves the significant name "Canal of the Común," in memory of its communal origin; for said canal was dug through personal service or *faena* imposed upon the citizenry of the Municipality of Mexquitic at the beginning of the last century.

Said canal, as such, was always used for the benefit of our community, until, with the assassination of our representative don Patricio Jiménez, the Hacienda dared to appropriate by force said spring, situated in land that legitimately belongs to the pueblo, as well as the canal built by our ancestors.[41]

The "Canal of the Común" the petitioners speak of is apparently the same one dug in 1797 and implicated in the Lozano dispute. The evidence in that case shows that the canal was appropriated by the precursors of the hacienda of Corte almost as soon as it was completed, and not after 1872. The later date was essential to the argument of the petitioners, for the land reform law applied only to land alienated after the passage of the national disentailment laws of 1856 (while much of the land alienated in Mexquitic was sold under the much earlier state law of 1827). Yet the conflation of these dates in the petition was not necessarily an act of deliberate dishonesty. Rather, I would contend, the memories of both Patricio Jiménez and of the struggle over the appropriation of the canal both derive from an oral tradition of recalling and reinterpreting acts of resistance to the power of the haciendas. The history presented in the petition may be chronologically inaccurate, even self-servingly so, but it faithfully depicts an enduring antagonism between the people of Corte and the large landowners.

A similar reinterpretation and conflation of history, less self-serving but equally political, came up in an interview with Tacho, a lifelong farmer from Corte. I was talking with Tacho and his friend Miguel, the school-teacher introduced in chapter 2, about the hacienda regime when the discussion turned to the great wall built in 1893 to divide La Parada between two heirs. The key image of the Patricio Jiménez story, his refusal to cross over into the hacienda, was strong enough to bind with the image of that dividing wall built twenty-one years after his death. "They say that later, when don Patricio Jiménez began the lawsuit, that was during the case when they were splitting La Parada in two parts," Tacho told us. Unlike don Raúl, Tacho has never been involved in municipal politics, and his phrases are correspondingly unpolished. "Then, over there belonged to don Pantaleón Ipiña. Then, that's why they put up a wall over there in that hill called El Pelón, half and half. And the house the same, half and half. And that was when don Patricio Jiménez, that was when the trouble started, and you see when they were going to do the doors of the house in La Parada, that was when the lawsuit started."

Miguel used his fluency in Revolutionary ideology to turn the conversation into an interview with his friend for my benefit. "Because don Patricio Jiménez must have been a peon, too, right?"

"Well, I think that is so, he must have been."

"And how did that lawsuit you speak of begin?"

"Well, that lawsuit began because of, well, since everyone went like to sell, like here for example, they might give permission for the peones to enter, for the people that lived there, to sell to them, to bring them, like onions, cabbages, since the haciendas didn't produce any of that. Back then they didn't produce that, they produced it here, the small proprietors." [42]

In this exchange Tacho gave a vision of how the haciendas depended on the productivity of the small proprietors, such as Patricio Jiménez, who survived in their midst. Leal and Huacujo have noted the "symbiosis," this "contradictory complementarity" of the hacendados with "the Indian pueblos, the renters, the sharecroppers and other minifundists" (1976 : 7 – 8), in terms of the hacendados' ability to regulate their control of the labor supply by letting the "minifundio sector" contract or expand. Here Tacho pointed out that the haciendas of La Parada and Corte also depended on the small proprietors for the very means of feeding their own workers. Tacho later pointed out that there were even years when the haciendas themselves would have disastrous harvests ("las haciendas también tenían sus quiebras") and were forced to borrow grain from the small proprietors. Within the context of their own rural communities, these "small" proprietors were the richest of the rich. Like the hacendados, they grew crops for a market, but their market was the hacienda. In Tacho's elliptical explanation, Patricio Jiménez did not rebel against hacienda land incursions, but against an apparent attempt of La Parada to cut the wealthy small proprietors off from their market. In his telling, the great dividing hacienda wall becomes a metaphor for this exclusion.

Later in the interview, Miguel (whose own mother was one of the largest "small" landowners in Carrizal and Corte) returned to the usual interpretation of Patricio Jiménez. "Say, so don Patricio Jiménez was one of the initiators [of the agrarian revolution], then?"

"The initiators. Yes, because my papa said that, I mean,—well, they were invading everything by then, lots of property, over in Carrizal. And that's when he said, 'Well, the thing is that here, this is my municipality and I'm in charge.' "

"The hacendados," Miguel tried to clarify, though Tacho had actually been reporting the speech of Patricio Jiménez. "And then don Patricio Jiménez came on the scene, he's the defender of private property, because I think they were invading even the small properties, weren't they?"

"Yes, invading, exactly."

"They no longer respected even the," Miguel began.

"No," Tacho agreed.

"No. Because they were the masters of lives and haciendas, weren't they."

"Right. As people say, they were the masters."

There were layers of irony in this exchange. Miguel introduced the image of Patricio Jiménez as he has been reshaped by contemporary political ideology and rhetoric, as the local "precursor of the Revolution." But in the same breath he presented him in a historically more accurate role, as "el defensor de la propiedad," fighting the haciendas to protect the property rights of the small proprietors. The double irony of this depiction is that it inverts the imagery of both supporters and detractors of the Revolution. In this 1988 reinterpretation of the agrarian struggles of the 1920s, it was the small proprietor, not the hacendado, who fought to protect private property; the enemy was not agrarian reform, but the omnivorous, monopolizing hacienda. The final irony, particularly considering the hostility of small-property partisans toward agrarian reform in the present (Frye 1994b), is how neatly this revisionist interpretation of Patricio Jiménez dovetails with standard revolutionary ideology. The key point of intersection is the assertion that the hacendados, those prodigious

builders of boundary walls, "no longer respected even the . . ." The unstated, understood end of the sentence: not even the boundaries of private
property.

AN AGRARIAN BRICOLAGE

It was only appropriate, then, when Prieto de la Maza's nightmare scenario of 1789 finally came to pass in 1924, when the haciendas were expropriated and the walls that had so long closed out the rabble suddenly
enclosed the fields of ejidatarios, that in this inverted world the first action
of the victorious *agraristas* of Mexquitic was to dismantle the heart of La
Parada—stealing cattle, tearing up the great house and the chapel, carting
off the private train track used to haul grain to the railroad line in Corte—
and to use the broken pieces to build up their own houses.

"When the agrarian movement began," Rosendo recalled, "they
grabbed the horses from the haciendas, eh. And over here, even people
from as far as Tapona, everyone brought back horses and cattle from the
hacienda, from La Parada, from Cerro Prieto. No, when the agrarian
movement broke out, over here in the hacienda La Parada they made *des-
garriates* (disorder, upheavals). These bricks are from there!"

"No, they aren't," Ofelia contradicted him.

"Aren't they? But the bricks in . . ."

"In the parlor."

"Yes, the bricks in the parlor. And in the house where Pedro lives, and
where Fulano lives, I know those bricks are from the hacienda La Parada,
because me and my papa went to get 'em ourselves. Not from the hacienda, we didn't take a single brick from the hacienda, rather the people
there sold it to us. These old bricks are still good!" he exclaimed, giving
one of them a hearty thump.

Ofelia took up the tale. "These people from Rincón del Porvenir are
the ones who tore up the hacienda. Even the chapel bells, they say, they
broke in half; the train tracks they carried off on burro back. . . . At three,
four in the morning, here they are on burro, Giddyap!, and there they go
with the sheaf of rails. To sell."

"Deformity of rails," Rosendo concluded.[43]

People in Mexquitic today explain that the great house of La Parada
was destroyed because everyone at the time assumed that a huge treasure
would be found there. The evidence of the desperate search is apparent in
the house and chapel—broken cabinets, lifted floorboards, great holes
gouged in walls where gold and silver might have been hidden in clay

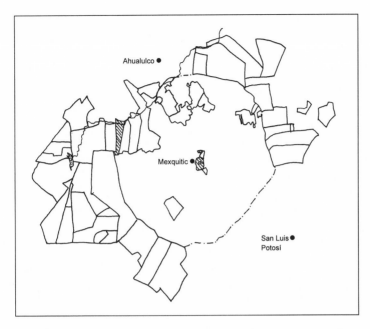

MAP 5.   The haciendas dismantled: ejidos granted to the communities of
Mexquitic, 1929–1980 (ejidos of the town of Mexquitic marked by
hatching)

pots. Rumors of treasures hidden and found are the stuff of everyday conversation in Mexquitic, and not without reason. There were no banks and
precious little for the rich to spend money on in Mexquitic until recently,
so that a well-hidden pot of gold coins spelled a certain security in uncertain times. The hacendados, for their part, put their wealth and power on
display. The walls, the great house, the ornate chapel, and the massive
granaries served to project a mystique of hacienda power that put all who
could see on notice of who was the "master of lives and haciendas." The
mystique carried over even after the Revolution. There were some who
refused to take part in forming the ejidos, certain that the days of the
haciendas would soon return. But in the inverted world of the 1920s, the
mystique of power the hacendados had cultivated was ultimately turned
against them and became the force behind their destruction. Where there
was power there had to be treasure. Even though the more systematic
destruction was undertaken by those satisfied with smaller treasures of
bricks, windows, and scrap metal, which they sold or used to build their
own homes, it is the lesser but somehow sacrilegious damage inflicted by
the treasure hunters that remains symbolic of the overthrow of La Parada.

Here is a description of the destruction of the hacienda penned by the Cabrera Ipiñas, two descendants of the hacendados:

> Of La Parada nothing was left, even the house was assaulted, robbed, and totally destroyed. Not even the handsome and well-appareled church was safe from the vandalic fury; from it they ripped the doors and windows, burned the paintings and images, violated the tombs, broke the altars, and carried off even the bells. It was not the people of the hacienda who did this, but the inhabitants of the neighboring ranchos and pueblos who, attracted still by the fabled wealth of the place, fell on it like the barbarians on Rome and did not leave one stone upon another in their search for treasure. They were the descendants of the ancient tribe of Maticoya, the bearers of the atavistic tendencies of those primitive Chichimecas who were coming to live again their ancestral customs of war and libertinage. . . . The proprietors begged for guarantees in every way and fashion but the authorities shrugged their shoulders.[44]

Quite aside from the images of atavistic Chichimecas and of barbarians falling on the Rome of hacienda civilization, it is only true from the hacendados' point of view that "it was not the people of the hacienda who did this." As noted in chapter 3, the hierarchical, multitiered labor system of La Parada acknowledged only the certain class of workers who were born and raised on the hacienda as being "of the hacienda." Most workers were classified as "sons of the pueblo" even if they spent most of their lives working on the hacienda, and even if, like Rosendo's father, they were born on land later taken over by hacienda expansion. The special treatment accorded to the first class of workers filled them with a lasting loyalty to the hacienda, but by the same token the injustices perceived by those of the lower tier filled them with the "fury" that turned their treasure search into a wave of destruction. This was not a blind but a focused fury, with a theme of redistributive justice. It was the hacienda workers who were called "of the pueblo" who destroyed La Parada.

When I asked Rosendo how the hacienda regime operated when he knew it in the early 1920s, he responded with stories about life in La Parada under the administrator Teófilo Torres that contrast with the portrait drawn by the Cabrera Ipiñas, who described Torres as a "man of great worth" who "helped put [La Parada] back on its feet" after the decline of the first years of Revolution.[45]

"In La Parada, that's what I was familiar with, all the fields irrigated with water from the dam were sown by the hacienda at their own expense, with peones. They'd bring in gangs of ox teams, as many as fifty teams. Eh? Fifty teams would work in one field and another fifty in another, and each gang came with its mayordomo. And the peones—not all of them, just the closest ones, the pampered ones, that is [*los más allegados, los consentidos*], like the mayordomos, the caporales, the granary guard; my maternal grandfather was a granary guard, he held the keys to the twelve granaries of La Parada—the most pampered people, let's say, the closest ones or to put it plainly, the brownnosers who spent all their time there gossiping with the boss, those were the ones who were given land to sharecrop."

"But not irrigated land," I guessed.

"No, not irrigated land, but sometimes they had better harvests without irrigation than on the irrigated land. My maternal grandfather sowed over there in El Arenal, and only on Sundays. They only gave them Sundays to go work, eh. It was a very delicate situation!" Rosendo laughed. "And who knows if there might still be one or two left in La Parada who didn't want to be agraristas, and hoped that the hacendado would come back instead. Because they were the pampered ones.

"My paternal grandfather was from a rancho over there called Rincón de Cabras. But the hacienda seized control of it and kicked the people out. They had fields there but the hacienda took all that over; and now the people sow it, all that. Over in Ojo Zarco, that was an enclosed pasture, eh. Nobody lived there, the hacienda of La Parada rented that pasture out to the poor people. The ones who had one or two little cows, and who worked there in the hacienda, that was their pasture, mm. And that was the reason why a renter there named Teófilo Torres ran off my papa. Because of the rent for some animals that he brought there."

"Why?" I wanted to know. "Did he claim that he hadn't paid?"

"Well, he was going to pay, only he didn't have the money!" Rosendo joked bitterly. "And after all, they only paid the peones 18 cents. A real and a half a day to work from five in the morning to sundown. Eh.

"So my papa didn't have the money, and he said he'd give Teófilo a calf instead, a nice little chile-red calf about so high." Rosendo marked the height of the calf with the palm of his hand as if he could still see it before him. "A calf in those days would have cost about 10 or 15 pesos. 'I'll give you this one.' 'That's fine.' 'Just do me the favor of loaning me a couple of cowboys to go catch it.' And he tells my papa, 'No, you go catch it by yourself.'

"So my papa went to see the Grimaldo brothers in Cenicera. They all had horses and knew how to handle a lasso; he went to see if they would help him catch the calf. But they were armed by the government, they were called *rurales*. They tell him, 'We just have to go to a review in Ahualulco this Saturday and then we'll come by.' Back then the hacienda charged the 'house' peones (*acasillados*) less to use the pasture. Since my papa was a son of the pueblo, he said, they charged him more. Even though he started working there in the hacienda as a youth, the man considered the 'house' people to be the ones who were born there. So the Grimaldos said, 'Wait for us there at the hacienda gate and we'll pass by around four on our way to Ahualulco, and we'll go see don Teófilo and see if he won't charge you like a house peón and not like a son of the pueblo.' And there was that Teófilo Torres in his office, and they went to see him. They discussed the point. 'Fine,' he says, 'in that case I won't charge him a thing. Nothing.' 'Fine. Don Teófilo, you have your friend in such-and-such a part,' and they shook hands.

"And he didn't charge him anything. But the next day, hurry it up and out with you! He ran him off. Eh. The Grimaldos had filled him with so much anger, he ran him off. He didn't charge him, but he didn't let him work there any more. My papa still went to sow for my grandfather, and that made Teófilo angry. 'Why do you bring that man here to me?' 'Well, who else? Otherwise, I won't work here. He's my son-in-law, who else is going to sow for me?'

"A few days later a horse killed that Teófilo. He was so bad. They were cutting down the corn stubble, and two boys—one of them told us himself: 'Hey, that old Teófilo, Fulano and me, we knocked him off.' He was riding around on his big horse and he came by to scold them while they were cutting cornstalks, and then one of them cut a piece of cornstalk and stuck the horse with it back here, and the horse reared up and knocked him off. The old man fell against a cornstalk back here, and he wasn't able to talk. If he could he would have sent them to prison." [46]

LAND AND IDENTITY: EL PUEBLO ESCOGIDO

Over the course of the eighteenth century, faced with constantly growing population and land pressure, the people of Mexquitic found themselves going to court more and more frequently both as individuals and as a pueblo. I have suggested that in the colonial courts they were forced to confront the most negative images of the Indian held by the colonial elite, respond to those images, and even adopt them, with whatever modifications they could make, in order for their voices to be heard.

An early lesson for the people of Mexquitic in the harshness of colonial images came in the disputes mentioned above with Tlaxcalilla over the overlapping three-league boundaries of the two pueblos. The suits began in 1721 with inconclusive results. When the problem arose again in 1744 it was settled by a voluntary compromise on the part of the officials of Mexquitic, once they became aware of how much land Tlaxcalilla was set to lose in the first legal measurement and demarcation of their common border. The Mexquitic contingent asked the San Luis officials in charge to suspend the demarcation at the time, "bearing in mind that they are all Indians descended from the Tlaxcalan conquerors and founders of the Evangelic Law among the Barbarians who inhabited these environs, and as such they have maintained a mutual fraternity." [47] As a result of the compromise, about a quarter of the overlapping land was retained by Tlaxcalilla, though three Tlaxcalan households—the objects of the original suit—were asked to move.

Twenty years later, the three households still remained on Mexquitic territory, and continued to be a thorn in the side of their neighbors from Mexquitic (they were accused of beating up the husband of Maria de Jesus in 1764 in the case discussed in chapter 4). Mexquitic officials again brought suit, and the households were again ordered to leave.

In a 1766 petition protesting this second ruling, the governor of Tlaxcala recalled the theme of fraternity that Mexquitic officials had raised in the earlier compromise. If the leaders of Mexquitic did not ask for the demolition of the houses back in 1744, he argued, it was "because they must have born in mind that brotherhood, union, and conformity with which these two Pueblos have lived since the time of their foundation, as sons of a single nature and a single Father, as witnessed by the act of possession made by Francisco Vásquez [the founding governor of both Mexquitic and Tlaxcalilla in 1591]." But his conclusion later in the same paragraph strikes a discordant note, evidence of the degree to which the urbanized Tlaxcalans of Tlaxcalilla considered themselves to have diverged from their country cousins in Mexquitic: "My parties are not the movers of this suit, but rather the natives of Mexquitic, stimulated by their lawyer, since he is the one who induces them, for they themselves are a bunch of impoverished country bumpkins and hillbillies." [48] These comments by the Tlaxcalan governor of the sister pueblo of Mexquitic point to the conflicted questions of the relations between Indian and *campesino* identity, and between racism and classism, in Mexico. These are questions the people of Mexquitic faced regularly in these colonial lawsuits and which their descendents continue to face in their daily lives and interactions.

In a late colonial case from 1810, the asesor in San Luis Potosí, presented with a petition over a land conflict between two people within Mexquitic, expressed his displeasure with what he saw as the readiness of Indians to go to court with such suits and his doubts that the plaintiff had a valid case. "Ordinarily the Indians, because of their natural imbecility, go ahead with lawsuits over the possession of land even after they have been completed and legal sentences passed on them," he reasoned.[49] In this case, the plaintiff did turn out to have a valid case, and he won back in the courts the bit of orchard that had been taken from him, but he won it at the price of official scorn, of being turned into an "Indian," and as such endowed with "natural imbecility."

There is no evidence that the people of Mexquitic ever considered themselves "Indians" in the first place. They were the Tlaxcalans of Mexquitic, with a specific local identity.[50] As cases such as this remind us, that identity no longer served them in late-colonial San Luis Potosí, where officials were not impressed by the record of their ancestors' service to the Crown three centuries before. Officially stripped of this identity, they were not about to take on another one, that of "natural imbecile," if they did not have to.

We had been talking for some time with our comadre Esperanza, who had come to visit us along with her youngest son, when she asked us how old we were. I told her that we were both born in 1956, the same year as her older son, Simeón. "Then how come Simeón looks older?" her fourteen-year-old son wanted to know.

"It depends on—," Esperanza searched for an explanation. "Simeón is short, dark. My compadre is a different person, not like someone from here, like—"

"Like the Mexicans," her son completed the thought.

"That's it. My compadres, on the other hand, they're big, fairskinned, and here one is dark and short. We are Indian-like (*indiados*). We here are the Indians, compadre and comadre. And besides, imagine, here we are in Mexquitic, where the Indians founded the church, right? We here are Indians."

"I'm Japanese!" her son exclaimed happily.

"We're Indians, the what? The Chichimecas? Or what? The Guachichiles? Don't you know, the Indians founded the church here. San Miguel appeared because the big wild Indian was here, the bad Indian. That's why, since they were all Indians, the Indians founded the church, then, because San Miguel appeared when he drove off that bad Indian who ate people. That is why we here are Indians. So then, who are you going to compare with us, son?" [51]

On another occasion we were sitting with doña Lala in the small, dark room where she sells Cokes, beers, and stale bread to the occasional customers, talking about the history of Mexquitic. She had just told us the story of the foundation of the pueblo and the apparition of San Miguel related in chapter 3. Then she began to tell us that the center of the town had once been down by the river, near her house, and that the present municipal office building, on higher land near the parish church, had only been built around 1910, the year of her birth. "Back then it rained a lot, more than it does now, and they say that once a lot of water ran down from the Sierra de San Miguelito, those hills [to the southwest of the town]. The water washed away the bridge and all these houses. That was when they must have cleared the monte up there and built streets and houses and moved the center of the pueblo.

"They say that around that time the *hacendado* of La Parada had a lot of cattle, and since it rained a lot back then, the land produced a lot. There were many plants and trees in the Sierra de San Miguelito—mesquites, yuccas, magueys, who knows what all, right?" Lala asked an old man from the community of Barbechos who had just come in.

"Yes," the old man agreed, "there were some flowers called *campanilla,* as big as this, very beautiful, that people would sell in San Luis."

"Well. With all that, the haciendero began to send his workers to take all his cattle to graze out there in the sierra. And when the cattle arrived and started to graze around the sierra, a señor on horseback appeared to the men who had brought the cattle, a señor on a white horse." Though Lala never mentioned this stranger's name, it is clear to everyone in her audience that he can only be a saint. We are tipped off by the fact that he is not described as just a man (*hombre*), but as a gentleman (*señor*), as well as by the use of the word "appeared," usually used only in referring to the apparition of a saint. His description seems to match that of Saint James or Saint Martin, but given his appearance in the Sierra de San Miguel, he must be no other than Saint Michael.

"And he asked them why they were grazing their cattle there, since that land was his. 'This land is mine,' he said. 'So you, remove your cattle from here.' So that night when they took the cattle back to the hacienda they all told the hacendado that this señor on horseback had appeared to them and had told them not to bring their cattle out there, because that land was his. But the hacendado said, 'Eh! And who was that?' And he

ordered them to bring the cattle back the next day. Then the next day
when they arrived with the cattle the señor appeared again and asked why
they had not done what he said. They said they had told the hacendado
but he had not paid attention, and that was when it began to rain."

The rain the señor San Miguel provoked in this story was the cause of
the flood that, according to Lala, swept away the old town center, and
presumably the cattle of the overweening hacendado as well. Though Lala
set the tale at the turn of the twentieth century, it is redolent of the conflicts between Mexquitic and La Parada in 1640, when the hacienda was
indeed sending its cattle to graze in the sierra. By declaring that "this land
is mine," San Miguel claimed his eponymous sierra as his own. "Was
that," I asked, "when this sierra got the name of San Miguelito?"

"No, no!" Lala explained, and she went on in a way that made clear
that from her point of view the parish and the pueblo of San Miguel Mexquitic were properly one and the same, as they had once been. "That was
from long, long before. All this territory belonged to the señor San Miguel, but now they're invading it. It used to reach right up to the door of
the church in Ahualulco, but now they've taken away land there, it just
goes up to the river, right?" she turned to the man from Barbechos for
support. "And El Saucito, Estanzuela, all that belonged to him, all those
lands used to recognize the señor San Miguel," though they had since
been separated from the parish to form separate vicariates. "Even the
name of the town," she continued. "Here it used to be called San Miguel
Mexquitic, you must know this; only when this law came, the agrarian
law, they said that now we don't use the names of saints any more, now it
has to be named after a valiant soldier who was from here, so now it's
Mexquitic de Carmona.[52] But my uncle refused to accept this change, and
he would always write San Miguel Mexquitic de Carmona. But it wasn't
the fault of this Damián Carmona, who was a valiant soldier in the Revolution; it was the people who came afterward who changed the town's
name. It wasn't his fault that they took away the name of San Miguel. In
any case," Lala concluded, with a nod of her head to the monumental
hilltop statue of Damián Carmona that had been damaged by lightning a
decade earlier, "he defended himself from the bomb but he couldn't defend himself from the lightning bolt, and he's still up there without a head,
which he could have used better than a rifle."

"And that happened because they changed the name of the town?"

"Many people think, many of us think, those of us who believe, that it
was because he offended the señor San Miguel," Lala answered. For, as

Lala and the man from Barbechos went on to tell us, "he defends his pueblo."

"When they were building the highway here around 1960," Lala said, "when they were cutting through the part that goes through the hill out here by La Campana, there used to be an image of San Miguel there, carved high in the rock. When you went to San Luis the old road went around like this to the left, and here in front was the hill, and here to the left of it, high up, was a mesquite. And around back—you could see it very clearly on the way back from San Luis—up high was the image of San Miguel in the rock, looking just like the painting in the church. Anyway, there was a man who worked on the highway who used to come here for dinner, but one day he said that he wasn't going to be working any more, and I asked him why not, what had happened, and he said that they had gotten to this hill but they couldn't go on, their dynamite charges wouldn't work, and finally the engineers had told everyone to go home, that they couldn't go on. And they also said that a señor on horseback had appeared to the people who were working on the highway when they got to this hill and had told them not to go on. So they stopped for a few days, but then they went ahead anyway, and they didn't have any more problems.

"And once they were digging a mine in Picacho—aren't you from there, from Picacho? You should know about this."

"Yes, it's true," said the old man, "some engineers were there in Picacho digging a mine, exploring for metal. I don't know how far in they had gotten when a señor on horseback appeared to the workers and told them to stop. And even though they tried to go on, they found the rock was too hard and the engineers finally gave up. It was San Miguelito, of course."

"Yes," Lala concluded, "he defends his pueblo. *Este pueblo es escogido por Dios.*" [53]

No one from Mexquitic appears in these stories. Instead, the tales portray San Miguel himself, alone, "defending his pueblo" against outsiders who have come to exploit it. The tales are well contextualized and told as contemporary history ("when they were building the highway"), yet their lack of individual actors from Mexquitic seems to situate them in the mythical time of the foundation stories. It is obvious that individual actors are unnecessary because, as in a textbook charter myth, the patron San Miguel is the embodiment of the community as a whole. The view that they present of "defending his pueblo" is not, as one might have expected, a political vision of the saint defending the people of the town, or the fields that they sow, from outside encroachment. What they all have in common is a defense of the physical integrity of the land. "This land is mine" is the key message: the land itself is sacralized by its dedication to San Miguel.

This comes through most forcefully in Lala's final sentence, which I have left untranslated, with its two interlacing meanings. *Este pueblo es escogido por Dios*. Given the context the phrase means, "This town-site was picked out by God." Such is the ultimate meaning of the story told in Mexquitic of the pueblo's foundation: San Miguel refused to leave the mesquite in which he appeared because that was the place where God had ordained that a pueblo should be built. At the same time it is a sterling example of the local pride inherent in the townspeoples' sense of self, and is thoroughly suffused with its original Biblical meaning: "This is God's chosen people."

The emphasis on maintaining the wholeness of sites dedicated to the saint relays a final message. While the land belongs to San Miguel, as the embodiment of the pueblo, in a deeper sense he is also one with the land. Land and community mutually define one another. An identification with the land is the central theme that runs throughout the history of identity in Mexquitic, sweeping away notions of "Tlaxcalan," "Indian," or "ethnic" identity.

Abbreviations

For a full explanation of these abbreviations see the section entitled "Primary Sources" in the Bibliography.

AGI　　　Archivo General de Indias, in Seville
AGN　　　Archivo General de la Nación, in Mexico City
AHESLP　Archivo Histórico del Estado de San Luis Potosí
AM　　　 Fondo Alcaldía Mayor
AOCI　　 Private archive of don Octaviano Cabrera Ipiña,
　　　　　　in San Luis Potosí
INAH　　 Instituto Nacional de Antropología e Historia
GSU　　　Genealogical Society of Utah
SGG　　　Secretaría General de Gobierno
SLP　　　San Luis Potosí

Appendix A

Population of Mexquitic

1. POPULATION ESTIMATES AND COUNTS

Year	Guachi-chiles	Pueblo	Juris-diction	Parish Total
1592	200	100	0	300
1622	121	384	269	774
1636	50	358	—	—
1674	2	457	—	—
1711		1,511	391	1,896
1727		1,624	—	—
1793		8,393	—	—
1800		9,814	3,014	12,828
1813		10,299	3,940	14,239
1819		—	—	9,947
1822		8,190	3,061	11,251

Year	Municipio Total
1832	13,900
1841	15,357
1869	16,598
1878	20,640
1900	16,565
1920	14,435

Year	Municipio Total
1940	18,924
1960	25,496
1980	36,587
1990	43,053

Early figures distinguish between the *pueblo* (the Tlaxcalans living within three leagues of the church) and the *jurisdiction* (the surrounding haciendas and ranches within the parish). The last Guachichiles recorded were "two old Guachichil women" in 1674.

Figures before 1792 are population estimates, from household or tributary counts culled from a variety of documents, and should be regarded as *extremely inaccurate.* A closer approximation to actual population can be derived from baptism records, below. The somewhat more reliable figures for 1792–1878 are from colonial and state "censuses," compiled by priests or local officials without undertaking any actual count, with the exception of the 1800 and 1813 figures from tributary lists. The drop in population between 1813 and 1819 reflects the high death toll in the 1814–1815 yellow fever epidemic, the last major mortality crisis of the colonial era. Figures for 1900–1990 are from official Mexican censuses.

A dash (—) indicates no data available. For sources, see Frye 1986 and 1989:79.

2. BAPTISMS AND CIVIL BIRTH RECORDS (TWENTY-YEAR TOTALS)

Years	Pueblo Indios	Juris-diction Indios	Esp	Mest	Cast	Parish Total
1644–1650	410	410	3	10	30	870
1661–1667	620	540	10	20	40	1,230
1676–1684	920	550	40	160	220	1,890
1695–1702	1,250	680	40	180	360	2,510
1708–1727	2,020	640	130	300	480	3,560
1728–1747	2,580	940	290	310	640	3,770

Years	Pueblo Indios	Juris- diction Indios	Esp	Mest	Cast	Parish Total
1748–1767	3,220	1,230	430	370	930	6,180
1768–1787	6,240	2,480	580	970	1,720	8,980
1788–1807	10,300	2,950	640	1,060	610	15,560
1808–1827	10,175	2,430	470	840	200	14,350
1828–1847						19,920
1848–1867						24,350
1868–1882						22,780
1883–1897						17,300
1898–1917						17,100
1918–1937						14,730
1938–1957						22,650
1958–1977						24,320

Figures for 1644–1897 are the total number of baptisms recorded in the Mexquitic parish archive, by category, for twenty-year periods (or for shorter periods, annual averages multiplied by twenty). I have rounded off the figures, including totals, to discourage a false sense of accuracy. Note that the parish may at times have covered a larger territory than the civil jurisdiction and the present municipality. After 1827 priests did not record the racial status of baptized children. Figures for 1898–1977 are from Mexquitic civil records and are included for comparative purposes.

These figures can serve as rough conservative estimates of total population. They reflect the average populations for the given periods, assuming that every child born was baptized *and* recorded (they were not), and assuming a crude birth rate of 50 (it is more likely to have been lower than higher, meaning actual population was somewhat higher than these figures, and in any case the rate would have fluctuated). Still, in my opinion these data are more trustworthy than the population estimates shown above, which were not based on actual counts, and they have the advantage of roughly indicating the distribution of the hacienda population by colonial racial categories. Especially interesting are the sustained growth of the pueblo and the rapid growth, then leveling off or decline, of the non-Indian categories in the jurisdiction.

The categories used here are:

Pueblo Indios: Tlaxcalans living within three leagues of the
church.

Jurisdiction Indios: people living on surrounding haciendas and
ranches, identified as Indians.

Esp: identified as *españoles* (Spanish or "creole").

Mest: mestizos and a small number of *castizos*.

Cast: *castas*, a category in which I include those identified in the
records as *mulatos* (the great majority) and *negros*, both free and
enslaved (the last baptism of a black is recorded in 1736; of an
enslaved mulatto, in 1787), as well as the minor categories of
lobos, *coyotes*, and *moriscos*.

Appendix B

Will of Sebastian Martin, 1714[1]

In the Name of the Father Almighty and of the ever virgin Mary our Mother and Lady with her life without original sin and of the blessed Saint Peter and Saint Paul, my Guardian Saint and that of the Heavenly Court.

I, Sebastian Martin, parishioner of the Pueblo of San Miguel Mexquitic, Jurisdiction of the city of San Luis Potosi: currently in the site of Salitrillo[2] in the territory of said Pueblo: legitimate son of Josephe Martin and of Juana de Jesus: being ill in bed from the illness which God Our Lord has seen fit to give me: And fully in my right mind, memory, and understanding, and free will, fearing death for it is a natural thing for all creatures, believing as I firmly and truly do in the ineffable mystery of the holy Trinity, God the Father, God the Son, and God the Holy Spirit, three distinct persons and one true God, and all the rest that our Holy Mother Roman Catholic Church holds, believes and confesses, in whose faith I have lived and profess to live and die as a Catholic and faithful Christian, I order this memorandum before the Governor Don Antonio Hernandez and witnesses, as there is no notary in this said Site and it is [several] leagues distance to the city of San Luis Potosi and fearing the gravity of the shock from which I suffer:

First I order that whensoever God sees fit to take me from this present life, my body should be buried in the Parish Church of this Pueblo shrouded with coarse woolen cloth without they should put more than that of a poor wretch made of earth, and buried in the humblest part of it, so is my will.

Item, I declare that I am married according to the rules of Our Holy

Mother Church to Maria Francisca, and when and at the time that we contracted said marriage she brought nothing.

Item, I leave, First, for my burial—27 pesos and 4 reales.

Item, I declare that I owe Captain Antonio Martin 12 pesos.

And I entrust my children to have two masses said for Our Lady of Charcas.

Item, another for Saint Sanicolas.

Item, my executors should be paid, I declare so that it shall be noted.

Item, I declare that Juan Angel, citizen of the pueblo of San Miguel, owes me six pesos four reales of gold, and I order this should be collected for my estate.

Item, I declare and name as my executors and holders of my estate, Maria Francisca my wife, and Miguel Sanchis, my legitimate son: may they enjoy it and have it in equal parts, with the blessing of God as well as mine.

Item, I declare and it is my will that my wife Maria Francisca, as mother of my children, be their legal guardian and representative because of the great faith that I have in her good works, and I ask and beg that the royal justice relieve her of deposits and bonds [. . .], this is my will.

First, I leave to Maria Francisca my wife, one small Holy Christ.

Item, and two canvases of Our Lady of Guadalupe.

Item, and a Cattle brand, with its registered mark.

Item, and sixteen cows.[3]

Item, and ten yearling calves.

Item, and four bulls.

Item, and six yearlings.

Item, and twelve oxen.

Item, and an oxcart; and five whips; and nine pairs of yoke straps; and four covers; and five buttons.

Item, and seven *ygus* [?].

Item, and two chisels; and one adze; and two fruit hooks.

Item, and four hoes, two large and two small.

Item, and a small chest; and a *gosa;* and a *rozadera.*

Item, and a plowshare; a silver spoon.

Item, and a rug with red and yellow fringes.

Item, and thirteen goats; and five sheep.

Item, and five he-goats; and six rams.

Item, and one dark burro, one year old.

Item, and a mare.

To my son, the oldest, married to Leonor de San Pedro, Miguel Sanchis I leave five cows with their calves.

Item, and two goats and a sheep.

Item, and a carbine and a dark burro.

Item, and a mare; and a whole saddle.

To my son, the bachelor, Domingo Martin, I leave five cows with their calves.

Item, and two goats and a sheep.

Item, and a dark burro with its harness.

Item, and two horses and a mare.

Item, and a saddle with its large stirrups.

To my son, the *jocoyote* [youngest], bachelor, Casimiro de Santiago, I leave five cows with their calves.

Item, and two goats; and a sheep.

Item, and a dark burro with its harness.

Item, and a bridle; and a piece of tanned leather.

To my daughter Raphaela, married to Antonio Rodriguez, I leave five cows with their calves.

To my daughter Dominga de la Cruz, married to Nicolas Barbosa, I gave her her part in life, for now I leave her a yearling one year old.

To my daughter Phelipa de Jesus +, married to Baltasar de los Reyes, I gave her her part in life, for now I leave her a yearling one year old.

I revoke, annul, and declare null and void any and every testament, codicil, power of testation, or any other final disposition I might have made or given in writing or word, in my right mind or not, I do not want any to be valid but this my memorandum which I now give before witness in this Place of Salitrillo in the parish of the Pueblo of San Miguel Mexquitic, jurisdiction of the city of San Luis Potosi. On 19 December 1714. Being witnesses, called here, Don Thoribio Diego, lieutenant Governor; Agustin Carmona, alcalde ordinario; Ignacio Lauriano, alguacil mayor; Diego Hernandez; Marcos Martin; Andres de Ordas; Domingo Hernandez; and since I do not know how to sign I asked one of the witnesses to sign for me, and he signed for all:

Don Antonio Hernandez Governor
Don Thoribio Diego lieutenant

For Agustin Carmona,
Gaspar Diego

For Ignacio Lauriano,
Thomas de Santiago

For Diego Hernandes,
Francisco Xavier

For Andres de Ordas,
Antoño Sevastian

For Marcos Martin,
Gaspar Diego

For Domingo Hernandez,
Thomas de Santiago

Appendix C

Summary of the Account Which
Merchant Don Augustin Navedo
Kept with Santiago Ortiz, Master
Shoemaker, Indio of Mexquitic,
from July 27 to December 23, 1798

Quantity	Object	Pesos	Reales
5 oz.	indigo dye, with son Esiderio	1	2
4 cups	*bria* (?), with son Esiderio		4
2 cups(?)	loose maguey fiber (*pita floxa*)	1	2
16 varas	coarse cloth (*manta*)	4	
—	ribbon		2
1 ounce	silk, for son Juan Jose	1	4
1	tribute cloths for (son?) Pascual Antonio	2	2
1	" for Maria Encarnacion,		
	less 2 reales	2	
1	blanket (*fresada*)	1	4
1	hat, for son Jose Trinidad	1	
2	strings of pearls, for daughter-in-law,		
	wife of Francisco de Sales	1	
1 ounce	coral, for Maria Encarnacion	2	
—	raw sugar, salt, mixed foods (*comistraxo*)	3	6.5
—	candles		1.5
2 cups	chocolate		4
3¼ fanegas	(8⅛ bushels, about 465 lbs.) corn	6	4
58	reales (cash advances)	7	2
	Total	36	6

The account reveals a fairly Hispanicized market operating in the middle of Mexquitic. At least half the goods listed were European or Asian in origin, though they were probably produced in Mexico. Several luxury goods are on the list, and if some (the indigo and perhaps the ribbon and silk) were used as raw materials for the Ortiz family business, others (the pearls and coral) were apparently for the personal use of family members.

The account was preserved in a civil suit (AHESLP, AM 1799 [25 junio]) in which Ortiz complained that Navedo forced his debtors to pay him in goats and sheep—also of Spanish origin—rather than cash. Navedo argued that payment in animals was customary from San Luis Potosí to Dolores and the Huasteca, but he finally agreed to accept a cash payment. Ortiz's debt added to 22 she-goats, 15 sheep, 10 he-goats, 8 year-old rams, and 2 reales cash. Subtracting 2 he-goats, 4 she-goats, and 5 sheep paid by son Esiderio and (son?) Ignacio Nieves, 32 pesos and 2 reales were left to pay (8 reales = 1 peso).

Navedo was not the only storekeeper in Mexquitic in the 1790s. Francisca de Sala, who described herself as an Indian born and living in the pueblo, had a food store (*tienda de comistrajo*) with 300 pesos worth of goods (AHESLP, AM 1793). We only know of her because of a challenged inheritance; there may have been others, and the presence of the shoemaker Ortiz also points to Indian commercial activity. But by 1819, eight years after Mexquitic was rocked by the Hidalgo movement, it had only one store (Navedo's?) with an inventory worth "at the most 200 or 300 pesos, since it contains nothing more than candles, soap, salt, and other small goods brought from the markets in San Luis" (Frye 1986:29).

Appendix D

Petition by Three Widows of
Mexquitic before the Alcalde Mayor
of San Luis Potosí, August 29, 1764

In the City of San Luis Potosi on the 29th day of the month of August of 1764.[1] Before Gen. Don Thomas Costa y Uribe, Alcalde Mayor [etc.] was presented the following————

Monica de la Cruz, Indian of the Pueblo of San Miguel Mexquitique, Widow of Phelipe de Santiago, in association with Doña Dominga de la Cruz, Widow, and with Catharina Lucia, also widow. We appear before you in the best and amplest form which accords with our right:

And we say that our governor, don Nicolas Lopez de la Puerta, without any cause wishes to take away the [house] sites that we have always occupied. In which we live as daughters of said pueblo, occupying ourselves in every office, as *tenanches* of the Church, our Sons as *fiscales*, as *ministros*, as *pastores*, which we have all done without anybody objecting. And on the present occasion, Antonia Juana as *tenanche*, with Maria Eufracia, *tenanche* as well. Juan Santos, former *Pastor*, and later *Fiscal topile*. In this present year [he was] again elected Pastor in his absence, which he was not able to fulfill because he arrived out of season, and they substituted another.

He is a son of the said Monica, who has been warned by the mayordomo of the hacienda of La Parada to vacate the site of Las Cabras,[2] together with said Doña Dominga and Cathalina. The mayordomo ordering me to see the governor, who is the one that sent him, I did so, I put myself in his presence to seek consolation, which I did not find. I did [find] mistreating me with insulting and indecent words, opening his hands to me, telling me "What do you want? What are you bringing before me? That son of yours, Juan Santos, I'm going to throw him out of the pueblo, he's turned out badly [here] and in the hacienda of La Parada too, and maybe I'll do the same with the rest of your sons." He didn't wish to give me his ear: I left, and my son Juan Santos, since he found out what had happened to me, out of fear has not wanted to go down to the pueblo, not even to hear Mass, dreading the whippings he gives or that he might shear him as he is used to doing and has done with others, no matter who they are, as is well known by everyone in this pueblo. Although he does it in [. . .][3] to hide his great cruelty from being known, since because he is intoxicated at all hours he has no charity. Unmarried women he whips, the married women he mistreats with improper words.

On this occasion, when my son Phelipe was taking part in the sheep-shearing,[4] the governor called him and told him, "Have you moved yet?" He responded, no; and once more he told him, "So as soon as you finish with your obligations here, go and move your mother nine *cordeles*[5] inside the Cañada, because there's no money for lawsuits," which I do not know which lawsuits they could be. The site that he is giving me produces nothing that I could support myself on, to the other widows he is giving another site named San Juanico that produces nothing with which they could bear the toils they are employed in, in which they have some expenses, and their children [could not pay] the tribute, just like mine.

We have been advised by Don Juan de los Santos, an old governor, that the territory of the pueblo has been harmed by the surveys which this past January the governor allowed, in which our [old] boundary markers remained behind [the newly drawn border] and the new markers robbed us of a great piece of land. And the said Don Juan de los Santos swears about these surveys, may he be called and he will tell the truth. We humbly beg your honor that said Don Juan de los Santos be called first, [and] that the said Governor have his declaration taken and that he tell what he knows about this point, with a proper swearing-in. Because for these surveys he did not summon anyone from the pueblo, he himself did what he felt like. Although some Sons [of the pueblo] were there, they had not been summoned, they came out of curiosity to see how one did a survey.

Your honor's true sense of justice must deign to order that the governor not sell nor rent out this land without the consent of everyone in the pueblo. For he is not an arbiter that he can dissipate or dismember our real estate, as presently there are rumors that he has sold several sites, since because he attends to the renters[6] the Sons of the Pueblo are harmed. Rather, he should guard over this property, so that it grows, without any harm at all, just as he should leave us in our house which we have always occupied, he should restrain himself, and should not mistreat us nor throw us out of this site, for it is not best for us to move because of the unfitness of the sites which he is giving us.

We file a criminal complaint against the governor for his bad conduct, for his bad governance, for the little respect he has for the elders, since even though he has them meet he does whatever his whims dictate, for even though someone else wishes to speak he pays no attention. Likewise we ask and beg that the governor appear before your honor and that this our [peti]tion be made known to him, that he not mistreat us, and that he look on us as a Father.[7]

Appendix E

Petition by a Friar to the Viceroy of
New Spain [1]

Excellent Sir:

Humanity trembles to see the sufferings of innocence, and the blood
freezes in one's veins when one notes with horror that the right [*razón*]
and the justice of the poor is almost always disregarded. The Indians of
the Pueblo of Mexquitic complained to this Intendant that, among other
things, there were twenty or more cofradías there (all condemned by
Law 15, Title 4, Book 1 of [the *Recopilación de*] *Indias*); that they work in
them all year without being given a single tortilla; that their priest assessed
contributions on them all with the pretext of the spiritual Funds of the
Church. These were the cardinal points, to which others were added.
Hearing this, the priest appeared in court, was offended by the charges,
declared that the cofradías were founded in the time of his predecessors
and that they had assessed the same contributions for the Church Funds.
He created a party of other Indians in his favor, and—these having accused the former of being seditious, rebellious, and disorderly, with no
more proof than their own declarations and sayings—Your Excellency
can see, imprisoned in these horrible jails, those who complained with
right and justice. They have also jailed the hapless Scribe [*Amanuense*]
who drew up the document of their first complaints, treating him most
cruelly as the inspirer and seducer; and the opposing party, the followers
of the Priest, prove whatever they want, because they are the illuminated
witnesses. The cofradías are allowed to keep running, twenty and more of
them—even if there were twenty thousand—and no one goes into the
fact that they are condemned by the Laws, with the most holy end that

the Indians should not suffer the tyranny and slavery that those of Mexquitic complain of. The exactions for the Church Fund continue, as if they were not also prohibited and the Indians freed of that obligation. The idea is that the just and the miserable should perish, and that those who have more power should triumph.

I am a poor Religious who loves truth, right, and justice, who sees that there is an endless number of these things to fix in this Kingdom, that many of these such cofradías are nothing but arbitrary inventions to benefit the pockets of the priests: and finally, I am a good Friend of my fellow men. If Your Excellency wishes to assure himself of the truth of what has happened in Mexquitic, he may ask for all the original documents in the state they are in, and that they be remitted by post without delay, or that the Royal Audiencia ask for them, because in truth they are innocent. God keep Your Excellency many years in his holy grace.

San Luis Potosi, 18 July 1798.

Alegria.

Notes

1. INTRODUCTION

1. Thus the description of the coast of Guerrero in the much recommended *Blue Guide,* the brevity of which indicates the peripheral nature of the region in the tourist map of Mexico: "For nearly three hours you will travel through charming scenery composed of *coconut groves* . . . ; you will go through *villages of straw huts* reminiscent of Africa and cross rivers busy with village women washing" (Boulanger 1979: 397; emphases in original). The only ethnography of Afro-Mexicans remains Aguirre Beltrán's remarkable *Cuijla* (1958), focusing on a village on the same Pacific coast.

2. Certainly not of Indians! An editor of the *Handbook of Middle American Indians* succinctly notes that "a great portion of this vast semi-arid and arid region bordering the United States is peripheral to our main concerns" (Cline 1972: 166).

3. See, for example, the emerging historical ethnographies of the far North by Alonso (1988, 1992), Koreck (1988), and Nugent (1993).

4. The phrase "moral dialogue" is from Burkhart's excellent history of the dialogic origins of Mexican Catholicism (1989).

5. The problem of unequal power relations between ethnographer (as field-worker and as writer) and "informant" (as friend and as source) has been much explored; see di Leonardo 1991: 31 – 32. For a deep consideration of this problem in the context of a project intertwined with the present one, see Behar 1993.

6. See Joanne Rappaport's comments on her efforts to share the results of her research with the people of Cumbal, Colombia (1994: 21 – 23); see also Rappaport 1990. On the uses of the past by the people of Mexquitic see chapter 3 of this book.

7. Here I am thinking of in-depth social histories of Mexican regions such as Taylor 1972; Altman and Lockhart 1976; Brading 1978; Morin 1979; Van

Young 1981; and Farriss 1984; and historical ethnographies such as Friedrich 1970, 1986; Warman 1976; and de la Peña 1980. Each of these works insists on the interconnectedness of the regions under study with the wider Mexican and world societies, without losing sight of their distinctiveness. Taylor, for instance, took up the problem of land tenure under the colonial regime addressed earlier by Chevalier (1966) in a national history and, by focusing on a particular region, was able both to show the variety of land tenure practices and to give a clearer picture of how that diversity worked on the ground, as it were.

In this attention to both connections and diversity these histories stand somewhat apart from their precursors, such as Gibson's monumental study of *Aztecs under Spanish Rule* (1964), a regional history of central Mexico which, in the absence of comparable accounts from other regions, came to stand as a definitive account of Mexican (i.e., national) history; Luis González's (1968) transformation of the local history, a long-standing Mexican genre, from a eulogy of local heroes (with scant attention to national connections) into a literary work in which one town stands, in its particularity, for the nation; and the ethnographic community study, criticized by Nugent (1988:15), among others, for reveling in the details of local difference without dealing with the fact that the communities they study are "situated within an embracing and very often brutal structure of power."

Since the early 1980s there has been an explosion of regional social histories; see the review articles by Super (1984), Gilderhus (1987), García (1987), Tutino (1987), and Chance (1988), and the collection of essays theorizing regional history in Pérez Herrero 1991. See also Lomnitz-Adler's innovative examination of the relations between regional and national cultures, which encompasses comparative ethnographies of Morelos and the Huasteca Potosina (1992).

8. See the critical studies in Clifford and Marcus 1986, Behar 1993b, Behar and Gordon (1995), and Fox 1991. Abu-Lughod has followed her article in the latter (1991) with an anti-ethnography that puts her critique into practice (1993).

9. This is essentially the position outlined and advocated by di Leonardo, which she calls "feminist culture and political economy" (1991:27–32).

10. Abu-Lughod (1991). These critiques have also been written within the emerging context of feminist anthropology. See Gordon 1988 and di Leonardo 1991 for two important collections of feminist anthropological theory. I thank Ruth Behar for bringing these works, which she has written about insightfully (1993a), to my attention.

11. Mora 1993. For an anthology of recent Chicana/Chicano criticism, see Calderón and Saldívar 1991.

12. Anzaldúa 1987:63.

13. For one cogent critique, in the context of a general examination of the "uses of time" in anthropological writing, see Fabian 1983:80–96.

14. I have pulled this brief description from a key phrase in E. Valentine Daniel's more extensive definition of "culture": "webs of relatively regnant and generative signs of habit, spun in the communicative act engaged in by the anthropologist and his or her informants" (1984:13). To this I would add that, just as history is not the private province of the historian, neither are anthropologists the only ones who reflect on and conceptualize cultures. This is perhaps particularly

the case in places such as Mexico, where rival "webs of signs of habit" publicly vie for primacy; compare Turner (1991) on the development of a Kayapo notion of "culture" in reaction to increased contact with Brazilians.

15. Bonfil Batalla 1987. Lomnitz-Adler (1992) cogently criticizes Bonfil Batalla's book as "more a symptom of a perceived political alternative than an analysis of national culture or of its true import" (252) and derides its "conservative" political implications. I agree that *México profundo* is more program than analysis, but I see the recent work of Lockhart and others as providing the historical basis for such an analysis.

16. *World Book Encyclopedia*, 1965: v. 19, p. 43.

17. Weisman 1990:32.

18. Herskovitz 1990[1941]:1–2, 298.

19. Though by no means the first step. For only a small handful of the many recent works that challenge old assumptions, especially as they have taken shape concerning the border between Mexico and the United States, see the essays in Romo and Paredes 1979; Cuello 1982; Limerick 1987; Montejano 1987; and the collection edited by Simonson and Walker (1988).

20. All Mexquitic comprised a single parish from 1591 to about 1975, when it was divided into three parts, and the main central church was the only house of worship apart from hacienda chapels. There are now auxiliary chapels in a dozen ranchos; in addition, about 5 percent of the municipality, mainly in the ranchos of Rancheria, Corte, and Jaral, are Evangelicals or Baptists and have their own chapels and prayer-houses.

21. Weber 1976. It is ironic that, as intellectuals and politicians in Mexico and other Latin American countries have tried to respond to their colonial legacy by removing the word "indio," which is now generally regarded as an ethnic slur, one of the euphemistic replacements they have offered is *campesino*, "peasant." (Compare Karen Spalding's *De indio a campesino* [1974] on Peru, another parallel title, and Friedlander [1975].) In so doing they have tried to shift the domain of discourse from race to class, but they have not succeeded in removing the pejorative connotations that surround rural life in urban thought. Bonfil Batalla, almost alone among Mexican intellectuals, has tried to confront this problem directly by emphatically using the word "indio" as a term of pride.

2. A WORLD IN CONSTRUCTION

1. Low-interest home improvement loans are generally available only to federal government employees, including the dozen or more schoolteachers from Mexquitic, who have used these loans to finance expansions of their homes.

2. This arrangement is strikingly similar to that of the Nahua "household compound" as described by Lockhart (1992:59–72). Since only the poorest of families now live in jacales in Mexquitic it is difficult to say how the richer families of the past might have lived. The oldest houses (as opposed to jacales) now standing in town date to the end of the nineteenth century, and it is possible that there have long been at least a handful of such houses in the town's center.

3. I asked Ramón if it would not be better to raise the pigs himself, but he quickly countered with calculations proving that his method was more profitable.

He bought pigs for 60 pesos a kilo (1983 prices), and sold the meat from them to the restaurant for 130 pesos a kilo, keeping the fat, organs, head, and skin to boil and sell as chicharrones in Mexquitic on the market days, Thursday and Sunday. On an investment of 6,000 pesos in a large pig he made a quick profit of 2,000 to 3,000 pesos, which he immediately reinvested. His profit doubled if he found a ranchero unaware of the pace of inflation, who would sell a grown pig for 3,000 pesos. If he instead bought six young pigs at 1,000 pesos each and raised them himself, he would not be able to touch that money for another six months, would have to put in constant care, feeding, and vaccinations, and in spite of all that one of them might die, wiping out the profit.

4. Thus Tim Golden (1991): "The ejidos, as both the communities and their lands are called, hark back to the land tenure of the Maya." To his credit, Golden observes that ejidos are "far more often [worked] as individual parcels" than communally. See Frye 1994b, which also analyzes some of the material in this chapter.

5. Santos supplied the seed, the fertilizer, the machinery, and the work, while Ramón supplied only the land. Santos made enough profit from this and other fields to own three trucks and in so doing helped to destroy my stereotypes about social and economic categories. The image of the poor sharecropper exploited by the absentee landlord was, in his case, inverted (cf. Finkler 1980).

6. CONASUPO (Compañía Nacional de Subsistencia Popular) runs a chain of stores throughout Mexico, with the object of bringing food and other basic goods to the people at a standardized price, usually slightly below the prices found at other stores. The PRI (Partido Revolucionario Institucional), the ruling party in Mexico under various names since the 1930s, began backing "CONASUPO del PRI" stores in 1984 in an attempt to shore up its political base among the "popular classes."

Benito did not remain long in control of the CONASUPO del PRI store; in late 1986 he was removed from the post after an audit showed some 30,000 pesos (about 30 dollars, or two week's wages for a peon at the time) missing from the till. This discrepancy did not, however, greatly tarnish his reputation. His family had, after all, been running the store for two years, while the next two administrators were removed after running up deficits of 60,000 and 80,000 pesos in a matter of two months each. Under the municipal president elected in 1985 Benito was finally paid back for his loyalty to the party, with a permanent job not for himself but for his eldest daughter. In 1987 Benito was working full-time as the guard and night-watchman for a dynamite warehouse he had allowed to be built on a piece of his land; realizing the danger to himself and his family, he soon gave up the job and forced the warehouse to close. Micaela and their daughters continue to sell enchiladas in the marketplace and more recently in front of their house, which is conveniently near a small private zoo that opened in Mexquitic in 1991.

7. Paredes identifies the popular music of the 1940s, which he calls "moving-picture corridos" after the singing-Western type movies that promoted them, specifically with middle-class taste: "When one says moving-pictures, one says middle class. These have been the songs of the man from an emergent middle class, a man who goes to the movies, has enough money to buy a car, and enough political influence to go around carrying a gun" (1971:24). By the 1980s these

songs and their ranchero descendents were more popular among the "common people" of rural communities such as Mexquitic than among the urban middle classes, who had turned to the urban pop music of Latin America, Spain, and the United States and had left behind the rural and Mexican themes of the Pedro Infantes and Jorge Negretes.

8. Which, in any case, is about 90 percent Catholic. The other 10 percent are Protestant, atheist, and assorted "other," with the Protestants concentrated in communities other than the town of Mexquitic. In a general study of the creation of "Mexicanness" I would have more to say about this issue. Conservative Catholics have been trying to use Catholicism as a defining Mexican national characteristic since Independence. Much has been written about the alternate paths of Mexican popular religion; see the ethnographies by Finkler (1985) and Behar (1993). For understandings of the Mesoamerican context and content of current religious thought and practice in Mexico, see López Austin 1993 and Burkhart 1989.

9. There were fifteen such small stores in Mexquitic in 1983, ten of which are run by families I would identify as being of this higher social stratum. In 1993, with the lessening of the economic crisis of the 1980s, there were about thirty stores and services in town, some of them quite specialized, such as a video rental, Yolanda and Miguel's office supply store, two auto part shops, the small public zoo, and a pleasure boat service for weekend outings on the lake behind the town dam. Again, about two-thirds of these were run by families of higher status.

10. My data for the town of Mexquitic are based on household surveys I conducted in 1983 and 1993; these are remarkably consistent with fecundity data for San Luis Potosí and indeed for Mexico as a whole, as reported in the official 1990 census.

11. Frye 1986:20.

12. Lockhart 1992:138; and see chapter 4 below.

13. For an example of early literacy in Spanish, see appendix B.

3. FOUNDING MEXQUITIC

1. The Spanish invasion of the north began somewhat earlier with Nuño de Guzmán's brutal 1530–1531 conquest of Nueva Galicia (modern Jalisco, which is actually west and not north Mexico) and the Pacific coast as far north as Culiacán, but Guzmán and his "savage hordes" (Gerhard 1993:5) were after Indian labor and land, not gold and silver. Subsequent Spanish inroads in Nueva Galicia laid the groundwork for the expansion described here.

2. On the growth of trade between the mines and central Mexico see Bakewell's important history of silver mining in Zacatecas (1971). The standard secondary sources on the Chichimeca War are Powell's well-documented histories (1952 and 1977); see also Naylor and Polzer 1986:33–145. For ethnohistorical accounts of the "Chichimecas" of San Luis, see Behar 1987 and Frye 1989:32–66 and Frye (forthcoming) includes a bibliographic essay on the subject. For a detailed history of Indian slavery in northeast Mexico, see Cuello 1988; see also Deeds 1989. On the price of enslaved captives, see Powell 1971 and Zavala 1967: 183–208; the average price for a Chichimeca captive was 80 to 100 pesos, com-

pared to 300 to 400 pesos for an enslaved African. Zavala has information on the participation of Nahuas from central Mexico in the system of reprisal and enslavement during the foundation of Durango (1560–1563) and their complaints about being despoiled of their captives by Spanish soldiers; see also the original document in Barlow and Smisor 1943.

3. The denunciation is published in Powell 1971:215–260. On the growth of hacienda agriculture in the north see Chevalier 1966 and the *relaciones geográficas* from the Zacatecas region, as cited by Gerhard (1993). The latter describe the plains stretching northeast of Zacatecas and Fresnillo, now an arid semidesert, as a prairie of high grasses (as also testified in its Nahuatl name, Zacatlan, or "Grassland," whence the name of its people, the Zacatecas). On the environmental and social consequences of the introduction of European cattle in Mexico see Melville 1994.

4. For details of the peace see the works of Powell. The *capitulaciones* of Viceroy Luis Velasco to the settlers are printed in Velázquez 1985 [1897]:177–183.

5. This is the self-characterization of Mexquitic officials, as for example in AGI México, legajo 1043, passim. Tepeticpac was the "barrio" (constituent altepetl) of Tlaxcala from which the settlers from Mexquitic (and probably neighboring communities in San Luis Potosí) came. Other northern Tlaxcalan towns founded in 1591 were San Luis Colotlán and San Andrés del Teul (the latter moved to Chalchihuites after a Tepecano uprising in 1592) among the Zacatecas in the west; Tlaxcala (which became the Indian barrio Tlaxcalilla of the Spanish town of San Luis Potosí) and Venado among the Guachichiles in the Mexquitic area; and San Esteban de Saltillo in the north, alongside an already existing Spanish settlement. See Gibson 1967:181–189; Adams 1971; Offutt 1982, 1992; Martínez Baracs 1993; and Frye (forthcoming).

6. This move both legalized Spanish authority in the region (important for the Spanish sense of justice) and made the Tlaxcalans directly dependent on the king for their land grant, rather than on the Guachichiles, whom they saw as their inferiors. The original description of the founding ceremony is printed in Velázquez 1985 [1897]:219–223.

7. Small Guachichil barrios existed well into the eighteenth century in Santa María del Río to the south (founded by Otomís in about 1589) and in Venado and Saltillo to the north. The Guachichil visita of Agua Hedionda (modern Moctezuma), founded in 1593 south of Venado, was the only surviving Guachichil settlement at the end of the colonial era. It is often supposed that the Guachichiles intermarried with the Tlaxcalans, succumbed to disease, or fled east into Tamaulipas. However, fragmentary baptism and marriage records from 1591–1700 reveal only one or two marriages with Tlaxcalans in Mexquitic, Tlaxcalilla, and San Luis Potosí (they may have been more frequent in Venado and Agua Hedionda) and suggest instead that many Guachichiles moved to the cities and mines and intermarried with Africans and Afro-mestizos rather than with Central Mexican Indians, becoming part of the mixed-race plebeian society.

8. On the altepetl see Lockhart's important work (1992:14–58 and 1991:2–64; see also Ouweneel 1990). The word "altepetl" is not used in any extant documents from Mexquitic—if Nahuatl records were ever kept there they were destroyed by the "revolutionary" Pedro García in 1914—but both the settlement

pattern and the general sense of "corporate self and history" in colonial Mexquitic were so similar to that described by Lockhart for Central Mexican altepetl that I read his work with an exciting sense of recognition. San Esteban de Saltillo, also founded in the 1591 Tlaxcalan expedition, was called an altepetl in Nahuatl testaments recorded there between 1611 and 1779 (Offutt 1992:411, 428, 442).

9. These figures yield an average annual growth rate of roughly 2.2 percent, a high rate for that era in world terms but not unheard of in the expanding economy of northern New Spain. Some of this growth may have come from migration into the pueblo, but there is no evidence for that (indeed there is evidence of some out-migration towards 1800). By contrast, in the "jurisdiction" of Mexquitic, the surrounding haciendas that belonged to the parish but not the pueblo, the highly unstable population grew from zero to about 4,000 in the same period mainly through in-migration. In northwestern New Spain frequent intervillage migration has been documented (Swann 1982, 1989; Deeds [forthcoming]).

10. Bazant 1975:10–11. I treat the land tenure history of Mexquitic at length in chapter 7.

11. In the alcaldía mayor of San Luis Potosí around 1750 there were five pueblos de indios and seven Indian barrios of San Luis (three of the latter also ranked as pueblos); see AHESLP, AM 1757, "Autos sobre bienes de comunidad." In addition, Venado and Agua Hedionda lay not far north of Mexquitic in a separate alcaldía; and between 1750 and 1800 a new, generic Indian pueblo, Ahualulco, sprang up north of Mexquitic on the hacienda Rancho de Bocas and was granted two square leagues of ejido. Non-Indian settlements in the area included San Luis, the mining center of Cerro de San Pedro and ore-processing centers at Armadillo, Valle de San Francisco (now Villa de Reyes), and Pozos. The main diagnostic features of a "pueblo de indios" were its form of government, by a república de indios (see chapter 4), and its possession of some form of inalienable pueblo land. After the 1767 revolt, in which all of the Indian pueblos but Mexquitic took part, their repúblicas were suppressed for many years and much of their pueblo lands confiscated (Castro Gutiérrez 1990). At the same time, the loose ranchero community of Soledad de Ranchos northeast of San Luis was incorporated as a generic Indian congregation, governed by a Spanish teniente and ayuntamiento.

12. For Spanish influence on material life in colonial Mexquitic, see appendixes B and C; for land tenure, chapter 7.

13. Castro Gutiérrez 1990.

14. AHESLP, AM 1771 and 1774, for don Pedro de Llanas, "alferes de cavalleria de la Legion de Sn Carlos," as "theniente del pueblo de San Migl Mesquitic y del partido de las Bocas"; both cases were homicide reports. In 1778 the alcalde mayor and the priest of Mexquitic, in a case discussed in chapter 5, requested that a Spanish teniente be imposed on Mexquitic, to supplant an allegedly corrupt Indian government. The request was flatly turned down by the viceroy, as contrary to laws strictly regulating Spanish tenientes in Indian pueblos, but ten years later a teniente was living in Mexquitic, as discussed below.

15. Parish priests are discussed at length in chapter 5. Sánchez de Bustamante is mentioned as renting a house ("unas casas . . . en las que tiene su comersio") in

AHESLP, AM 1778 (8 mayo). Lozano mentioned "Dn Joaquin Sanchez Busta-mante y Vizente su hermano criados en este Pueblo [des]de pequeños" in an 1804 lawsuit over pueblo elections (AGN Tierras 1402, exp. 2, f. 17v); I assume they were sons of don Francisco. Navedo appeared as teniente de justicia ordinario in AHESLP, AM 1788 (20 jul). A year later don Domingo Caro appeared as teniente (AM 1789 [1 jul]); Caro was also mentioned in later lawsuits (AM 1791 [30 jun and 20 jul]; 1798 [11 enero], where he is called "el Teniente Español") as having come to Mexquitic in 1784 to straighten out conflicting land claims within the pueblo, but the impression is that he came as an impartial outsider and did not reside there. In 1791 a suspicious outsider claiming to be an "Oficial Real" and carrying falsified papers was ejected from the town (AM 1791 [11 sep]). Navedo's mercantile career is attested in AHESLP, AM 1799 (25 jun), his parish burial record, and elsewhere; he is listed as comisario of elections in AGN Tierras 1402, exp. 2, f. 17v; in the same file, f. 38v, opponents of the governor criticize him for "tolerating the house of a merchant"; the priest Lozano describes Navedo in AGN Tierras 1363, exp. 1, f. 14v. Other known comisarios and tenientes (an overlapping group) resided outside Mexquitic, such as don Juan Nepomuceno Oviedo, the energetic administrator of Bocas who died in 1812 combatting the Hidalgo insurgency. The maestro de escuela López García—there is no indica-tion of his racial status, but he could not have been considered an Indian—briefly outlined his career and his marriage to a "Desendiente immediata de los mas Principales Governadores, y Republicanos" in a petition for a new schoolteacher which he wrote from San Luis in 1806, a mere eighteen years after he had aban-doned the post (AGN Intendencias 51, exp. 6). He also appeared in AHESLP, AM 1788 (20 jun), in which, calling himself a *defensor* (defense attorney), he suc-cessfully argued for the release of three Indians from charges of incest and bigamy. Perhaps that was his "better destiny" (as teacher he had been paid 21 pesos a month).

A curious footnote to the question of non-Indians in Mexquitic is the sur-name Quixtiano (now spelled Quistián), which was Nahuatl for "Christian," that is, "Spaniard" (Lockhart 1992:298). It originated in a colonial nickname (as in "Pedro de Santiago, el quistiano," AHESLP, AM 1778, referring to a man living in 1736), which conceivably referred to the person's "Spanish" appearance or background. Ironically, it is the only surviving "Nahuatl" surname in Mexquitic.

16. Frye 1986:29.

17. Gibson showed that the image of the Tlaxcalans as the first and best allies of the Spaniards in New Spain was largely created by the Tlaxcalans themselves in their successful drive for special privileges (Gibson 1967:158–161). For the suits between Mexquitic and La Parada see chapter 7; for the imposition of tribute on the Tlaxcalans of San Luis Potosí, see AGI México, legajo 1043. Most Indians, free blacks, and mulattos in New Spain were subject to annual tributes of 13 to 22 reales in the eighteenth century (Gibson 1964:209); the Indians of central San Luis Potosí were eventually forced to pay 10 reales (one and a quarter pesos).

18. Arlegui 1851:136. Arlegui was referring here to the Tlaxcalans, Mexicans (Nahuas), and Otomís as a group, for he considered these Indians all to be essen-tially the same. By the eighteenth century the Spanish elite of San Luis increas-

ingly thought of the people of Mexquitic not as *tlaxcaltecas,* as they still called themselves, but simply as indios.

19. Frye 1986:32.

20. I take the concepts of syllogisms of association and arguments of images from Fernandez 1986.

21. Taylor 1979:123.

22. AHESLP, AM 1599 (4 mayo). The notion that labor scarcity should lead to an improvement in the working conditions of laborers, a commonplace in Western economic theory, has sometimes been applied to Mexican colonial history (as in Brading 1978:8), but I have yet to see any convincing evidence to support the idea, especially in the late sixteenth and early seventeenth centuries, when the shortage of labor was most acute (see Gibson 1964:233). For an extreme case of responding to labor shortage with cruel treatment, see Taussig 1984.

23. The case, from 1780, is mentioned in chapter 5 and analyzed in Frye 1994a.

24. AHESLP, AM 1779 (6 feb).

25. Ruth Behar has told and analyzed Esperanza's story in Behar 1993.

26. Tape recorded interview, August 10–11, 1985. I have cut the story to a third of its original length, mainly by removing some of the multiple repetitions.

27. The painting was heavily "restored" in 1799 and again in the early 1900s. A caption on the painting claiming that the image dates to 1546 is among the more obviously repainted features.

28. Christian 1981:75–77.

29. I have no way of knowing or discovering how old the story might be. The other stories that old Matías told and that his relatives Esperanza and Atanasia have retold to us are: the boy whose father was the Devil; the priest who wanted to find out where the world ends (the house of the wind); "El Pedro de Ardimales," who had some pebbles that could make water boil; the woman who wanted to know what dogs see at night; the origin of weeds; the happy childless couple; and the man who unwittingly married a witch. The last of these is a common tale throughout Mexico and the U.S. Southwest (Parsons [1927] collected a version of it in New Mexico in the 1920s, and I have seen published Nahuatl versions from Veracruz and central Mexico—for a rather different version, see Paredes 1970:27); it is also the only one of the stories that anyone else in Mexquitic has told us.

30. Fernandez 1986:11.

31. Fieldnotes, March 30, 1984.

32. The most important works are Powell 1952 and 1977. Behind the allegory is a comparison, sometimes explicit, between Caldera's methods in "pacifying" the north of New Spain and those U.S. methods in the "Indian Wars" of the contiguous Southwest. The comparison, always unfavorable to the U.S., places Powell in the Hispanophile camp of the U.S. Borderlands historians of his generation.

33. Velázquez 1982 [1946]: I, 417. The works mentioned have all been republished: Torquemada 1969 [1615], Arlegui 1851 [1737], and Velázquez 1985 [1897].

34. In his own brief history of the town (Escalante 1919). The name of Fray Diego de la Magdalena does not, however, appear in the document relating the official foundation of Mexquitic, nor in fact in any document concerning the pueblo. Torquemada placed Fray Diego in Santa María del Río in the years immediately following the conquest and in Tlaxcalilla for the remainder of his life (see Frye 1989:423).

35. The statement on the plaque was actually taken verbatim from Padre Escalante's brief *Historia de Mexquitic* (1919; based in turn on Peña 1979 [1894]), where it is surrounded by accolades to Fray Diego. The plaque contains a few minor factual errors. Mexquitic was actually founded in 1591; "Guachichiles and Chichimecas" were not separate groups; Miguel Caldera was never a "don"; the "future founders of San Luis," a Spanish town, did not hail from the Tlaxcalan town of Mexquitic.

36. This is my rendering of one popular view of Revolutionary agrarian ideology; the legal practice is quite different, and in fact appeals directly to Spanish colonial title. The haciendas surrounding Mexquitic were redistributed as ejidos partly on the strength of the concessions granted to the Tlaxcalans by King Philip II in 1591.

37. Fieldnotes, translated, February 9, 1983.

38. Fieldnotes, translated, August 18, 1993.

39. Fieldnotes, parts translated, March 3, 1984.

40. Fieldnotes, parts translated, March 3, 1984. Her derivation of the local racial insult *teco* is right on target; compare Santamaría 1978, s.v. "Teco."

41. Taped interview, August 11, 1985.

4. COLONIAL POLITICS

1. Lockhart 1992:30.

2. From the early baptism records of Mexquitic, we know that the first Tlaxcalan governor, don Francisco Vásquez Coronado, remained in office until at least 1593 and probably until his death. The next governor, don Diego Sánchez— he appeared without the "don" in 1593 and 1594—was in office in both 1604 and 1610, perhaps continuously. (Curiously, don Diego was one of the few Tlaxcalans appearing in the baptism records who did not figure among the 227 settlers from Tepeticpac; he may have been a late recruit from Tlaxcala, or he may have moved to Mexquitic from San Esteban del Saltillo, where three Tlaxcalans named Diego Sánchez—none married to the same woman as the don Diego of Mexquitic, however—were among the settlers in 1591.) By 1640 the rule of one-year terms without successive reelections was in place, but in that year don Bernabe de San Juan successfully petitioned the viceroy for a four-year term as governor (AGN Indios 12, exp. 120, f. 237). In the early years there was a parallel Guachichil pueblo of Mexquitic that shared the space of the Tlaxcalan pueblo; the Guachichil governor Pedro de Torres was also one of the Guachichil "captains" who had negotiated the end of the Chichimeca War.

3. After Independence the title but not the function of the governor was changed, first to "alcalde constitucional" and later to "presidente municipal." The term of office continued to be one year until about 1920, when it was ex-

tended to two years. In 1941 it was extended again to three years, now the standard length in all Mexican municipalities. Elections have been moved from December 31 to the first Sunday in December, but New Year's Day is still the first day of office for the new administration, though the inauguration ceremony is now held at midday rather than at the stroke of midnight, and officials no longer pass on the *vara de justicia,* which was still used early in this century.

4. Compare Lockhart 1992:49.

5. All thirty-seven principales signed this petition, an indication of spreading literacy among the elite (AGN Tierras 1402, exp. 2, ff. 32–32v). A generation earlier, in 1776, the former officials protesting the governor's actions had to ask two sons of the pueblo (non-nobles, in this context) to sign their petition for them (AHESLP, AM 1776).

6. Cargo systems (civil-religious hierarchies, fiesta systems, etc.) are described in virtually every ethnography of Mesoamerican Indian communities, from Tax 1937 to Watanabe 1992. Since the 1960s a number of ethnographies have focused directly on the cargo system, including Cancian's pioneering economic study (1965), Nash's behavioral study (1970), Smith's study of the impact of economic change (1977), Greenburg's survey and evaluation of ethnographic models of system (1981), and Mathews's gender analysis (1985); see also Stephen's gender/class analysis (1991).

Given the fact that most ethnographers, at least from the time of Wolf's theorization of the system (1957), attribute to the cargo system a colonial if not a pre-Hispanic origin, there has been surprisingly little attention paid to it by historians. Farriss (1984:320–351) is an important exception. Historical studies of cofradías, one part of the total picture of modern civil-religious systems, include Lavrin 1990 and Gruzinski 1990. The only investigation of the historical validity of claims made about the system is Chance and Taylor's fundamental article (1985), which establishes the chronology of its development out of colonial religious and civil governing systems and dates the emergence of joint civil-religious "ladders" from the nineteenth-century breakdown of the colonial regime. The fact that such a ladder never formed in Mexquitic, where the pueblo elite did not lose political power, indirectly confirms the Chance and Taylor thesis.

7. This description of powers and duties is based on general impressions from dozens of documents. The role of the governor is evident in almost every document concerning Mexquitic; of course, some governors may have been mere figureheads for more influential bosses who preferred to work behind the scenes, as was alleged in more than one lawsuit. Rental of community land to non-Indians, around the edges of the pueblo, began at least as early as the 1640s, when the "hacienda de Mexquitic" (modern Corte and Carrizal) appears in the earliest surviving parish records. By 1783 pueblo land was rented annually to twenty-five outsiders for a total of 109 pesos (AHESLP, AM 1783; also 1782). In 1806 the pueblo treasury held 1,065 pesos in cash, 2,061 pesos in the Casa de Consolación, and 412 pesos in the Banco Nacional de San Carlos; but rental of community land had fallen to 22 pesos (AGN Intendencias 51, exp. 6). On the alguaciles or ministros, who are rarely mentioned, AHESLP, AM 1788 (20 jul) mentions a ministro de vara arresting a suspected murderer; and in AHESLP, AM 1778 (19 nov), where the alcalde mayor of San Luis unsuccessfully requested that a

Spanish teniente oversee Mexquitic government, he stipulated that "los que le hubieran de servir de Ministros o Topiles tengan obligacion de acarrearle la Agua y Leña nesesaria."

8. "A las tenanches del pueblo, de las cofradias u hermandades les há quitado dinero" (AHESLP, AM 1776).

9. A petition of 1804, however, lists "mayordomos" among the servants provided to the priest by the pueblo, along with topiles and cooks. But this may merely indicate a devaluation of the position, at a time when the priest was accused of inventing nonexistent cofradías to increase his income, systematically plundering cofradías funds and cattle herds, and forcing cofradías members to work for him (see chapter 5). Today all sponsors of the fiesta of San Miguel (anyone who contributes any money or time) are called "mayordomos"; informal sodalities, without the name of cofradías, organize the celebration of such major feast days as Corpus Christi.

Some information on colonial cofradías is to be found in an account book (1800–1815) kept in the parish archive. I was only permitted to consult this book once, for a period of an hour. There is some data in a tithe document from 1754 in the Archivo de la Casa de Morelos, Diezmatorios (copied in INAH microfilm 776614). Two cofradías, honoring San Diego and La Exaltación de la Sma. Cruz, dated from 1616 and 1664 respectively; ten more were founded by 1754, and another ten within a few years after the parish was secularized in 1769.

The alcalde municipal of Mexquitic abolished all cofradías in 1836 (some continued to operate for another year or two) and turned their land and assets over to the priest. But a note in the parish account book dated 1846 complains that the funds "of the Cofradías have been arbitrarily usurped by the citizens of the town, in spite of the judicial possession of them which was given to the current parish priest by sentence of the Supreme Tribunal of Justice and by order of the Superior Gobierno of the Department." At least one piece of cofradía property— about sixty hectares of scrubland once used to pasture the sheep of San Diego— was handed out in 1839 by municipal judge don José María Vásquez, to don Félix Vásquez (a relative?) who claimed it "because the cattle . . . for which it was destined no longer existed." Two decades later, in 1860, Félix Vásquez (who had meanwhile been presidente in 1858) sold the land to the hacienda of La Parada for 500 pesos (AOCI, Titulos de Santa Teresa, vol. 7, lista de "Rusticos," no. 176).

10. This is the position that most recalls the literature on the Mesoamerican "cargo system." A related religious cargo, or perhaps another name for the same one, was that of Gran Turco ("Great Turk"—the stereotyped leader of the "Moors" in the dance of *moros y cristianos*). This also entailed some expenses, as we know from an inscription on the painting of the parish patron, San Miguel: "It was retouched . . . for the second time in 1799 . . . at the expense of the Turco Augustín Banegas and the other *fiesteros*" (Escalante 1919). See also AHESLP, AM 1759 (28 jul), in which the governor of the pueblo of Santiago (an Indian neighborhood of San Luis) petitioned to hold a bullfight as a fundraiser to defray "los cresidos costos que tienen las compañías de Moros y Christianos, cuyos principales Jefes se eligen de un año para otro."

11. AHESLP, AM 1799 (25 jul). A summary of the shoemaker's debts appears in appendix C.

12. Chance and Taylor 1985:2.

13. From a transcript of the original in a 1797 case, in which San Luis was again trying to prohibit bullfights. AHESLP, AM 1797 (copy in INAH microfilm roll SLP series no. 13).

14. Gibson 1964:404. I follow Lockhart's critique here, in his genial appreciation of Gibson's achievement (1991:173–174).

15. This is essentially the same office described by Cutter as the "protector de indios" (1986); see also Borah 1983.

16. Pastores (shepherds) might have been either the herders of the sheep and goats kept by cofradías, or the actors in *pastorelas* (shepherd dramas) put on during the Christmas season (between early December and Lent). Through putting on a pastorela (which are rarely performed now; we saw one in Cerro Prieto in March 1984) one can fulfill a *manda,* a promise to God or a saint, and receive spiritual benefit but not social prestige or authority.

17. One of the widows is given the title "doña," indicating a higher social position, yet she is not otherwise distinguished in the petition. I do not know what to make of this fact, or of the fact that untitled Mónica de la Cruz rather than doña Dominga presented the petition (except to suggest that Mónica herself might have added the latter's name to her petition in order to bolster her own credibility).

18. By contrast, in rural Spain only friars or monks are called "padre," and then only in direct address. Perhaps it is significant that most Mexican parishes, including Mexquitic, were originally held by friars rather than by secular priests. On the Spanish normative literature on patriarchalism, theorizing the father as the archetypal authority figure, see Boyer 1989.

19. Sánchez Unzueta 1982:7.

20. The witnesses were presented in order of rank: a governor, a lieutenant governor, a fiscal mayor, two alcaldes primeros, and two alcaldes. Regarding the accusation that don Nicolás did not listen to "those more elder [*mas antiguos*] than he," he was forty-six years old and all but one of the witnesses were in their fifties and sixties.

5. PEOPLE AND PRIEST

1. AHESLP, AM 1776. As is often the case with colonial documents there is no indication of how the authorities responded to this petition. Perhaps they listened, for the next governor elected (Urbano Sánchez) proved to be no favorite of the priest, while the governor from 1776 (Eusebio Hernández, who had already been governor in 1766 and 1769) was trying to have his house, which had been seized by the alcalde mayor for unstated reasons, returned to him in 1778; the new owner of La Parada was his *fiador* (guarantor).

2. AHESLP, AM 1780 (7 nov).

3. Of the other significant social powers in the region, miners found no ore here, the merchant class had only a minor presence, and even though the alcalde

mayor of San Luis resided only five leagues away he preferred to rule indirectly—through the Indian governor, the priest, and hacienda administrators.

4. This portrait of priests and friars is based on documents in AHESLP, AM, and on conversations with William B. Taylor, who will soon publish a broad study of parish priests in colonial Mexico; see also Taylor 1988:234–235. In another important essay Taylor places the endemic conflict and litigation between priests and parishioners of late-colonial Mexico in the context not only of secularization but of the Bourbon redefinition of the functions of parish priests (Taylor 1994). On intergenerational differences in "priestly styles," another aspect of the idiosyncrasy of the secular parish, see Behar 1990. I do not wish to overemphasize the impact of secularization on the relations between priest and people in Mexquitic; as with other major administrative reforms such as disentailment, secularization merely hastened the pace of social transformations already well under way. Comparable conflicts occurred between the Indians of San Martín de la Cal (near Guadalajara) and the Franciscans who were still in charge of their parish in 1803, some thirty years after the conflicts began in Mexquitic (Van Young 1984:75).

5. This and the following quotes are from AHESLP, AM 1778 (28 feb).

6. AHESLP, AM 1778 (28 feb).

7. AHESLP, AM 1779 (3 feb).

8. "Padre" is a formal term in Mexican Spanish, and generally used in this sense only in the legalistic phrase "padre de familia," male household head. (The common term for "father" is papa or papá, or in colonial documents from Mexquitic, tata, from Nahuatl tahtli.)

9. AHESLP, AM 1780 (7 nov).

10. This case is analyzed at length in Frye 1994a, where I explore the question also addressed in this chapter of how documents of arguable factual value can be read for a history of racial and power relations.

11. Florescano and Gil Sánchez 1976:539.

12. Taylor 1984.

13. AHESLP, AM 1785 (8 nov).

14. AHESLP, AM 1785 (sin fecha).

15. On the donation, see Escalante 1919. The testament was published (as a political move against Lozano's antifederalist siblings) in El Yunque de la Libertad 108, 3 mayo 1834 (AHESLP, Hemeroteca; Montejano y Aguiñaga 1971:74), showing a net worth of 41,718 pesos. Of interest in the testament is the list of books in Lozano's library valued at 866 pesos, including La recopilación de Indias, El Conde de la Cañada, La nueva recopilación, and Las leyes de partida. Loans totaling 30,000 pesos to don Pantaleón Ipiña of La Parada, of which only 6,000 had been repaid by 1834, listed in AOCI, Títulos de Santa Teresa, vol. 7, lista de "Rústicos," nos. 49–54. (For comparison, the 51,000 hectares of La Parada, with houses and animals, sold in 1822 for 121,737 pesos [Bazant 1975:41].)

16. Cases cited below, and AHESLP, SGG 1812 (8 enero); AGN Tierras 1412, exp. 4; Mexquitic parish archive, Libros de Bautismos.

17. AHESLP, AM 1797; AGN Tierras 1402, exp. 2, f. 44v–45v (petition from 1806 summarizing the 1797 case). The canal, measuring 2,473 varas (2,070 meters), is still in use in Corte under the name "sanja del común." Ventura died in

1799 and his role as Lozano's proxy landowner was taken over by José María Ji-ménez, a once and future governor.

18. Ventura obviously had help in drawing up his petition, since he himself was illiterate, but his opponents felt he was helped by a lawyer and not simply a scribe. In fact, one of the references in this document (to Juan de Nevia, *Curia filipica*) was also cited in a letter that Lozano wrote the same year to the owner of La Parada while trying to cover up his role in the irrigation affair (see AGN Tie-rras 1402, exp. 2, f. 46). I suspect Lozano had a hand in Ventura's defense, whether or not he was the actual author.

Regarding "the use of reason," *cuando tenía uso de razón* ("when I had the use of reason") is a common phrase used in Mexquitic today to refer to the time around the age of eight when a person suddenly becomes conscious of his or her surroundings and life conditions. The appellation *gente de razón* for non-Indians is not used in central San Luis Potosí, nor have I found it to figure in the docu-ments, though it clearly comes out of this colonial image and probably was used here in the colonial period.

19. AHESLP, AM 1797, f. 25v.

20. AHESLP, AM 1797, f. 28.

21. AGN Tierras 1363, exp. 1, f. 15 (April 26, 1805). Thanks to Tutino (1986: 163) for this reference.

22. AGN Tierras 1402, exp. 2, f. 14.

23. Ibid., f. 16v.

24. Hamnett 1986:4.

25. Lozano, AGN Tierras 1363, exp. 1, f. 9v–17v; witness, f. 20v.

26. Ibid., f. 10.

27. AGN Intendencias 51, exp. 6 (dated 1803). In addition to the sources listed elsewhere, cases involving Lozano include: AGN Clero Secular 72, exp. 20, f. 383–465, a report on cofradías elsewhere in the province of San Luis Potosí in 1798 carried out as a result of the accusation in AHESLP, Poder Ejecutivo 1798, of exploiting cofradías (thanks to William Taylor for this reference); and AHESLP, AM 1799 (27 marzo), (2 nov), (3 dic), and AM 1800, continuations and complications of the suits over the canal and the alleged exactions, which spilled over into lawsuits concerning the election of Lozano cronies as governors.

28. Tutino 1986:162.

29. AGN Tierras 1363, exp. 1, f. 1–6. Ironically, the petitioners proposed that, in order to remove the influence of Lozano and of his commissioner friends, the elections should be supervised by the royalist officer don Felix Calleja, who a few years later made his name by suppressing the Hidalgo insurrection. Lozano vehemently denied the charge of neglecting his pastoral duties, but the intendant Bruno Díaz de Salcedo (who incidentally strikes me as an unusually balanced and judicious official) had noted in 1798 that "this same Priest has been here [in San Luis] much of this year, when in previous years he only came on August 25 to greet his father and returned that afternoon or the next morning" (AHESLP, Poder Ejecutivo 1798).

30. AGN Tierras 1402, exp. 2, f. 40 (September 1, 1806).

31. AGN Tierras 1385, exp. 7, f. 10–14 (September 15, 1807), from which the quotations in the following paragraphs are taken.

32. AGN Tierras 1363, exp. 1, f. 10 (April 26, 1805); AGN Tierras 1402, exp. 2, f. 72 (April 8, 1807); and AGN Tierras 1385, exp. 7, f. 10 (September 15, 1807).

33. AHESLP, Poder Ejecutivo 1798 (September 5, 1798).

34. AGN Tierras 1385, exp. 7, f. 4 (August 27, 1807); f. 10–14 (September 15, 1807); and f. 18v (September 24, 1807).

35. AGN Tierras 1402, exp. 2, f. 7 (January 2, 1804).

36. AHESLP, Poder Ejecutivo 1798.

37. In the following section I reinterpret the conclusions of Tutino, who has used the Lozano conflict and the subsequent involvement of Mexquitic in the Hidalgo insurrection as a case study in his penetrating history of "the social bases of agrarian violence" (1986:159–164). Tutino argues that by increasing and controlling irrigation and renting pueblo lands to outsiders, Lozano "forced many residents long sustained by subsistence production" into "making firewood, charcoal, and pulque" or working in his textile and rope businesses to make ends meet. Faced with "insecure dependence on wage labor and the commercial economy," many from Mexquitic joined the insurgency (1986:161–163). Although my interpretation of the case is somewhat different, I do not feel that it affects Tutino's valuable general theory of agrarian insurrection, the essence of which can be summarized as follows: the grievances that can lead peasants to insurrection are not the droughts or famines that can bring sharp but temporary losses in material well-being, but systemic changes in the economy that threaten to reduce their social and economic standing permanently. "Long-autonomous peasants suddenly forced into dependence without security, and long-secure dependents rapidly made to face insecurity without mobility, tend to become outraged at the injustices imposed upon them by the powerful" (1986:31).

38. Tutino (1986:161).

39. In this century a long succession of priests and state governors have been credited with reintroducing textile production and other small industries to Mexquitic, but each attempt has risen and ultimately failed according to rhythms utterly beyond the control of temporary paternalism or the local market.

40. For a measure of growth in Mexquitic see appendix A. Such growth (averaging nearly 2 percent per year from 1590 to 1790) was not peculiar to Mexquitic; crude annual growth rates of 1 to 2 percent were registered in this period all over Spanish America, as population recovered from the catastrophe of conquest and disease, or (on borderlands such as Mexquitic) settled agriculture moved into zones previously occupied by nomadic groups, with additional economic stimulation from the mining economy.

41. After the suppression of the Hidalgo insurrection and the military destruction of the opposition to Lozano in 1811, the priest engineered the removal of his former ally Melecio Sandate (compared by his assistant priest to "Nero and Caligula," AHESLP, SGG 1812 [8 enero]) and imposed José Olayo Mendoza, who remained in power until at least 1823. In that year Olayo Mendoza and Lozano were denounced by a single citizen of the municipio: "The current alcaldes and all those who have been in the past, are all godchildren of the Priest, and therefore although there is National and Independent rule, the poor citizens of

the town get nowhere, because it is as if the inhuman despotism had never been destroyed" (AHESLP, SGG 1823).

42. Brian Hamnett has also briefly interpreted the late colonial history of Mexquitic in his important work on the "roots of insurgency" in Mexico (1986: 91–92). Hamnett emphasizes struggles with the hacienda of La Parada over the usurpation of community land, but he minimizes the importance of land pressure and emphasizes the alleged loss of traditional land rights, taking at face value the claims of Mexquitic opposition leaders who alleged that La Parada had violated local custom by forcing the rental of pueblo lands.

43. Tutino 1986:163.

44. Montejano y Aguiñaga 1981:64.

45. Fieldnotes, translated, August 31, 1983.

46. On "pious anticlericalism" see Behar 1990, and for a general perspective on the strained relations between official doctrine and popular practice in European religion see the entire collection edited by Badone (1990).

47. Taped interview, August 13, 1985.

48. There is absolutely no evidence of any wrongdoing or impropriety in this cooperative. Still, in any situation where one person is put in charge of someone else's money (treasurers for the water board or the school board, for instance), there is an overwhelming tendency in Mexquitic to assume corruption until proven otherwise.

49. Though I speak of "the priest" here in the singular, to be precise, in the Franciscan years there were two or three friars at a time, and later priests often hired vicarios or assistant priests to aid them in their considerable duties. In the present, as noted in chapter 1, the parish has been divided into three parts, but the priest still has over 20,000 souls in his flock.

50. Ramón's theory was that the melino's constant state of drunkenness had made him less attached to this world, more open to visions. The melino's image of the afterlife, largely based on an interpretation of traditional Catholic imagery and religious paintings, seems to contradict the commonly expressed view (which the melino himself also voices) that death is a definitive end. As one man put it, "They say that when we die we'll go to heaven, but they don't say what heaven is: a hole six feet deep!" No one in Mexquitic, however, seems particularly interested in resolving or even acknowledging this contradiction.

51. This narrative is based largely on the fieldnotes of Ruth Behar, who wrote a much more complete account of this incident than I did.

52. Taped interview, September 14, 1987; I have edited out many repetitions for reasons of space.

53. Burkhart 1989.

6. MODERN POLITICS: MEXQUITIC AND THE NATION

1. This situation recalls Trouillot's description of the " 'fetishism' of the state" in the "blocked political system" of Haiti. Trouillot quotes Alain Touraine to the effect that such a system "pushes a good part of all political and class relations back inside the state. If it is completely closed, political life is replaced by

rivalries between individuals, clans, cliques, and interest groups within the state itself" (Trouillot 1990:85–86). This is a good description of the political industry in Mexquitic. It is important, however, to note that in Mexico as a whole, in contrast to Haiti, a civil society has continued to function independent of the state throughout the social disruptions of the past two centuries. Politics and the state may be the principal paths to a professional class identity in a rural municipality, but the alternative remains of leaving that circumscribed world behind for the broader professional horizons of urban Mexico. For an important new study of the complex relations between popular cultures and state formation in Mexico, see Joseph and Nugent 1994.

2. The most promising of which are in the San Luis Potosí state archive (AHESLP, SGG). The Mexquitic municipal archives were destroyed in 1914, and I was unable to consult more recent documents.

3. *El Momento de San Luis Potosí,* 23 agosto 1987.

4. For an account of the San Luis case, see Bezdek 1984.

5. In the midst of these activities, Pedro García was listed by Wilber L. Bonney, the local U.S. consul, as a rebel leader in September 1913, commanding (together with a certain Justina Cervantes) 150 men, and operating around Salinas, to the east of Mexquitic (Ankerson 1984:65).

6. This account is based on Falcón 1984:146–150 and Ankerson 1984:102–105. I use both of these excellent studies of Cedillo's cacique rule in San Luis and its relations with national politics extensively in the account that follows. The early career of Cedillo (1910–1920) is also treated in Rojas 1983. For a more general view of personalistic-militaristic cacique rule in Revolutionary Mexico and its connections with the new national politics, see the collection of essays on Mexican regions edited by Brading (1980); and for a parallel examination of the Santos cacicazgo in the Huasteca, see Lomnitz-Adler 1992.

7. Ankerson 1984:105.

8. Ankerson 1984:106; Falcón 1984:151–152.

9. Ankerson 1984:107, 109–110; Rosendo S., interview.

10. Ankerson 1984:110–111.

11. Ankerson 1984:119; Falcón (1984:186–187).

12. Other factors in the lack of support for the Cristeros in Mexquitic were the long-standing antagonism between the parish priests and an influential sector of the local elite (see chapter 5) and the fact that Catholicism as it came to be practiced in Mexquitic functions quite well without priests, except on sacramental occasions (baptisms, weddings) that require their services.

13. For a history of the war, with a brief mention of Tepatitlán, see Meyer 1973:302–303.

14. Ankerson 1984:160–161.

15. Quoted in Falcón 1984:192; for a similar denunciation of Pilar García from 1935, see ibid., p. 201.

16. Velázquez 1982:4.336.

17. Velázquez 1982:4.2, my translation. Velázquez gives a comprehensive account of Bustamante that is also layered with his own antiliberal sentiments.

18. Ibid. pp. 1–21. The Mexquitic disturbance is detailed in a long document in AHESLP, SGG 1869 (marzo, leg. 2) entitled "Espediente relativo al motin que

tuvo lugar en Mesquitic por los partidarios del C. Juan Bustamante, la tarde del dia 14 de marzo del presente año," written in part by municipal president Patricio Jiménez.

19. For a broad ethnographic treatment of the themes of this section see Greenburg 1989.

20. See the "murder map of the Texas-Mexico border" in Montejano 1987: 124.

21. As one woman in the town whose mother was from Ojo Zarco told us: "Tengo descendencia mala por parte de mi madre, que en San Pedro Ojo Zarco son muy matones, tienen sangre muy matona" (I have bad ancestry on my mother's side, 'cause they're real killers in San Pedro Ojo Zarco, they have real killer blood).

22. Archivo de la Secretaría de Reforma Agraria, SLP, leg. 779.

23. This chronology is basically supported by documents in the Reforma Agraria archive in San Luis, though it seems the problems between the two communities arose as early as the 1920s and became serious by the 1930s.

24. See Falcón 1984:269 for Santos's takeover of Cedillo's land in the Huasteca; ibid., p. 242 for his agrarian reform base. For a subtle reading of the roots of Santos's politics in the "ranchero localist ideology" of the Huasteca in tropical eastern San Luis Potosí, and the way that "Gonzalo successfully utilized ranchero culture in a national forum" to back up his monopoly of power in the state, see Lomnitz-Adler 1992:189–204 (the quote is on p. 200).

25. According to the analysis of Bezdek (1984).

26. "The village president is said to be 'the father of the village,' and in dealings with higher officials the phrase 'as a father to his children' is common. . . . This paternalistic conception of power and leadership coexists with the ideal of equal rights and obligations among the citizens" (Dennis 1987:25–26).

27. For an insightful ethnography of the 1988 PRI presidential campaign, see Lomnitz, Lomnitz-Adler, and Adler 1993.

7. LAND, HISTORY, AND IDENTITY

1. AGI, México 1043, cuaderno 1a.

2. Compare Van Young on the neighboring Guadalajara region around 1600: "Agriculture was relatively unimportant compared to livestock-raising, however. . . . An extensive, wasteful livestock economy developed, not dissimilar to that of the Argentine pampas in the days before the advent of the *saladeros*. Animals were slaughtered for their hides and tallow, the meat left to rot on the carcasses" (1981:25).

3. This was a significant and perhaps exaggerated amount. The previous year, 1621, was a year of great shortage in which prices reached 3 to 5 pesos in central Mexico (Gibson 1964:454). In spite of wild price swings throughout the colonial period, any price over three pesos was high. Neither Gibson (1964:452–459, for the valley of Mexico, 1525–1809) nor Van Young (1981:82, for the Guadalajara region, 1710–1820) records a price as high as 6 pesos before 1786. See Florescano 1969.

4. AGN Indios 9, exp. 365, f. 181v.

5. AOCI, Libro, f. 119v.

6. A key difference in the land tenure histories of central Mexico and the San Luis area is that in the former colonial land titles such as the mercedes were superimposed on a complicated, preexisting web of land title (both private and communal) that in many cases was maintained, though usually in modified form, under colonial rule (Gibson 1964; Taylor 1972; Osborn 1973; Lockhart 1992). Here, colonial land tenure began with a clean slate.

7. AGN Indios 12, exp. 47, f. 189, 21 marzo 1640.

8. AGN Indios 13, exp. 11, f. 11v and 12v.

9. As for the wisdom of concluding the suit promptly, note that the legal costs for both sides (which the Jesuits of La Parada were forced to pay) came to about 1,400 pesos, almost as much as the 1,500 pesos the land involved was judged to be worth. The Jesuits immediately asked the nephew and heir of the former owner of La Parada to repay them the 1,500 pesos for the censo plus the 1,400 pesos for court costs. I do not know whether they were successful (AOCI, Libro, f. 196).

10. AOCI, Libro, f. 388v–394.

11. Escalante 1919.

12. AOCI, Libro, f. 433.

13. AOCI, Libro, f. 191v.

14. Area, in AOCI, Libro, f. 1050 (cf. Bazant 1975:16); boundaries, listed in AOCI, Libro, f. 1244–1263.

15. I discuss the specifics of the case below. At the same time the pueblo set out to reclaim its territory in the "hacienda" of Estanzuela. Over the century that had passed since Estanzuela had been auctioned off for an annual censo of 25 pesos, the original agreement had apparently been forgotten by both sides, and the case was renegotiated in the colonial courts. From what I can tell, part of "Estanzuela" may have been annexed to the hacienda of Peñasco, and the rest may have become part of the "communal land" that Mexquitic rented out in the late eighteenth century; altogether, this relatively arid and unpopulated corner attracted little attention before it was transformed by the Mexquitic dam in the 1920s.

16. AHESLP, AM 1798, 11 enero.

17. According to a history of the hacienda written by descendants of its last owner, contemporary rumor held that divine wrath would be visited upon anyone daring to make a bid (Cabrera Ipiña and Cabrera Ipiña 1978:70).

18. The hacienda was valued at 62,434 pesos: 32,025 for the land and buildings (a price Bazant considers to have been very undervalued), the rest for tools, grain, and (above all) cattle on the hoof, especially goats. The hacienda also had debts of 25,952 pesos, mainly in mortgages taken out from various *obras pías* (religious foundations). Prieto was to pay the difference between the assets and the debts, and he did so in part by taking out further mortgages (Bazant 1975:16–17).

19. Frye 1989:84–89.

20. Real Academia Española 1979:353, (s.v. "censo perpetuo"), my translation.

21. Bloch (1966:181, quoted in Behar 1986:191); Behar 1986:198.

22. AOCI, Libro, f. 377v, emphasis added.

23. Ibid., f. 395–396.

24. Ibid., f. 409.

25. Ibid., f. 432v–433v.

26. Ibid., f. 1261. A century later, in 1886, the matter of the censo was settled once and for all: the heirs of La Parada rid themselves of the bothersome annual payments by "redeeming" the censo, "paying back" the 1,000 pesos that was the basis of the fifty-peso-a-year payments, as well as another 500 pesos "which the Señores Ipiña generously give," presumably to relieve lingering bad feelings over the lost 25 pesos a year. Ibid., f. 430, marginal note.

27. AGN Tierras 1363, exp. 1, f. 9v–17v.

28. AOCI, Libro, f. 1186–1189v.

29. Ibid., f. 1339v.

30. Ibid., f. 1169–1170.

31. Though the population did not continue to grow geometrically, as in his argument. To answer his rhetorical question, if the population of Mexquitic had continued to grow at the same rate as it had from 1640 (population about 350) to 1789 (about 8,500), then 149 years later, in 1939, it would have reached about 200,000.

32. Ibid., f. 1336v; f. 1342v–1343.

33. AGN Tierras 1412, exp. 4, f. 8–8v. See Van Young (1989) on "campanilismo." Escalante (1919) confirms the executions mentioned here and others as well: "On March 11, the insurgents José Puerta, Martín Francisco, Lorenzo Flores, and Fermín López, leading citizens of this pueblo, were hanged at the four cardinal directions of this town by the royalists, they having been the first to respond to the *grito de Dolores.* . . . A few days later, don Félix Ma. Calleja passed by this pueblo on his way to Zacatecas; he remained here only a few hours but nevertheless ordered seven individuals hanged without trial or charges, solely because there were suspicions that they were devoted to the cause of Independence." Escalante also notes the execution in San Felipe, Guanajuato, in 1819 of "the Insurgent Colonel Pedro M. Vázquez, of Mexquitic."

34. San Luis Potosí n.d.:88.

35. Debts and land purchases are listed in AOCI, Títulos de Santa Teresa, vol. 7, libro de "Rústicos," which also notes the settlement of "overdue salaries" in 1836 after seven and a half years of nonpayment. Land parcels purchased from 1837 to 1873 totaled about 1,300 hectares in Mexquitic (total of 10,986 pesos paid), 200 hectares in Ahualulco (3,174 pesos), and the 400-hectare ranch of Tomates north of Ahualulco (1,500 pesos). In addition, in 1832 Ipiña bought the 20,000-hectare hacienda of San Nicolás de Ardila, a ragged stretch of monte north of La Parada, for an unrecorded amount of money.

36. The evidence for this is indirect but compelling. The population of Mexquitic appears to have fallen from more than 20,000 around 1865–1875 to about 15,000 in 1910 (see appendix A). I suspect that this drop in population was almost entirely due to outmigration and that most of the migrants went to La Laguna, which was the fastest-growing region in Mexico during the same period. Several present-day residents of Mexquitic were born in La Laguna and returned to their parents' hometown as children in the mid-1920s. Others recall that their parents

made annual journeys to La Laguna to work in the cotton harvest as late as the 1940s; see Behar 1993:31–32 for one account.

37. AOCI, Libro, f. 1249.

38. Taped interview, August 13, 1985.

39. AOCI, Títulos de Santa Teresa, vol. 7, libro de "Rústicos."

40. Fieldnotes, translated, January 4, 1984.

41. Archive of the ejido of Corte Segundo.

42. Taped interview, Corte Segundo, August 23, 1988.

43. Taped interview, August 13, 1985. This interview continued with the observations quoted at the end of chapter 5.

44. Cabrera Ipiña and Cabrera Ipiña 1978:124–125; ellipsis in original, my translation.

45. Ibid., 124.

46. Taped interview, August 23, 1988.

47. AHESLP, AM 1744.

48. "Por ellos son unos miserables campestres serriles y montarases," AHESLP, AM 1766.

49. AHESLP, AM 1810 (6 abril).

50. Compare Taylor's observations about Tonalá and Tlajomulco, as well as his incisive observations on colonial "Indian" identity in pueblos of central Jalisco (1988:243 and 230–232).

51. Taped interview, September 14, 1987.

52. In 1947 the municipality of San Miguel Mexquitic was officially renamed Mexquitic de Carmona in honor of the soldier and native son Damián Carmona, a hero of the siege of Querétaro in 1867 (Montejano y Aguiñaga 1979). A commemorative statue of Carmona was built on a hill overlooking the town in 1967, but was hit by lightning that knocked off its head a few years later. It was not repaired until 1985.

53. Fieldnotes, translated, March 3, 1984.

APPENDIX B

1. AHESLP, AM 1715. I include this, a literal translation of the earliest will produced in Mexquitic that I have so far found, to give an indication of the early hispanization of the pueblo. The will was written in a fully literate and fluent Spanish, though in an unschooled hand (which seems to be that of Gaspar Diego, one of six signers of the will, who appears as governor in 1735). It is, unremarkably, full of unorthodox spellings (aside from *b* for *v* and so on, the text has *bura* and *tiera* for *burro* and *tierra,* and *anego* for *añejo*), but no more than would be found in a text written in a small pueblo in Spain itself at the same time, and it is hard to infer from these few alterations a distinctive pronunciation. The only ungrammatical phrase in the text is "sin mas pongan que" (rendered as "without they should put more than") where standard Spanish would have "sin que pongan mas que"—this level of error, again, is common in untutored Spanish documents. The only Nahuatlism is *jocoyote,* "youngest child," which had entered Mexican Spanish, though the concern with birth order could itself possibly be considered a Nahua emphasis.

The list of items in Sebastian's estate, too, is entirely Spanish, consisting mainly of horses, cattle, Spanish iron tools, and even a *carabina* (carbine or rifle); the absence of land, even a house site, in the will, however, is equally noteworthy, and points both to the continuing surplus of land in 1714 and to the land tenure system of the pueblo de indios. It is also interesting that, though the will favors sons over daughters and the oldest son over all, Sebastian's wife receives by far the largest portion, and all children receive an equal number of cows, the most valuable single items in the estate.

2. There are several places called Salitrillo in Mexquitic.

3. Described as "bacas oras"—gold-colored cows?

APPENDIX D

1. AHESLP, AM 1764 (29 agosto). I have taken the liberty of adding paragraph breaks, which are lacking in this and most other colonial documents, and adding clarifying comments within brackets, but I have generally respected the typically idiosyncratic sentence divisions, capitalization, and spelling of proper names.

2. Las Cabras (now Ranchería de Guadalupe) was a disputed site on the border between Mexquitic and the hacienda of La Parada.

3. About three words are lost here at the bottom of the first page.

4. Probably on an hacienda, though many families in Mexquitic owned small herds of up to a hundred sheep.

5. A *cordel* was a knotted rope used to measure either 50 *varas* (about 42 meters) or 50 *pasos* (70 meters).

6. That is, to the Spaniards and castas who annually rented out a portion of Mexquitic's communal land known as the hacienda of Mexquitic, to satisfy a number of colonial taxes and to help fund the fiestas. This rented land became, towards the end of the eighteenth century, the basis of the hacienda of Corte.

7. Concluding legal formulas, partially cut from the page, follow. There is no signature.

APPENDIX E

1. AHESLP, AM 1798 (11 agosto). Paragraph breaks and punctuation as in the document, which is a copy of the original letter.

Bibliography

PRIMARY SOURCES

The major source for the historical information in this book was the delightful Archivo Histórico del Estado de San Luis Potosí (AHESLP), which opened its doors in 1980. In it I surveyed all of the documents from the years 1750 to 1810 and a sampling of half the years from 1700 to 1749 and 1811 to 1823 for information about Mexquitic. These documents are now all incorporated into the fondo Alcaldía Mayor (AM) and organized by year (I have not been able to find some documents formerly classified under "Poder Ejecutivo," of which I have photocopies). Seventeenth and late-nineteenth-century materials, the latter in Secretaría General de Gobierno (SGG), are still being organized, and my consultation of them was much more erratic. I also consulted the Hemeroteca of rare nineteenth-century Potosino newspapers.

Other archives consulted were:

Archivo General de Indias, in Seville (AGI), ramo México.

Archivo General de la Nación, in Mexico City (AGN), ramos Indios, Tierras, Historia, and Intendencias.

The private archive of don Octaviano Cabrera Ipiña, in San Luis Potosí (AOCI), series of hacienda records labeled "Títulos de Santa Teresa," of which volumes 1 ("Libro de Títulos" or "Libro") and 7 ("Rústicos") were particularly useful.

Archivo de la Secretaría de Reforma Agraria, San Luis Potosí, expedientes 773–806, my main twentieth-century archival source and an unexplored gold mine of cartographic information.

Mexquitic parish records, 1592–1898 (the first book, recording baptisms from 1592 to 1605 and marriages from 1599 to 1613, has disappeared from the parish archive but was consulted on INAH [Pompa microfilms] rollo 39 de la serie SLP).

Mexquitic municipal records (civil birth and death registers, 1875–1983; some have disappeared or been destroyed, but duplicates are kept in AHESLP).

Archive of the ejido of Corte Segundo.

Archivo de la Parroquia Sagrario de la iglesia Catedral de San Luis Potosí, bautismos de hijos españoles, bautismos de castas, 1593–1651, consulted in Genealogical Society of Utah (GSU), microfilm no. 640576.

Archivo de la Parroquia Nuestra Señora de la Asunción de Tlaxcalilla, Bautismos y matrimonios, 1594–1654, consulted in GSU, microfilm no. 709750.

Archivo de la Casa de Morelos in Morelia, containing the archives of the bishopric of Michoacán to which Mexquitic belonged until 1854; at the time we attempted to work in this archive its records were more easily consulted in the GSU microfilm copies at the Instituto Nacional de Antropología e Historia (INAH).

Several important primary sources are transcribed and published in Velázquez 1985 and Frye 1986.

REFERENCES

Abu-Lughod, Lila. 1991. "Writing against Culture." In Richard G. Fox, ed., *Recapturing Anthropology: Working in the Present*, pp. 137–162. Santa Fe: School of American Research Press.

———. 1993. *Writing Women's Worlds: Bedouin Stories*. Berkeley: University of California Press.

Adams, David B. 1971. "The Tlaxcalan Colonies of Spanish Coahuila and Nuevo León: An Aspect of the Settlement of Northern Mexico." Ph.D. diss., University of Texas at Austin.

Aguirre Beltrán, Gonzalo. 1958. *Cuijla: Esbozo etnográfico de un pueblo negro*. Mexico City: Fondo de Cultura Económica.

Alonso, Ana María. 1988. "'Progress' as Disorder and Dishonor: Discourses of *Serrano* Resistance." *Critique of Anthropology* 8 (1): 13–33.

———. 1992. "Gender, Power, and Historical Memory: Discourses of *Serrano* Resistance." In Judith Butler and Joan W. Scott, eds., *Feminists Theorize the Political*, pp. 404–425. New York: Routledge.

Altman, Ida, and James Lockhart, eds. 1976. *Provinces of Early Mexico: Variants of Spanish American Regional Evolution*. Los Angeles: UCLA Latin American Center.

Ankerson, Dudley. 1984. *Agrarian Warlord: Saturnino Cedillo and the Mexican Revolution in San Luis Potosí*. DeKalb: Northern Illinois University Press.

Anzaldúa, Gloria. 1987. *Borderlands/La Frontera: The New Mestiza*. San Francisco: Aunt Lute Books.

Arlegui, José. 1851 [1737]. *Crónica de la Provincia de N. P. S. Francisco de Zacatecas*. Mexico City.

Badone, Ellen, ed. 1990. *Religious Orthodoxy and Folk Belief in European Society*. Princeton: Princeton University Press.

Bakewell, P. J. 1971. *Silver Mining and Society in Colonial Mexico: Zacatecas, 1546–1700*. Cambridge: Cambridge University Press.

Barlow, R. H., and George T. Smisor, eds. 1943. *Nombre de Dios, Durango: Two Documents in Náhuatl Concerning Its Foundation.* Sacramento: The House of Tlaloc.

Bazant, Jan. 1975. *Cinco haciendas mexicanas: Tres siglos de vida rural en San Luis Potosí (1600–1910).* Mexico City: El Colegio de México.

Behar, Ruth. 1986. *Santa María del Monte: The Presence of the Past in a Spanish Village.* Princeton: Princeton University Press.

———. 1987. "The Visions of a Guachichil Witch in 1599: A Window on the Subjugation of Mexico's Hunter-Gatherers." *Ethnology* 34:115–138.

———. 1990. "The Struggle for the Church: Popular Anticlericalism and Religiosity in Post-Franco Spain." In Ellen Badone, ed., *Religious Orthodoxy and Folk Belief in European Society,* pp. 76–112. Princeton: Princeton University Press.

———. 1993a. *Translated Woman: Crossing the Border with Esperanza's Story.* Boston: Beacon Press.

———, ed. 1993b. Special issue on "Women Writing Culture," *Critique of Anthropology* 13 (4).

Behar, Ruth, and Deborah Gordon, eds. 1995. *Women Writing Culture.* Berkeley: University of California Press.

Bezdek, Robert R. 1984. "Electoral Opposition in San Luis Potosí: The Case of Nava" (epilogue). In Kenneth F. Johnson, *Mexican Democracy: A Critical View,* pp. 242–263. New York: Praeger.

Bloch, Marc. 1966 [1931]. *French Rural History: An Essay on Its Basic Characteristics.* Berkeley: University of California Press.

Bonfil Batalla, Guillermo. 1987. *México profundo: Una civilización negada.* Mexico City: SEP.

Borah, Woodrow. 1983. *Justice by Insurance: The General Indian Court of Colonial Mexico and the Legal Aides of the Half-Real.* Berkeley: University of California Press.

Boulanger, Robert. 1979. *Mexico, Guatemala: A Complete Guide.* David B. Castledine, trans. Mexico: Fomento Cultural Banamex.

Boyer, Richard. 1989. "Women, *La Mala Vida,* and the Politics of Marriage." In Asunción Lavrin, ed., *Sexuality and Marriage in Colonial Latin America,* pp. 252–286. Lincoln: University of Nebraska Press.

Brading, D. A. 1978. *Haciendas and Ranchos in the Mexican Bajío: León, 1700–1860.* Cambridge: Cambridge University Press.

———, ed. 1980. *Caudillo and Peasant in the Mexican Revolution.* Cambridge: Cambridge University Press.

Burkhart, Louise M. 1989. *The Slippery Earth: Nahua-Christian Moral Dialogue in Sixteenth-Century Mexico.* Tucson: University of Arizona Press.

Cabrera Ipiña, Octaviano, and Matilde Cabrera Ipiña. 1978. *Historia de la hacienda San Francisco Javier de la Parada.* San Luis Potosí: Editorial Universitaria Potosina.

Calderón, Héctor, and José David Saldívar, eds. 1991. *Criticism in the Borderlands: Studies in Chicano Literature, Culture, and Ideology.* Durham: Duke University Press.

Camp, Roderic A. 1988. *Memoirs of a Mexican Politician.* Albuquerque: University of New Mexico Press.

Cancian, Frank. 1965. *Economics and Prestige in a Maya Community: The Religious Cargo System in Zinacantan.* Stanford: Stanford University Press.

Castro Gutiérrez, Felipe, ed. 1990. *José de Gálvez, Informe sobre las rebeliones populares de 1767 y otros documentos inéditos.* Mexico City: Universidad Nacional Autónoma de México.

Chance, John K. 1988. "Recent Works on Colonial Mexico." *Latin American Research Review* 23 (3): 213–226.

Chance, John K., and William B. Taylor. 1985. "Cofradías and Cargos: An Historical Perspective on the Mesoamerican Civil-Religious Hierarchy." *American Ethnologist* 12:1–26.

Chevalier, François. 1966. *Land and Society in Colonial Mexico: The Great Hacienda.* Berkeley: University of California Press.

Christian, William A., Jr. 1981. *Local Religion in Sixteenth-Century Spain.* Princeton: Princeton University Press.

Clifford, James, and George Marcus, eds. 1986. *Writing Culture: The Poetics and Politics of Ethnography.* Berkeley: University of California Press.

Cline, Howard F. 1972. "Ethnohistorical Regions of Middle America." In Howard F. Cline, ed., *Guide to Ethnohistorical Sources,* pp. 166–181. Vol. 12 of *Handbook of Middle American Indians* (Robert Wauchope, General Ed.). Austin: University of Texas Press.

Cuello, José. 1982. "Beyond the 'Borderlands' Is the North of Colonial Mexico: A Latin-Americanist Perspective to the Study of the Mexican North and the United States Southwest." *Proceedings of the Pacific Coast Council of Latin American Studies,* 9:1–24.

———. 1988. "The Persistence of Indian Slavery and Encomienda in the Northeast of Colonial Mexico, 1577–1723." *Journal of Social History* 21: 683–700.

Cutter, Charles R. 1986. *The Protector de Indios in Colonial New Mexico, 1659–1821.* Albuquerque: University of New Mexico Press.

Daniel, E. Valentine. 1984. *Fluid Signs: Being a Person the Tamil Way.* Berkeley: University of California Press.

Deeds, Susan. 1989. "Rural Work in Nueva Vizcaya: Forms of Labor Coercion on the Periphery." *Hispanic American Historical Review* 69:425–449.

———. Forthcoming. "Legacies of Resistance, Adaptation, and Tenacity: History of the Native Peoples of Northwest Mexico." In Murdo MacLeod, ed., *The Cambridge History of the Native Peoples of the Americas: Mesoamerica.* Cambridge: Cambridge University Press.

de la Peña, Guillermo. 1980. *Herederos de promesas: Agricultura, política y ritual en los Altos de Morelos.* Mexico City: Ediciones de La Casa Chata [INAH].

Dennis, Philip A. 1987. *Intervillage Conflict in Oaxaca.* New Brunswick: Rutgers University Press.

di Leonardo, Micaela, ed. 1991. *Gender at the Crossroads of Knowledge: Feminist Anthropology in the Postmodern Era.* Berkeley: University of California Press.

Escalante, Br. Albino. 1919. "Historia de Mexquitic." (Broadside.) No place, no publisher; reprinted in *El Heraldo de San Luis,* September 19–27, 1956.

Fabian, Johannes. 1983. *Time and the Other: How Anthropology Makes Its Object.* New York: Columbia University Press.

Falcón, Romana. 1984. *Revolución y caciquismo: San Luis Potosí, 1910–1938.* Mexico City: El Colegio de México.

Farriss, Nancy M. 1984. *Maya Society under Colonial Rule: The Collective Enterprise of Survival.* Princeton: Princeton University Press.

Fernandez, James W. 1986. *Persuasions and Performances: The Play of Tropes in Culture.* Bloomington: Indiana University Press.

Finkler, Kaja. 1980. "Land Scarcity and Economic Development: When Is a Landlord a Client and a Sharecropper His Patron?" In Peggy F. Bartlett, ed., *Agricultural Decision Making,* pp. 265–286. New York: Academic Press.

————. 1985. *Spiritualist Healers in Mexico: Successes and Failures of Alternative Therapeutics.* New York: Praeger.

Florescano, Enrique. 1969. *Precios del maíz y crisis agrícolas en México (1708–1810).* Mexico City: El Colegio de México.

Florescano, Enrique, and Isabel Gil Sánchez. 1976. "La época de las reformas borbónicas y el crecimiento económico, 1750–1808." In Centro de Estudios Históricos, *Historia general de México,* pp. 471–589. Mexico City: El Colegio de México.

Fox, Richard G., ed. 1991. *Recapturing Anthropology: Working in the Present.* Santa Fe: School of American Research Press.

Friedlander, Judith. 1975. *Being Indian in Hueyapan: A Study of Forced Identity in Contemporary Mexico.* New York: St. Martin's Press.

Friedman, Jonathan. 1992. "The Past in the Future: History and the Politics of Identity." *American Anthropologist* 94 (4): 837–859.

Friedrich, Paul. 1970. *Agrarian Revolt in a Mexican Village.* Englewood Cliffs, N.J.: Prentice-Hall.

————. 1986. *The Princes of Naranja: An Essay in Anthrohistorical Method.* Austin: University of Texas Press.

Frye, David. 1986. *Descripciones geográfico-estadísticas de Mexquitic, S.L.P.* San Luis Potosí: Academia de Historia Potosina.

————. 1989. "Local Memory, Local History, and the Construction of Identity in a Rural Mexican Town." Ph.D. diss., Princeton University.

————. 1994a. "Telling Histories: A Late-Colonial Encounter of 'Spanish' and 'Indian' in Rural Mexico and in the Archives." *Colonial Latin American Review* 3:115–138.

————. 1994b. "Speaking of the Ejido: Three Modes of Discourse about the Salinas Reforms." *Urban Anthropology and Studies of Cultural Systems and World Economic Development* 23:307–330.

————. Forthcoming. "The Native Peoples of Northeastern Mexico." In Murdo MacLeod, ed., *The Cambridge History of the Native Peoples of the Americas: Mesoamerica.* Cambridge: Cambridge University Press.

García, Alma M. 1987. "Recent Studies in Nineteenth- and Early-Twentieth-Century Regional Mexican History." *Latin American Research Review* 22 (2): 255–266.

Gerhard, Peter. 1993. *The North Frontier of New Spain.* Norman: University of Oklahoma Press.

Gibson, Charles. 1964. *The Aztecs under Spanish Rule: A History of the Indians of the Valley of Mexico, 1519–1810.* Stanford: Stanford University Press.

————. 1967. *Tlaxcala in the Sixteenth Century*. Stanford: Stanford University Press.

Gilderhus, Mark T. 1987. "Many Mexicos: Tradition and Innovation in the Recent Historiography." *Latin American Research Review* 22 (1): 204–213.

Golden, Tim. 1991. "The Dream of Land Dies Hard in Mexico," *New York Times*, November 27, p. A1.

González, Luis. 1968. *Pueblo en vilo*. Mexico City: El Colegio de México.

Gordon, Deborah. 1988. *Feminism and the Critique of Colonial Discourse*. Special issue of *Inscriptions*, no. 3/4.

Greenburg, James B. 1981. *Santiago's Sword: Chatino Peasant Religion and Economics*. Berkeley: University of California Press.

————. 1989. *Blood Ties: Life and Violence in Rural Mexico*. Tucson: University of Arizona Press.

Gruzinski, Serge. 1990. "Indian Confraternities, Brotherhoods, and *Mayordomías* in Central New Spain: A List of Questions for the Historian and the Anthropologist." In Arij Ouweneel and Simon Miller, eds., *The Indian Community of Colonial Mexico*, pp. 205–223. Latin American Studies series, no. 58. Amsterdam: CEDLA.

Hamnett, Brian R. 1986. *Roots of Insurgency: Mexican Regions, 1750–1824*. Cambridge: Cambridge University Press.

Herr, Richard. 1974. "El significado de la desamortización en España." *Moneda y crédito* 131:55–94.

Herskovitz, Melville J. 1990 [1941]. *The Myth of the Negro Past*. Boston: Beacon Press.

Joseph, Gilbert M., and Daniel Nugent, eds. 1994. *Everyday Forms of State Formation: Revolution and the Negotiation of Rule in Modern Mexico*. Durham: Duke University Press.

Koreck, María Teresa. 1988. "Space and Revolution in Northeastern Chihuahua." In Daniel Nugent, ed., *Rural Revolt in Mexico and U.S. Intervention*, pp. 127–148. San Diego: Center for U.S.-Mexican Studies, University of California-San Diego.

Lavrin, Asunción. 1990. "Rural Confraternities in the Local Economies of New Spain: The Bishopric of Oaxaca in the Context of Colonial Mexico." In Arij Ouweneel and Simon Miller, eds., *The Indian Community of Colonial Mexico*, pp. 224–249. Latin American Studies series, no. 58. Amsterdam: CEDLA.

Leal, Juan Felipe, and Mario Huacujo R. 1976. *Fuentes para el estudio de la hacienda en México: 1856–1940*. Centro de Estudios Latinoamericanas, Serie Bibliográficas no. 1. Mexico City: UNAM.

Limerick, Patricia Nelson. 1987. *The Legacy of Conquest: The Unbroken Past of the American West*. New York: W. W. Norton.

Lockhart, James. 1991. *Nahuas and Spaniards: Postconquest Central Mexican History and Philology*. Stanford and Los Angeles: Stanford University Press and UCLA Latin American Center.

————. 1992. *The Nahuas after the Conquest: A Social and Cultural History of the Indians of Central Mexico, Sixteenth Through Eighteenth Centuries*. Stanford: Stanford University Press.

Lomnitz, Larissa Adler, Claudio Lomnitz-Adler, and Ilya Adler. 1993. "The

Function of the Form: Power Play and Ritual in the 1988 Mexican Presidential Campaign." In Daniel H. Levine, ed., *Constructing Culture and Power in Latin America*, pp. 357–401. Ann Arbor: University of Michigan Press.

Lomnitz-Adler, Claudio. 1992. *Exits from the Labyrinth: Culture and Ideology in the Mexican National Space*. Berkeley: University of California Press.

López Austin, Alfredo. 1993. *The Myths of the Opossum: Pathways of Mesoamerican Mythology*. Bernardo Ortiz de Montellano and Thelma Ortiz de Montellano, trans. Albuquerque: University of New Mexico Press.

Martínez Baracs, Andrea. 1993. "Colonizaciones tlaxcaltecas." *Historia mexicana* 43 (2): 195–250.

Mathews, Holly F. 1985. " 'We Are Mayordomo': A Reinterpretation of Women's Roles in the Mexican Cargo System." *American Ethnologist* 12(2): 285–301.

Melville, Elinor K. 1994. *A Plague of Sheep: Environmental Consequences of the Conquest of Mexico*. Cambridge: Cambridge University Press.

Meyer, Jean. 1973. *La cristiada*. Vol. 1: *La guerra de los cristeros*. Mexico City: Siglo Veintiuno Editores.

Montejano, David. 1987. *Anglos and Mexicans in the Making of Texas, 1836–1986*. Austin: University of Texas Press.

Montejano y Aguiñaga, Rafael. 1971. *El clero y la independencia en San Luis Potosí*. San Luis Potosí: Academia de Historia Potosina.

———. 1979. *Damián Carmona: Rectificaciones históricas*. San Luis Potosí: Academia de Historia Potosina.

———. 1981. *Documentos para la historia de la Guerra de Independencia en San Luis Potosí*. San Luis Potosí: Academia de Historia Potosina.

Mora, Pat. 1993. *Nepantla: Essays from the Land in the Middle*. Albuquerque: University of New Mexico Press.

Morin, Claude. 1979. *Michoacán en la Nueva España del siglo XVIII: Crecimiento y desigualdad en una economía colonial*. Mexico City: Fondo de Cultura Económica.

Nash, June. 1970. *In the Eyes of the Ancestors: Belief and Behavior in a Mayan Community*. New Haven: Yale University Press.

Naylor, Thomas H., and Charles W. Polzer, eds. 1986. *The Presidio and Militia on the Norther Frontier of New Spain: A Documentary History*. Vol. 1, *1570–1700*. Tucson: University of Arizona Press.

Nugent, Daniel. 1988. "Rural Revolt in Mexico, Mexican Nationalism and the State, and Forms of U.S. Intervention." In Daniel Nugent, ed., *Rural Revolt in Mexico and U.S. Intervention*, pp. 1–21. San Diego: Center for U.S.-Mexican Studies, University of California–San Diego.

———. 1993. *Spent Cartridges of Revolution: An Anthropological History of Namiquipa, Chihuahua*. Chicago: University of Chicago Press.

Offutt, Leslie Scott. 1982. "Urban and Rural Society in the Mexican North: Saltillo in the Late Colonial Period." Ph.D. diss., UCLA.

———. 1992. "Levels of Acculturation in Northeastern New Spain: San Esteban Testaments of the Seventeenth and Eighteenth Centuries." *Estudios de cultura náhuatl* 22:409–443.

Osborn, Wayne S. 1973. "Indian Land Retention in Colonial Metztitlán." *Hispanic American Historical Review* 53 (2): 217–238.

Ouweneel, Arij. 1990. "*Altepeme* and *Pueblos de Indios*: Some Comparative Theoretical Perspectives on the Analysis of the Colonial Indian Communities." In Arij Ouweneel and Simon Miller, eds., *The Indian Community of Colonial Mexico*, pp. 1–37. Latin American Studies series, no. 58. Amsterdam: CEDLA.

Paredes, Américo, ed. and trans. 1970. *Folktales of Mexico*. Chicago: University of Chicago Press.

———. 1971. "The United States, Mexico, and *Machismo*." *Journal of the Folklore Institute* 8:17–37.

Parsons, Elsie Clews. 1927. "Witchcraft among the Pueblos: Indian or Spanish?" *Man* 27:106–112, 125–128.

Peña, Francisco de la. 1979 [1894]. *Estudio histórico sobre San Luis Potosí*. San Luis Potosí: Academia de Historia Potosina.

Pérez Herrero, Pedro, ed. 1991. *Región e historia en México (1700–1850): Métodos de análisis regional*. Mexico City: Instituto de Investigaciones Dr. José María Luis Mora.

Powell, Philip Wayne. 1952. *Soldiers, Indians, and Silver: The Northward Advance of New Spain, 1550–1600*. Berkeley: University of California Press.

———. 1971. *War and Peace on the North Mexican Frontier: A Documentary Record*. Vol. 1, *Crescendo of the Chichimeca War (1551–1585)* (transcriptions by María L. Powell). Madrid: Ediciones José Porrúa Turanzas.

———. 1977. *Mexico's Miguel Caldera: The Taming of America's First Frontier, 1548–1597*. Tucson: University of Arizona Press.

Rappaport, Joanne. 1990. *The Politics of Memory: Native Historical Interpretation in the Colombian Andes*. Cambridge: Cambridge University Press.

———. 1994. *Cumbe Reborn: An Andean Ethnography of History*. Chicago: University of Chicago Press.

Real Academia Española. 1979. *Diccionario manual e ilustrado de la lengua española*. Madrid: Espasa-Calpe.

Rojas, Beatriz. 1983. *La pequeña guerra: Los Carrera Torres y los Cedillo*. Zamora, Mich.: El Colegio de Michoacán.

Romo, Ricardo, and Raymund Paredes, eds. 1979. *New Directions in Chicano Scholarship*. La Jolla: Chicano Studies Monograph Series, University of California–San Diego.

Sánchez Unzueta, Horacio. 1982. *Un motín de campesinos en la Hacienda de Bocas, S.L.P., 1847–1853*. San Luis Potosí: Academia de Historia Potosina.

San Luis Potosí. n.d. *Legislación potosina*. No place, no pub. [presumably San Luis Potosí: Imprenta del Estado, about 1835].

Santamaría, Francisco J. 1978. *Diccionario de mejicanismos*. Mexico City: Editorial Porrúa.

Scott, James C. 1976. *The Moral Economy of the Peasant: Rebellion and Subsistence in Southeast Asia*. New Haven: Yale University Press.

Simonson, Rick, and Scott Walker, eds. 1988. *Multicultural Literacy: Opening the American Mind*. The Graywolf Annual 5. Saint Paul: Graywolf Press.

Simpson, Eyler. 1937. *The Ejido: Mexico's Way Out*. Chapel Hill: University of North Carolina Press.

Simpson, Lesley B. *Many Mexicos*. New York: Putnam.

Smith, Waldemar R. 1977. *The Fiesta System and Economic Change*. New York: Columbia University Press.

Spalding, Karen. 1974. *De indio a campesino: Cambios en la estructura social del Perú colonial*. Lima: Instituto de Estudios Peruanos.

Stephen, Lynn. 1991. *Zapotec Women*. Austin: University of Texas Press.

Super, John C. 1984. "Recent Studies on Eighteenth-Century Mexico." *Latin American Research Review* 19 (2): 163–170.

Swann, Michael. 1982. *"Tierra Adentro": Settlement and Society in Colonial Durango*. Boulder: University of Colorado Press.

———. 1989. *Migrants in the Mexican North: Mobility, Economy, and Society in a Colonial World*. Boulder: University of Colorado Press.

Tannenbaum, Frank. 1929. *The Mexican Agrarian Revolution*. New York: Macmillan.

Taussig, Michael. 1984. "Culture of Terror—Space of Death: Roger Casement's Putumayo Report and the Explanation of Torture." *Comparative Studies in Society and History* 26:467–497.

Tax, Sol. 1937. "The Municipios of the Midwestern Highlands of Guatemala." *American Anthropologist* 43 (1): 27–42.

Taylor, William B. 1972. *Landlord and Peasant in Colonial Oaxaca*. Stanford: Stanford University Press.

———. 1979. *Drinking, Homicide, and Rebellion in Colonial Mexican Villages*. Stanford: Stanford University Press.

———. 1984. "Conflict and Balance in District Politics: Tecali and the Sierra Norte de Pueblo in the Eighteenth Century." In Ronald Spores and Ross Hassig, eds., *Five Centuries of Law and Politics in Central Mexico*, pp. 87–106. Nashville: Vanderbilt University Press.

———. 1988. "Banditry and Insurrection: Rural Unrest in Central Jalisco, 1790–1816." In Friedrich Katz, ed., *Riot, Rebellion, and Revolution: Rural Social Conflict in Mexico*, pp. 205–246. Princeton: Princeton University Press.

———. 1994. "Santiago's Horse: Christianity and Colonial Indian Resistance in the Heartland of New Spain." In William B. Taylor and Franklin Pease G. Y., eds., *Violence, Resistance, and Survival in the Americas: Native Americans and the Legacy of Conquest*, pp. 153–189. Washington: Smithsonian Institution Press.

Torquemada, Juan de. 1969 [1615]. *Monarquía indiana*. Mexico City: Porrúa.

Trouillot, Michel-Rolph. 1990. *Haiti, State against Nation: The Origins and Legacy of Duvalierism*. New York: Monthly Review Press.

Turner, Terence. 1991. "Representing, Resisting, Rethinking: Historical Transformations of Kayapo Culture and Anthropological Consciousness." In George W. Stocking, ed., *Colonial Situations: Essays on the Contextualization of Ethnographic Knowledge*, pp. 285–313. Madison: University of Wisconsin Press.

Tutino, John. 1986. *From Insurrection to Revolution in Mexico: Social Bases of Agrarian Violence, 1750–1940*. Princeton: Princeton University Press.

———. 1987. "Peasants and Politics in Nineteenth-Century Mexico." *Latin American Research Review* 22 (3): 237–244.

Van Young, Eric. 1981. *Hacienda and Market in Eighteenth-Century Mexico: The*

Rural Economy of the Guadalajara Region, 1675–1820. Berkeley: University of
California Press.

———. 1984. "Conflict and Solidarity in Indian Village Life: The Guadalajara
Region in the Late Colonial Period." *Hispanic American Historical Review* 64:
55–79.

———. 1989. "The Raw and the Cooked: Elite and Popular Ideology in Mex-
ico, 1800–1821." In Mark D. Szuchman, ed., *The Middle Period in Latin
America: Values and Attitudes in the 17th–19th Centuries,* pp. 75–102. Boulder:
Lynne Rienner Publishers.

Velázquez, Primo Feliciano. 1982 [1946]. *Historia de San Luis Potosí,* 4 vols. San
Luis Potosí: Archivo Histórico del Estado.

———. 1985 [1897]. *Colección de documentos para la historia de San Luis Potosí.*
Vol. 1. San Luis Potosí: Archivo Histórico del Estado.

Warman, Arturo. 1976. *. . . Y venimos a contradecir: Los campesinos de Morelos y el
estado nacional.* Mexico City: Ediciones de La Casa Chata [INAH].

Watanabe, John M. 1992. *Maya Saints and Souls in a Changing World.* Austin: University of Texas Press.

Weber, Eugen. 1976. *Peasants into Frenchmen: The Modernization of Rural France,
1870–1914.* Stanford: Stanford University Press.

Weisman, Alan. 1990. "An Island in Limbo." *New York Times Magazine,* February 18, 1990, pp. 28–40.

Wolf, Eric. 1957. "Closed Corporate Communities in Mesoamerica and Central
Java." *Southwestern Journal of Anthropology* 13 (1): 1–15.

———. 1959. *Sons of the Shaking Earth.* Chicago: University of Chicago Press.

Womack, John, Jr. 1968. *Zapata and the Mexican Revolution.* New York: Vintage
Books.

World Book Encyclopedia. 1965. Chicago: Field Enterprises Educational
Corporation.

Zavala, Silvio. 1967. *Los esclavos en Nueva España.* Mexico City: El Colegio
Nacional.

Index